An Introduction to Library and Information Science

An Introduction to Library and Information Science

(In Accordance with C.B.S.E. Syllabus)

Class XI

Shiva Sukula

Ess Ess Publications
New Delhi

An Introduction to Library and Information Science

ISBN : 978-81-7000-733-3

₹ 295/-

First Published 2014

Published by:
Ess Ess Publications
4831/24, Ansari Road,
Darya Ganj,
New Delhi-110 002.
INDIA
Phones: 23260807, 41563444
Fax: 41563334
E-mail: info@essessreference.com
www.essessreference.com

Cover Design by *Patch Creative Unit*

Printed and bound in India at Salasar Imaging Systems.

Contents

Preface

The library and information science education is intended towards creating professionally trained librarians and information professionals. The education at various levels has been envisaged the designing of syllabi and contents to show the role of the LIS professional as manager. The education gives an in dcpth understanding of the technical, human, conceptual skills, and communication skills for LIS professional and manager. The library and information science education helps in building up a student a knowledgeable person to understand the intricate tasks of a library and the student emerges as a LIS professional for library. The education at higher level in library and information science enables a trained graduate to learn the innovative strategies for where it's needed.

Libraries are an integral part of any academic system. Of late, they become vigorous and purposeful as the present period is a period of digital libraries, electronic libraries and virtual libraries. These changes demand development of modern skills to both library professionals as well as users. The skills for the library professional in the role of resource worker help users to return to library alongside their classrooms or workstations. In this context, the library management and information services related education provide a future library professional the basic learning such as knowing the use of types of resources, the lending procedure of documents, and provisions of Library Services etc. The efficient use of library personnel resources maximizes the library performance.

It has been observed that for a library and information system to run efficiently, the manager must know managing technical services as well as providing good leadership to other library information staff members to ensure that library goals are achieved and that users are satisfied. Library functions with the aims and objectives of the same. It evaluates their relevance in comparison to the objectives of its parent organization. As reflected, librarians are path breakers, but the paths they break will be characterized more by their divergence than their similarity. In order to achieve the goals of organization through the services of library, the motivational forces, managerial style and other behavioral approaches are considered to maximize the efficiency of staff.

The present book introduces a learner to the elementary concepts of library and information science and the concerned services. The chapters have been designed to give a clear and comprehensive insight into the intriguing topics. More than century old concepts and practices have been explained simply yet explicitly. The book plans to cover the prescribed concepts as the chapters range from the conventional techniques of libraries to applications of modern information technology into library and information services.

—Shiva Sukula

1
Library And Society

INTRODUCTION

The historical and future roles have been played by public, private, academic and special libraries in supporting and shaping society at local, regional, national and international levels. There are factors affecting people in different niche; such as globalization, economic turmoil, political and ethnic tensions, rapid technology development, global warming etc. Libraries and Society are related with each other from hundreds of years in serving diverse communities. Libraries play a fundamental role in society. They have been acting like gateways to knowledge and culture; the libraries provide learning resources and services which further create opportunities for learning, support literacy and education. They have myriad ways to shape the new ideas and perspectives that are central to a creative and innovative society. They have been responsible ensuring an authentic record of knowledge created and accumulated by past generations. Libraries have been an agent to advance research and human knowledge or preserve the world's cumulative knowledge and heritage. Libraries offer a means by which we can gain access to knowledge.

WHAT IS THE MEANING OF LIBRARY?

How we perceive, a library may depend on the use or the services it offers. But how a library is in real? What makes an organization or institution as a library? A library refers to a place where literary and artistic materials are kept for the purpose of reading and research. This material includes books, pamphlets, records, and periodicals. It also refers to a collection or set of books issued by a publisher.

Literary way shows that the word Library is derived from the Latin word "liber" which means-A BOOK. In the past a library was considered "a place where books were written or kept". This term was frequently used as a "collection of books" and à librarian was considered and assigned duties as a keeper or guard of books. The developments taken place during last two centuries have transformed the libraries and their functions and the services have changed. The entire outlook has been changed due to the way it started offering its services in the society and the way people expected it to function.

In a layman's understanding, it is a place in which literary and artistic materials, such as books, periodicals, newspapers, pamphlets, prints, records, and tapes, are kept for reading, reference, or lending.

As explained in literature, ignoring the physical, technological underpinnings for now, we assert that the library is, at root, a collection of information selected for use of, and made useable for, a particular community. That community may be large or small, physically proximate or not, present or future, homogeneous or not, but it is essential that it be identified and at least partially understood. That is, proverbially like politics, all collections are local.

A quote from past is sufficient to state the value of libraries in society and the state:

If this nation is to be wise as well as strong, if we are to achieve our destiny, then we need more new ideas for more wise men reading more good books in more public libraries. These libraries should be open to all — except the censor. We must know all the facts and hear all the alternatives and listen to all the criticisms. Let us welcome controversial books and controversial authors. For the Bill of Rights is the guardian of our security as well as our liberty. —*John F. Kennedy, Saturday Review (29 October 1960), p. 44.*

TYPES OF LIBRARIES

Libraries are offering their services to the kind of people exist in the society. The people have different professions, varied requirements and expectations from the library. Broadly there are four types of libraries:

1. Public Library
2. Academic Library: It can be categorized in to three types:
   a. School Library
   b. College Library
   c. University Library
3. Special Library; and
4. National Library

INFORMATION AND ITS CHARACTERISTICS

Information is that which informs, i.e. that from which data can be derived. Information is conveyed either as the content of a message or through direct or indirect observation of some thing. That which is perceived can be construed as a message in its own right, and in that sense, information is always conveyed as the content of a message. Information can be encoded into various forms for transmission and interpretation. For example, information may be encoded into signs, and transmitted via signals.

Information resolves uncertainty. The uncertainty of an event is measured by its probability of occurrence and is inversely proportional to that. The more uncertain an event, the more information is required to resolve uncertainty of that event. The concept that *information is the message* has different meanings in different contexts. Thus the concept of information becomes closely related to notions of constraint, communication, control, data, form, instruction, knowledge, meaning, understanding, mental stimuli, pattern, perception, representation, and entropy. Information is any type of pattern that influences the formation or transformation of other patterns.

Information is considered as a "difference that makes a difference". Information includes both electronic and physical information. The information lifecycle involves regardless of source or format (data, paper documents, electronic documents, audio, video, etc.) for delivery through multiple channels that may include cell phones and web interfaces. In this way the information requires its collection and management. The Information Management means the organization of and control over the structure, processing and delivery of information.

ROLE OF LIBRARIES IN MODERN SOCIETY

The information society revolves around the position and objectives of all the institutions which work with information, knowledge, and culture. The information society is a kind of an institution which is always busy in collecting and organizing information and offering general access to it. In the information society, the libraries are especially important now when the whole idea of education is stressing more and more independent learning and acting. Libraries are providing the knowledge resources in an orderly manner. Emergence of the information society requires reassessment of the role of libraries and increased understanding of the meaning and economic manifestations of information. It is urged that widespread professional attention be directed to emerging public information policy and to clarifying a library role in prevailing economic terms. Though the main function of a library is to collect and store information, resources, sources and services which are to be used by individuals yet more fall in its ambit such as:

Organization of knowledge and Preservation : The unique function of libraries is to acquire, organize, offer for use and preserve publicly available material irrespective of the form in which it is packaged (print, cassette, CD-ROM, network form) in such a way that, when it is needed, it can be found and put to use. No other institution carries out this long-term, systematic work. Libraries are organizing information and offering access. The libraries are meant for life-long learning.

Supporting education : Libraries are synonymous with education and offer countless learning opportunities that can fuel economic, social and cultural development. Libraries make interlibrary loans possible, providing local access to materials that normally reside in a library hundreds, or even thousands, of miles away.

Integrating and Preserving Culture : Culture has an important and unique role in mobilizing resources of human beings. It has been described: To some extent, culture makes its influence felt more indirectly than knowledge, but it is impossible to imagine how people's creative powers could be fully activated without the impact of culture, which extends into the depths of the mind. Recognizing the cultural importance of sharing, Mahatma Gandhi said that, "no culture can live, if it attempts to be exclusive". The stimulus to share and reuse information and knowledge comes in many guises. The desire to preserve our culture for future generations has also become one of the important functions of libraries.

Repositories : Libraries are rich repositories of historically and culturally significant collections, many of which are not available anywhere else in the world. Today, many works are only "born digital" websites, electronic journals etc.) , and are unavailable in print format. It requires legal framework to preserve and replace works in a variety of media and formats to save for future generations of historians.

Library and information Society

Libraries are one of the leading supporting institutions which present the knowledge and materials to the people according to their needs. Libraries function as to support individual learning efforts at independent library halls and virtual platforms. Hence, the libraries have an important and unique role in the education of the society. Specifically, libraries are one of the important axes of the transformation to the information society. The individually emphasized library usage (physical or virtual) is derived from the information society concept. The characteristics of information society are as following:

i. In the information society, the information and information economy takes the lead.
ii. Individuals access to the information, generate, update.
iii. People use information in addition to the need of developing lifelong learning abilities.
iv. The information literacy skills are essential for people in information society.
v. The libraries have an important place in the information society as the libraries are the institutions where in the information is gathered, compiled and distributed.
vi. Libraries have a vital role in raising the individuals that the information society needs.

vii. There is a transformation to a production form which is based on the computers and information technologies.

viii. Information society indicates a new social structure that is shaped on the foundations of the information factor and the information and communication technologies contribute as the driving force.

The main features of this formation of society are described as:

i. The information centered and patented technological production as well as the utilization of the produced information in every field of the economy.

ii. Information society expresses a society formation in which the information flows in a rapid pace at a global scale in every aspect of life and the trained individuals make a difference.

iii. This information is ruled by the concepts as flexibility, diversity, creativity and innovation and a network comprised of sophisticated influences.

iv. There is a massive growth and activity of information in globalization and speed.

v. Due to speed of scatter of information, specialization and multi discipline, economical value and social division are at increase.

vi. Change in the status of the information.

LIBRARY MOVEMENT IN INDIA: GENESIS OF RRRLF

The Raja Rammohun Roy Library Foundation (RRRLF) is an autonomous organization fully financed by the Ministry of Culture, Government of India. It is registered under the West Bengal Societies Registration Act, 1961. The basic idea behind establishing the foundation was to take the library movement not only to small towns and villages but also to the remotest corner, in cooperation with the state governments, union territory administrations and other organizations engaged in the library service and mass education.

When, in the year 1972, country was celebrating the silver jubilee of independence, the same year keeps an important place in the history of library movement in India due to following reasons:

i. The year 1972 was the bicentenary year of the birth of Raja Rammohun Roy, a pioneer social reformer who had stressed the need for modern education for the progress of the nation.

ii. The year was also being celebrated as an International Book Year with the slogan BOOKS FOR ALL. Emphasis was laid on promotion of reading habit among the masses for betterment of their lives.

iii. In 1972, Raja Rammohun Roy Library Foundation (RRRLF) was established by the Ministry of Culture, Govt. of India to spread library services all over the country in cooperation with State Governments, Union Territory Administration and Organisation is working in the field.

Some important objectives of the Raja Rammohun Roy Library Foundation (RRRLF) are:

- To promote library movement in the country;
- To enunciate a national library policy and to help build up a national library system;
- To provide financial and technical assistance to libraries;
- To provide financial assistance to organizations, regional or national, engaged in the promotion of library development;
- To publish appropriate literature and to act as a clearing house of ideas and information on library development in India and abroad;
- To promote research in problems of library development;
- To advise the government on all matters pertaining to the library development in the country.

The RRRLF functions as a funding body and national agency for coordinating, monitoring and developing public library service in the country. The RRRLF is vested with the responsibility of promoting library movement in the country. The RRRLF works in close association and active cooperation with different State Govts. and Union Territory Administrations through a machinery called State Library Planning Committee (SLPC/SLC) set up in each state at the instance of the Foundation. To participate in RRRLF's Programme, a State Government/ U.T. is required tc contribute a certain amount fixed by the RRRLF.

Role of RRRLF for the development of Public Libraries

i. Promotion of reading habit being the primary concern, the major share of assistance is allowed for increasing the book stock of libraries.

ii. Assistance is also rendered under different schemes towards construction of library building, and purchase of furniture, equipment, audio-visual materials and computer. A scheme of assistance towards development of mobile library service and rural book centres was also introduced in order to extend library facilities to the disadvantaged sections of the people.

LIBRARIES AND NATIONAL KNOWLEDGE COMMISSION

A library is not a building stacked with books – it is a repository and source of information and ideas, a place for learning and enquiry, and for the generation of thought and the creation of new knowledge. Public libraries in particular have the potential to bridge the gap between the 'information poor' and the 'information rich' by ensuring that people from all sectors and settings of society and the economy across India have easy access to knowledge they seek. In establishing the Commission in 2005 – the world's first such body/entity – India seized the challenge of making access to knowledge a reality for all. Implicit in this assignment is the opening up of knowledge resources and institutions, and the improvement of access and dissemination. At the inception of the Commission's work, the Prime Minister pointed to the key role public libraries can play "as an extremely important element of the foundation of a knowledge economy."

The Commission thus took it as one of its first initiatives to review library services, and to examine the present standards of public, private, institutional and specialized libraries and other information centres and resources, in order to formulate and create mechanisms and institutions that will serve the people. The Commission therefore set up a Working Group on Libraries to initiate objective review of current services and standards and to recommend the changes India needs. An honest review of how libraries now function has highlighted the need for changes in the mindsets of those who own, manage and operate libraries, starting with their perceptions of their responsibilities.

The Commission's first recommendations on libraries were forwarded to the Prime Minister in December 2006. The development of libraries and their accessibility to those in search of knowledge also implies the translation of books and information into all major languages in use in India and their appropriate conversion into user-friendly versions for the varied ages, interests, needs and knowledge levels of present and potential clients of library and information services. The Commission's integrated approach to its mandate is already reflected in its initiation of working groups and consultative enquiry on language, translation, literacy, open education and information and knowledge networking – all of which can connect to the gateways that the opening up of libraries can yield. The Commission has already submitted recommendations on language and translation, to enrich and enhance the availability of knowledge.

Terms of Reference of the Working Group on Libraries

The Working Group on Libraries has carried out a process of consultative review, analysis and recommendation under terms of reference flagging nine priorities:

1. To redefine the objectives of the country's Library and Information Services sector;
2. To identify constraints, problems and challenges relating to the sector;
3. To recommend changes and reforms to address the problems and challenges to ensure a holistic development of information services in all areas of national activity;
4. To take necessary steps to mobilize and upgrade the existing library and information systems and services, taking advantage of the latest advances in Information Communication Technology (ICT);
5. To explore possibilities for innovation and initiate new programmes relevant to our national needs, especially to bridge the gap between the information rich and the information poor within society;

6. To suggest means of raising standards and promoting excellence in Library and Information Science education including re-orientation and training of working professionals;
7. To assist in setting up facilities to preserve and give access to indigenous knowledge and the nation's cultural heritage;
8. To set up adequate mechanisms to monitor activities for securing the benefits of acquisition and application of knowledge for the people of India;
9. To examine any other issues that may be relevant in this context.

In order to reach the goal of creating a knowledge society, the majority of the people of India must be helped to overcome 'information poverty.' The knowledge deprived have to be given access to relevant and timely information and knowledge to address the roles they should play in the developmental process. It is critical that the Library and Information Services sector is given the necessary fillip to ensure that people from all walks of life and all parts of India have easy access to knowledge relevant to their needs and aspirations. Keeping in mind the fact that the stakeholders of all the focus areas of the NKC mandate will need well-organized and systematic library and information services to support all their activities, it was felt that the existing institutions and services are ready for significant change.

The Commission has therefore made the following recommendations to ensure sustained attention to development of libraries:

Set up a National Mission on Libraries : There is need of a permanent, independent and financially autonomous statutory body to address all the library-related concerns and measures that require attention if the information and learning needs of the citizens of India are to be met. To launch the process in a mission mode, the Central Government should set up a National Mission on Libraries immediately, for a period of three years. This Mission should subsequently be converted into a permanent National Mission.

Prepare a National Census of all Libraries : A national census of all libraries should be prepared by undertaking a nation-wide survey. Collection of census data on libraries would provide baseline data for planning. The Task Force that has been set up by the Department of Culture for this purpose should be given financial and administrative support to implement this activity and complete the survey on a priority basis (within one year). Survey of user needs and reading habits should be periodic at the national level as part of the National Sample Survey.

Revamp Library and Information Science education, training and research facilities : The proposed Mission on Libraries must assess as soon as possible the manpower requirements of the country in the area of Library and Information Science management, and take necessary steps to meet the country's requirement through Library and Information Science education and training. To keep the sector abreast of latest developments, necessary encouragement should be given to research after evaluating the research status in this field. Establishing a well equipped institute for advanced training and research in library and information science and services would provide the necessary impetus to this task.

Re-assess staffing of libraries : In the changed context, it is necessary to assess the manpower requirements for different types of libraries and departments of library and information science, keeping in mind job descriptions, qualifications, designations, pay scales, career advancement, and service conditions.

Set up a Central Library Fund : A specified percentage of the Central and State education budgets must be earmarked for libraries. In addition, a Central Library Fund should be instituted for upgrading existing libraries over a period of three to five years. Initial funding from the Government sector may be Rs. 1,000 crores, which may be matched by the private sector through corporate philanthropy. This fund should be administered by the National Mission on Libraries.

Modernize library management : Libraries should be so organized and the staff so trained that they become relevant to user communities (including special groups) in every respect. Also, to optimize resources, efforts should be made to synergize the strengths of different types of libraries through innovative collaboration. A proposed outline for this modernization1 includes a model Library Charter, a list of services to be performed by libraries, and proposals for a library network and a National Repository for Bibliographic Records.

Encourage greater community participation in library management: It is necessary to involve different stakeholders and user groups in the managerial decision-making process of libraries. Public libraries must be run by local self-government through committees representing users of the library.

2

The Trinity of Library: Documents, Staff And Users

For the cultural advancement of the society and world, the role of library is unquestioned. Library and information services are key actors in providing unhindered access to essential resources. The libraries are contributing effectively to the development and maintenance of intellectual freedom, safeguarding democratic values and universal civil rights. In this context the IFLA documents describe:

- A library is a means of access to information, ideas and works of imagination.
- The library experience may be the key to understanding your place in the world, the pleasure of a children's story, advice on securing a safe water supply, or the record of the healing wisdom of an elder.

Libraries are perceived by different communities and user groups as:

- place of wide-eyed discovery tool or life-long learning
- support for political and social enquiry
- bank of ideas and inspiration
- source of answers to factual questions
- place to acquire new skills
- community centre
- a place of sheer pleasure and enjoyment.

From the academic institutions to government departments, research institutes, museums, or in many different environments in the private sector, libraries are storing documents, having staff to render services to the respective users. A study states that in the area of the current member states of the European Union there are 90,000 libraries. On that basis, it is assumed that there must be well over 250,000 around the world.

DOCUMENTS IN LIBRARY

Libraries are store house of various kinds of documents, especially books. When we talk about book, we mean that a book is a set of written, printed, illustrated, or blank sheets. These sheets are made of ink, paper, parchment, or other materials, usually fastened together to hinge at one side. More describing, a single sheet within a book is called a leaf, and each side of a leaf is called a page. There are various kinds of documents in a library other than book, for example, e-books. A set of text-filled or illustrated pages produced in electronic format is known as an electronic book, or e-book. Other documents are monographs, serial periodicals such as magazines, journals, newspapers. The various types of documents are equally popular depending on the user types and their needs and purpose of reading.

There are various kinds of documents in libraries:

- **Print** - books, documents, journals, magazines
- **Visuals** - maps, photographs, charts
- **Audio media** - audiotape, CD
- **Motion media** - videotape, DVD, streaming video
- **Web** - web pages, video, audio, visuals
- **Electronic databases** - local and remote server
- **Software** - productivity tools, reference materials, instructional materials
- **Tactile** - kits, games, manipulative, stuffed toys, realia, globes
- **Hardware** - cameras, handheld devices, electronic keyboards, laptops, learning devices

There are different types of Books' sections and services in libraries such as:

Fiction

i. **Adult fiction collection :** The adult fiction collection encompasses works by all major English-language fiction writers and recognised non-English authors in translation. The library can select books on the basis of high usage by the library members are received on standing order. Also the suppliers automatically send all new titles from authors on the library's list. Usually the list is reviewed annually.

ii. **Bestseller collection :** The Bestseller collection provides quick access to the most popular, newly published books.

Non-fiction

The general non-fiction Collection aims to provide a lending collection of up-to-date and stimulating books on a wide range of subjects for the general reader.

Stack collection : Books more than 10 years old that have continuing value are moved to the Stack collection.

An example of General Documents Collection

The general collection contains books, journals, videos and other resources in many of the subject areas of interest to users, including:

- Business
- Education
- Public policy
- Social sciences
- Technology

There are other kinds of documents and collections such as:

- Online Resources
- Standards
- Civil Service Exam Study Guides
- Historical Collection
- World Languages Collection
- Services to State Government

Various Types of Documents and Their Collections

Usually the Libraries are rich in their documents collection. In addition to the physical collections, the libraries provide online access to periodicals, reference databases, and a growing number of e-books in the form of following:

Curriculum Materials : The Curriculum Materials refer the resources for students and researchers in the field of education.

Government Publications : The Government Publications collection consists of publications produced by both the central government and the state government.

Media Resources : The Media Resources are inclusive of dramatic, documentary, entertainment and educational media. This kind of collection is available in electronic non-print (audio and visual) formats.

Special Collections : The Special Collections are comprised of unique research collections, including primary and secondary resources.

The Purpose of the Documents and Their Collection in Library

- to provide, preserve, develop and promote collections in the most appropriate formats and to act as a gateway to both printed and electronic resources in an integrated way;
- to collaborate with other institutions at local, regional, national and international levels for mutually beneficial resource sharing and access provision whilst fulfilling the Library's role in areas of specialization.

Collection Assessment

Collection assessment and evaluation has been defined as:

> "the systematic evaluation of the quality of a library collection to determine the extent to which it meets the library's service goals and objectives and the information needs of its clientele. Deficiencies are addressed through collection development."

According to Greiner (2010), the approach to collection analysis you select will depend on the mission of the library. While some librarians focus their energies on analyzing the collection itself, others stress the needs of users. Let's explore these two areas of focus. A number of tools have evolved to assist in collection analysis.

DOCUMENT COLLECTION MANAGEMENT AND POLICIES

Purpose : Purchased material, is selected for the collections to support and benefit the teaching, learning and research needs of the users.

Format : Information Services preferences purchasing its resources in electronic format to ensure access from anywhere at anytime. Exceptions to this may be due to issues of accessibility, quality, suitability for purpose, and cost.

Language : When determining whether to acquire material in foreign languages, issues of accessibility, quality, and relevance to the current teaching, learning and research needs of the staff and students of the University, are considered.

Special collections : Information Services has a responsibility for the ongoing collection of all organisational publications and theses for higher degrees by research.

Formed collections : Collections of information resources that have been assembled by individuals or groups (formed collections) are only acquired and retained as discrete collections when they have a value as a coherent collection which they would not have if dispersed.

Affordable and open access to information : Information Services will support and promote affordable and open access to information and will resist unreasonable publisher and vendor price increases.

Document Collection maintenance

Retention : Material in collections is usually retained indefinitely if it is deemed to be of continuing historical or research value. Textbook material selected to support the teaching needs of the organisation is not normally retained once it ceases to be current and relevant. Reference works are not normally retained where the information is outdated, misleading or inaccurate, unless the specific edition has intrinsic historical or research value.

Preservation : Material becomes unusable in its current format is withdrawn and replaced with a usable format, where possible. Appropriate preservation measures are applied to ensure that material which is intended to be retained can continue to be used without difficulty.

PRINCIPLES IN SELECTION OF DOCUMENTS

Selection involves looking for the strengths and weaknesses in an item and how it might or might not match the needs of the collection. Literature shares the following general rules:

1. Library materials are best selected on the basis of suitability for inclusion in the collection.
2. The collection should be an unbiased source of information that represents as many points of view as possible.
3. Subjects should be covered in a manner appropriate to the library's anticipated users' needs.
4. No materials should be excluded from the collection because of the race, religion, gender, nation origin, individual preference, or political view of the author, the materials, or the user.

Fundamental Principles in Book Selection

During the 1930s, Helen Haines provided a list of fundamental principles in book selection; few of them are listed here:

1. Community : Study your community and know its general character. Without this basic information, you have little direction.

2. Current Interest : be familiar with subjects of present interest – general, national, and local. So what do you think are these current topics, whether you are in a school, public, academic, or special library? Can you be a visionary to determine what this will be before the patrons start to walk in the door?

3. Comprehensive : represent all subjects that apply to community conditions and reflect community interests.

4. All Ages & Formats : provide for all age groups whose activities and interests can be related to books. In 1950, libraries were limited to books, but this principle could be extended to all relevant media formats.

5. Anticipate : provide for actual/potential readers – existent/anticipated demand, foreshadowed by events and conditions, increasing use. Who would have predicted the demand for resume writing and other job seeking resources?

6. Demand : avoid selecting books for which no demand is evident; eliminate books that have definitely outlived their usefulness. That may sound obvious, but sometimes we get carried away.

7. Best : do not try to build a complete collection. Select the best books: on a subject, by an author, the most useful of a series.

8. Trends : keep abreast of changing current thoughts and opinions. Represent the scientific, social, and intellectual forces that are shaping the modern world.

Selection Criteria for Documents

The library's general criteria for selection should be based on the mission, budget, users, and strengths and weaknesses of the current collection:

Current Selection : This type of selection involves purchases of titles that are new or recently released.

Retrospective Selection : Retrospective acquisitions means library is filling in gaps or buying historically significant resources that it should have in the collection. For retrospective acquisitions, the library considers the following criteria:

- Research value
- Importance to the collection
- Cost of acquisition and preservation

ODLIS defines selection criteria as:

"the set of standards used by librarians to decide whether an item should be added to the collection, which normally includes a list of subjects or fields to be covered, levels of specialization, editions, currency, languages, and formats (large print, nonprint, abridgments, etc.). Selection criteria usually reflect the library's mission and the information needs of its clientele, but selection decisions are also influenced by budgetary constraints and qualitative evaluation in the form of reviews, recommended core lists, and other selection tools."

Common criteria for types of libraries

The following aspects are considered significant for school, public, academic, and special libraries:

- Authoritativeness
- Accuracy
- Impartiality
- Recency of data
- Adequate scope
- Depth of coverage
- Appropriateness
- Relevance
- Interest
- Organization
- Style
- Aesthetic qualities
- Technical aspects
- Physical characteristics
- Special features

- Library potential
- Cost and cost-effectiveness

Acquisition of Documents

i. Subjects collected and criteria for acquisition : The range of subjects covered by the collections is very wide. The acquisition policy for particular subject areas will adapt both to changes in the usage patterns. Academic libraries concentrate on the document collection according to the courses taught and related researched. So, the multiple copies of items which are identified as core textbooks are bought wherever possible and the use of e-versions of core textbooks as a viable alternative to print copies is investigated. Multiple copies are acquired using the following formula based on the number of students on the course, unit or programme for which the title is required as a guide. An example is given as:

- 1 copy for courses with 11-20 students
- 2 copies for courses with 21-30 students
- 3 copies for courses with 31-50 students
- 4 copies for courses with 51-70 students
- 5 copies for courses with 71-90 students
- 6 copies for courses with 91-110 students
- 7 copies for courses with 111-130 students
- 8 copies for courses with 131-150 students
- 9 copies for courses with 151-180 students
- 10 copies for courses with 181-210 students

ii. Language : The library takes care of language as the medium. With the exception of the specialist language and area-studies collections, the usual language of the documents collections is the most preferred one of the user community.

iii. Format and medium : Usually the documents in a library are collected in print, electronic, audio-visual or other formats as appropriate. Where there is a choice of formats preference is given to users' choice and preferences through subscriptions. When selecting material in electronic formats, technical requirements, ease of use and access and the existence of appropriate licensing and archiving arrangements are taken into account to ensure a high-quality and reliable service.

iv. Retention : Books and monographs, journals and periodicals are retained where they are:

- Required for current teaching, learning or practice
- Support current school / faculty research profiles
- Reinforce existing heritage collections or areas of known strength
- Included in a contractual or collaborative agreement requiring retention
- 1st editions

- Part of a limited edition
- Required for current and future teaching or research
- Titles which are not available electronically
- Titles where electronic access is not secure or where licence agreements do not guarantee access to archives if a subscription is cancelled

Selection Tools for Documents

To help with the process, a number of sources are available. Selection aid has been defined as:

> "a publication used by librarians to develop a balanced collection of materials to meet the information needs of library users. The category includes bestseller lists, best books lists, core lists, national bibliographies, and review publications intended specifically for librarians (Booklist, CHOICE, Library Journal, School Library Journal, etc.)."

Review Sources : Tools for review include sources that provide background information, varying points of view, critiques, and suggestions for use.

Retrospective Tools : There are a few retrospective sources such as Book Review Digest, published by H.W. Wilson and Book Review Index, published by Gale.

Tools by Library Type : for example, H. W. Wilson (EBSCO) has published a range of "core collection" tools to help librarians build a collection. These include

- Fiction Core Collection
- Middle and Junior High Core Collection
- Public Library Core Collection: Nonfiction
- Senior High Core Collection

Also the American Library Association develops an annual list of Outstanding Reference Sources "for small and medium-sized libraries".

Tools by User Type/Age : Another type of selection tool looks at the type or age of the user.

Tools by Literature, Format, or Genre : For a specific type of literature, format, or genre, for example, H. W. Wilson (EBSCO) provides support.

Tools for Academic and Special Libraries : Many of the selection tools are specific to the area of an academic library collection. For example,

- Global Books in Print (Bowker)
- Livres Disponibles (French Books in Print)

Another source is the scholarly and professional journals for specific subjects. This will be very discipline specific in terms of usefulness; however, a number of general sources include:

- Ulrich's International Periodicals Directory

- Serials Review
- Library Journal
- Choice Reviews Online
- Publisher's Weekly

There are few other selection tools such as:

- Publishers
- Authors
- Recommendations
- Patron-driven acquisition (PDA)

LIBRARY STAFF

The library is not only a building to collect the documents but also it provides services to users. The question arises, how? The library staff is responsible for management of library and its resources as well as making those resources utilized by users. The library staff has very important position in the development and maintaining the library services. It is the library staff which is the mediator between the library documents and users. They lead to users to the documents of library as well as help, support them in locating and finding the desired documents in the library as well as outside the library. Without library staff, the library cannot function.

Various Library Staff posts and their duties

Librarian : The duties of librarian are concerned to supervise and co-ordinate the work of Library system. The emphasis is on planning of book acquisition programme of the library and select books for orders. He is also responsible to develop programme of library management for improving the efficiency of the library.

Deputy Librarian : the deputy librarian generally assists the Librarian in planning of academic and professional work in the Library.

Assistant Librarian : The Assistant librarian interacts with the user and academic community in order to determine their requirements of reading materials, and acquires the same for the library. He also does various technical functions.

Documentation Officer : Performing and supervising all professional work relating to books, periodicals, electronic database and other formats of documents, collection, development, reference documentation and information services etc.

Professional Assistant : The professional assistants classify and catalogue the documents. They also help in acquiring the reading material. They provide reference and documentation services. They are responsible for preparing bibliographies and indexes. They supervise the activities of a unit in the section

Reprographic/Xerox Assistant : They render assistance to all users in reprographic work and to maintain equipments etc.

Library Attendant : The library attendant performs various duties such as:

i. Shelving of books.
ii. Preparation & pasting jobs.
iii. Shifting of books.
iv. Display of journals etc.
v. As assigned by the Librarian/Deputy Librarian/Assistant Librarian from time to time.

Role of Library Staff in Changing Times

A growing consensus suggests that the roles of librarians as well as support staff must be redefined. It has become increasingly clear that before librarians can resolve the issues of support staff, they need to put their own house in order. Increasingly, librarians suggest that the resolution of the profession's staffing dilemmas may require nothing less than a redefinition of librarianship itself. In the "Strategic Vision for Professional Librarians" document, the "visions" group of librarians has formulated a statement that redefines service, outlines innovative leadership roles for librarians, and articulates the values of the profession. The new roles for library staff are envisaged effectively in:

- The library staff develops specialized subject knowledge about the purpose of the organization.
- Relating user needs to information availability;
- Designing interconnected technical systems, organizational structures, and human interfaces;
- Flexible in adapting to new situations, systems, tools, environments
- Anticipating accepts, adapts and manages change effectively
- Managing complex technological, financial, and bureaucratic systems;
- Identifying materials appropriate to customers' requirements and their abilities
- Expert knowledge in the content of information resources and ability to critically evaluate and filter them
- Developing and delivering convenient, easily accessible and cost effective information services to the users
- Remaining knowledgeable in current events and technologies
- Selecting and organizing information resources; teaching and consulting;
- Articulating logical and intuitive insights about information; and
- Interacting with the external environment through the formulation and articulation of information policy.

To clarify the roles of all library staff, many issues remain to be resolved such as:

i. Adequate compensation
ii. status
iii. continuing education opportunities
iv. addressing the differences between support staff and librarians

There have been various factors that have redefined the roles of library staff:

i. Automation
ii. Rapid change due to ICT implementation
iii. Competition for control within the information
iv. Changing documents pattern (format, media)
v. Varied demands due to information explosion

Library Staff and the Managerial Skills at Various Levels

Library staff should exercise a unique set of skills like managers. There are various types of skills required at different positions in library:

- technical skill,
- human skill,
- conceptual skill,
- leading skills,
- planning level,
- organizing skills,
- decision-making skills.

The various positions in library staff are defined to perform different kinds of duties and functions. As one moves up in the hierarchy of the managerial positions, the responsibility increases. The fundamental functions of a manager such as planning, organizing, leading, controlling and decision-making are the skills required to be mastered by the managers. In order to exercise these functions, the library staff needs to keep in mind, the type of job, the size of organization, the skills and experiences of the people one works with and the time available at his or her disposal to do these management functions.

Core Professional Competencies for Library Staff

Professional competencies can be thought of as flexible knowledge and skills that allow the library staff to function in a variety of environments and to produce a continuum of value-added, customized information services that cannot be easily duplicated by others. Professional competences enable librarians to respond effectively and efficiently to the constant development of new technologies. Some of the unique competencies of the library staff are discussed as:

Technical Skills : In the current scenario library professional must have the knowledge of HTML, Networking, scripting languages, the ability to deal with the back-end of the OPAC, the ability to translate library services into the online medium, the ability to troubleshoot basic computer and printer problems, or just a good healthy knowledge of emerging technologies.

Ability to easily learn new technologies : Learning about new technology is definitely a skill. Library staff needs to learn how to learn about new technologies without having to ask other people for help all the time.

Time Management Skills : Time management refers to a range of skills, tools, and techniques used to manage time when accomplishing specific tasks, projects and goals. This set encompass a wide scope of activities, and these include planning, allocating, setting goals, delegation, analysis of time spent, monitoring, organizing, scheduling, and prioritizing.

Presentation Skills : Library staff should have highly effective presentation skills in this age of marketing and ICT developments. Through the presentation skills, the library staff can increase awareness of the role of libraries and librarians in promoting information literacy.

Communication Skills : Communication has a great importance in providing better services to users. Communication is not only must be effective with users only but must have ability to negotiate effectively with publishers, customers, management and vendors.

Knowledge of Policies and Procedures : The library staff maintains current awareness of professional issues impacting libraries. They also demonstrate knowledge of library policies, procedures and service standards by providing proper services to library users.

LIBRARY USERS

Library users are customers with desires, demands, wants, needs, and interests; they visit libraries to satisfy their information needs.

User characteristics reflect

Demographic characteristics, geographic location, and psychological indicators. In addition, ability, access, and interest in using technology impacts digital and virtual library needs and use.

Relation between Documents Collection and Users

The relationship between the collection and users is known by Collection mapping. It helps in determining selection and weeding needs, and justifies expenditures on materials. After examining the quantity and quality of a collection, a graphic representation can be produced to show the strengths and weaknesses of the collection. There are three basic assumptions about collections that relate to users:

1. The collection should have breadth. There should be something for everyone.
2. It should have depth based on the needs of the students and teachers.
3. The collection should be well understood in order to be effectively developed and used.

In 1981, Richard Gardner developed a list of criteria for judging materials, specifically in the selection of nonfiction materials.

- Is the item considered authoritative?
- This can be determined in part by the credentials of the author.
- Is it accurate and impartial and include recent data?
- Is the scope and depth of coverage of the item adequate for the purpose and audience?
- Is it appropriate and relevant for the intended purpose and audience?
- Is it of interest to and well organized for the intended audience?
- Are the style, aesthetic qualities, technical aspects, and physical characteristics appropriate?
- Are there special feature considerations?
- And if all these characteristics are thumbs up for the collection, what is the library potential and how much does it cost?

Applications of Collection Maps for Users' Services

Collection maps are used to show the strength for users' services: These include:

- showing strengths and weaknesses in the collection
- evaluating whether the strengths of the collection match the curriculum focus
- tailoring purchasing decisions
- planning for future directions
- suggesting areas of weeding
- demonstrating areas of need and areas of excellence
- developing short and long term goals
- building a budget plan to match curriculum goals
- creating selection procedures that material collection goals

Relation between Library Staff and the Library User

- Library staff pays attention to the need to analyze the ways in which it can more effectively carry out the role of making library resources available to the readers.
- They take care of the bibliographic control of the material.
- Library staff is equipped to ensure that aim of library is achieved.
- Library staff ensured that readers are provided with the best possible service.
- Library staff emphasizes on management with methods of improving the efficiency of libraries.
- The library staff welcomes the introduction of computer-based procedures to facilitate practical bibliographical work and thereby improve the technical efficiency of a library.
- The library staff take cognizance of the revolution of industrial

relations practices and takes interest of making their libraries happy places in which to work and therefore effective in providing the human and physical environment in which their resources could be exploited.

User-centered Collection Analysis

The user centered collection analysis is based on following aspects:

- Who are the library clients?
- What are their interests, preferences, and needs?
- What are the trends and how are the users changing?

This information is essential in making collection decisions.

Example : If a majority of the library users are affluent, there may be more demand for high-tech download options than other communities.

Example : If you reside in German speaking community, it's important to consider the need for German language materials.

Many libraries examine in a routine manner the user population trends. It is helpful in selecting documents for users as well as deigning services for the library users.

Understanding User needs

Understanding user needs must go beyond one-shot surveys and observations. It's important to have on-going, open communication with clients. They need opportunities to make requests, share ideas, and express concerns.

User-centered approaches compare the collection against user needs, interests, and requests. How is the collection being used by the library patrons? This approach is demand-driven. Analysis focuses on whether the collection reflects the needs of the library users.

Nixon, Freeman, and Ward (2010, 120) state that : "from today's perspective, the ease and effectiveness of what is now commonly called patron-driven acquisitions, or user-initiated collection development, seem so obvious. What better way to build at least a portion of the collection than by letting the users' directly expressed needs guide the expenditure of scarce collection development funds? Not only are the requesting patrons' needs satisfied, but also it is highly likely that those books will interest other patrons in the future."

Various Kinds of Traditional and Web-Based Services for Users

Using Libraries

- Borrowing Information
- Using the Catalogue
- Inter Library loans
- Pay Services
- Housebound Service

Books, Movies and Music currently selected

- Books
- Talking Books
- eBooks
- Magazines
- Newspapers
- Movies
- Music

Information and Research

- Reference Resources

Online Services

- General Reference
- Art, Music and Literature
- Business
- Dictionaries and Encyclopedias
- Health and Science
- Library In-House Services
- Newspapers and Magazines

3
Academic Library

INTRODUCTION

The academic library has been described as the "heart" of the learning community, providing a place for students and faculty to do their research and advance their knowledge. The librarians and library staff provide numerous services to the users, addressing their diverse needs, characteristics, and interests. Academic libraries serve colleges and universities and schools also. Academic libraries play vital and varied roles in the life of the university, guiding students and faculty at the reference desk, instructing library research sessions, and developing library collections.

An Academic Library is defined as: "A library which is associated or attached with any educational institution to support its educational programmes".

Academic library is an integral part of formal education system which provides time bound education from primary school level to university level. An academic library works as a base for teaching, learning, research etc.

We can categorize academic libraries in to following three categories:

1. School Library
2. College Library
3. University Library

Academic Libraries are much more than a place to read books and journals. Libraries also house advanced electronic resources, including the Internet, digital library collections, remote access to a wide range of technology and instruction. Most academic libraries focus on the following services:

- **user services** (connecting people to the information they need)
- **technical services** (ordering, cataloging, and preparing materials)

- **computer services** (maintaining library databases, software programming, web page design)
- **administrative services** (managing the library and services, negotiate contracts with vendors, supervise library employees, prepare budgets etc.)

However, with the advent of online catalogs, CD-ROMs, online databases, other electronic resources, new methods of document delivery, and access to information, the role of the academic library has begun to change. Students do not have to be physically present in the library in order to access the library's resources. With the Internet and the availability of new technologies and numerous indexes, abstracts, and databases, the range of services that academic libraries can provide has increased dramatically. Users can access the libraries' resources without stepping into the library building. They can also access other libraries' resources, such as online catalogs and unrestricted databases. The Internet has opened the resources of libraries to students and faculty worldwide.

THE SCHOOL LIBRARY

At the outset we can say that the School Library is the library provided in a school, meant for its student to enhance their learning apart from the class room teaching and learning. School libraries are part of a wider information landscape. The school library is an ideal place to learn about the way that libraries work and how to use libraries. The school library includes a wide range of genre and text types, and different media: books, magazines, newspapers, and online resources.

As stated by Jill Powell, the School libraries serve students from Kindergarten to grade 12. In the direction of defining the functions and services to be given by the school libraries, various associations have come forward. As the School Library Association, UK believes that the purpose of a school library is to provide a wide range of books and multimedia resources to support teaching and learning throughout the key stages, and foster a reading and information culture that promotes independent motivated readers and learners for life. It will be appropriately staffed and funded and accessible to the whole school community during and outside the school day. Little further, the American Association of School Librarians has various "Position Statements" on the role of the Library and Librarian. Going through the policy statements of ASLA, Australia, the Australian School Library Association has a range of policy documents on its site, including this School Library Bill of Rights.

The International Federation of Library Association's (IFLA) Manifesto states:

"The school library provides information and ideas that are fundamental to functioning successfully in today's information and knowledge-based society. The school library equips students with lifelong learning skills and develops the imagination, enabling them to live as responsible citizens" (2008).

Assumptions for School Libraries

Cooperative relationships improve library services and ultimately provide children and youth better access to information, knowledge, and learning. Cooperative relationships in the institutional settings are essential ingredients in achieving educational reform leading to improved student learning; the use of literature in educational programs such as:

i. both in reading programs
ii. the whole language approach
iii. across curriculum areas

These aspects are meant to increase the need for expertise in children's literature (through well-qualified children's and school librarians), and for rich fiction collections in libraries. Computer-assisted instruction and learning, as well as computer-based information databases such as CD-ROM encyclopedias, have revitalized the use of the school library for better access to these resources and as an introduction to information literacy skills for students. It serves the purpose as:

- In the library, students become active seekers and users of information.
- Library users are supported in their inquiry learning and the school inquiry model is displayed prominently in the library and referred to regularly.
- All learners develop and use searching skills effectively based on careful choice of information. Students and educators learn to discriminate useful and valid information relevant to their task.
- The library encourages all learners to reflect on their own learning and to challenge their own assumptions and perceptions.
- The library is a place where curiosity and creativity are encouraged.

Functions of School Libraries

Enhancing the Learning : The school library provides a model for inquiry learning and building knowledge and confidence in seeking and processing information.

Motivational : There is a large and growing body of evidence showing the impact of the school library on student achievement. The school library is pivotal to developing 21st century learners.

Support to Teaching : It is a fundamental resource for supporting students' learning, and a key support for teaching staff. The school library reflects and encourages collaborative learning and sharing of ideas.

Literacy and Reading : School libraries are places for learning and thinking, and play a key role in supporting and developing enjoyment of reading and multiple literacies.

The Role of School Library

It is well stated that, when Teacher-Librarians and teachers work together, students achieve higher levels of literacy, reading, learning, problem-solving and technology skills. The Teacher-Librarian is responsible for both initiating and participating in the teaching of information literacy in the context of the total curriculum, and managing the school's information resources and services to facilitate learning/teaching. The various aspects are as following:

- The key lies in the phrases "to support teaching and learning" and "whole school community". The school librarian promotes the Library as a whole school resource for use by everyone.
- The role of the school library is impressive as a space (both physical and virtual) where learning can happen, where information can be transformed into knowledge and understanding, where students and staff feel secure and safe and thus able to focus on the activity they have chosen "to do". Due to motivating behavior and efficient services of school librarian, the students see the library as a safe place to visit where they can find the useful information apart from their classroom teaching.
- With the pastoral role as school librarians often have very different relationships with students to those that they have with teaching staff. Also, the student helpers that many school librarians nurture gain a great deal from working with us.
- The school library promotes all kinds of literacy such as Emotional, Information and Reading. The tasks are providing a current awareness service for staff, providing targeted reading materials for classes and encouraging reading for pleasure and purpose.

(***Source :*** *International Federation of Library Associations and Institutions, Section of School Libraries and Resource Centres, The School Library in Teaching and Learning for All, IFLA/UNESCO School Library manifesto.*)

Teacher-librarians support in school environment

- Resource-based teaching and learning
- Individual and group research
- Individual and group reading, viewing and listening
- Development of lifelong learning skills
- Development of information literacy skills
- Development of technological skills
- Development of media literacy skills
- Development of the love of reading and appreciation of literature
- Implementation and enrichment of the curriculum
- Diverse needs and interests of the students

(***Source:*** *Achieving Information Literacy: Standards for School Library Programs in Canada p.24*)

Resources and Technology in School Libraries

In addition to staffing problems in school libraries, collections are often dated and lack sufficient fiction and recreational reading. At the same time, much of the funding is now being allocated to the installation of computer hardware and software. The schools have books and encyclopedias in a CD-ROM format. The national and statewide initiatives to provide youth with access to technology have had an impact on both school and public libraries. School libraries are receiving major funding for technology. In this context, the role of the school library media center can be defined as that "supports and furthers the purposes formulated by the school or district of which it is an integral part, and its quality is judged by its effectiveness in achieving program purposes."

COLLEGE LIBRARY

A college library is a library attached or associated with a college and used by teachers, students and staff of the college is known as COLLEGE LIBRARY. Commonly referred to as research libraries, they are often used by students as a quiet place for study and research. In fact, majority of students use academic libraries as a place for study, using their own materials. The same user behavior is common to most academic libraries. Since academic libraries rely heavily on collections of print material, as opposed, for example, to the large variety of video, audio, and other forms of media commonly found in school libraries, compact shelving to house growing collections is equally an important design consideration in college libraries as adequate reader seating. As a result, when planning academic libraries, it is imperative for the design team to incorporate quiet, comfortable, and adequate space for study.

FUNCTIONS OF COLLEGE LIBRARIES

To achieve its objectives, a college library performs the following functions:

- In order to help in all educational and instructional programmes of the college it develops its collection by acquiring different documents like textbooks, audiovisuals etc. related to various courses offered by the college.
- It also procures a good amount of more advanced books other than text books on different subjects to develop a habit of deep and advanced studies among college students.
- It acquires reference books such as encyclopedias and other books on each and every aspect of different subjects to enhance the understanding of subjects among students on their own besides class-room teaching and text-books.
- It prepares the students for different professions and occupations and to develop their skills. It procures self-learning material,

competitive exam books etc.

- It procures newspapers, weekly and monthly magazines on current events, general knowledge books etc. to make aware its users about their surroundings.
- It subscribes useful journals, research bulletins on different subjects as per the recommendations of faculty (teachers) for research work and to keep the teachers abreast with the latest in their disciplines.
- If some document is not available in the library it brings it on inter-library loan on demand of its users.
- It also provides light reading material like fiction, biographies, magazines, travel book guides, audio-visuals etc. to give healthy leisure time to its users.
- It procures general reference books such as dictionaries, directories, encyclopedias, yearbooks as well as some subject specific reference books.
- It makes library and its use more accessible and easy. It makes proper classification, cataloguing, shelf arrangement, display of new arrivals and provides services like bibliographical, indexing, abstracting etc.
- It provides orientation training to its new users to use the library and disseminate information time to time regarding new library services and latest books.

UNIVERSITY LIBRARY

A library attached or associated with a university and used by students, teachers, researchers, administrative staff etc. of the university as well as by the other research workers, alumni outside the university is known as university library. It is also known as the heart of university. It works like an axis of all educational and research activities in all disciplines.

According to Dr. Krishan Kumar "a university library is a part of a university set up. Therefore, it exists to serve the objectives of its parent organization. Every library programme must support university's total programme. In other words, a university library should aim to advance the functions of its university. It should reflect character of the university". He also states that the major distinction between a college library and university library that a university library lays emphasis mainly upon research. Thus we find that research is a major objective of a university library. In others words, it circulates knowledge to generate new knowledge.

University library is significant and the educational environment of academic library is characterized by the academic specificity:

- It is an integral part of university's educational system;
- It has to interact with all the educational environments of academic study programmes;
- Its regular clients (students, teachers, researchers, administration

staff) interact with each other;

- The selectivity of university library learning environments depends on the clients and the educational environment as well as research programme (it is important for students in particular).

Objectives of the University Libraries

A University Library has the following objectives:

- To provide facilities for all teaching, learning, educational and research programmes of the university
- To cater to the information needs of teachers, students, researchers associated with the university
- To provide facilities to its users for intellectual development which is a power of acquiring ideas through individual efforts
- To conserves knowledge
- To put knowledge to use for research purpose it makes extension of knowledge
- To provide latest knowledge to teachers in their field for effective teaching
- To make transmission of knowledge possible

An academic library plays a significant role in the context of this new learning paradigm. According to this new understanding of learning, a university library as a subsystem of university organization has not been a division only providing services for studies and research any longer. Instead, it has become an important unit of university's information infrastructure and an active participant in the learning process of the particular study programme. Together with the university departments and teaching staff, the academic library strives to realize the study aims. The library becomes one of the potential learning environments that function at the university. It is characterized by the abundance of information sources.

Functions of the University Libraries

The universally recognized basic functions performed by a University Library are:

- It conserves knowledge and ideas, by procuring comprehensive range of documents including books, manuscripts, journals, magazines, newspapers etc. on varied subjects.
- It gives easy and open access to knowledge to its users, by processing the procured documents with the help of classification, cataloguing, proper shelf arrangements.
- It provides facility of inter-library loan to its users if document desired by user is not available in the library.
- It interacts with different information networks to give easy access to e-sources/ data to more users so that they could access the desired information even from their workplace.

- It also provides entertainment and healthy leisure to users by providing different newspapers, magazines, short story books, fiction, internet facility etc.
- It gives the user orientation training to new enrolled users to make them feel at home and to acquaint them with the library system so that they could make maximum use of library services.
- It keeps the users updated with the library activities with the help of display of new arrivals, old book exhibitions, information bulletins about new library services etc.
- It provides reference service through reference section to establish a contact between the right reader and the right document in a personal way to attract more users.

The college and University libraries play very important role in education and research purposes of user. In year 2010, Ithaka S&R gave criteria to judge an academic library through [six] functions as below:

- "The library supports and facilitates faculty teaching activities."
- "The library helps undergraduates develop research and information literacy skills."
- "The library provides active support that helps increase the productivity of faculty research and scholarship."
- "The library pays for resources faculty members need, from academic journals to books to electronic databases."
- "The library serves as a repository of resources; in other words, it archives, preserves, and keeps track of resources."
- "The library serves as a starting point or 'gateway' for locating information for faculty research."

CHANGING SCENARIO IN ACADEMIC LIBRARIES

It is perceived that libraries now take on the key role of providing the "competitive advantage" for the parent university. In the changing times, the libraries are establishing themselves to be the learning and research centres of universities. Their transformation into the "learning building" is happening due to various factors:

i. Services and Access : Due to advent of the networked online environment, libraries are forced to exploit all forms of digital and telecommunication technologies. The academic libraries, especially university libraries are searching new ways and means to provide feasible forms of collections, services and access to library materials. their policies and planning have been centered on providing digital information services in following ways:

a. using email, Web forms or videoconferencing
b. Online reservation and renewal of library materials
c. Library automation systems

d. Web-based systems
e. Online document delivery service
f. Improvement in computer security and authentication techniques
g. electronic resources and services

ii. User Education and Research : Information Literacy and competency in fact, is giving guidance in the selection, use and evaluation of information. This can have a significant impact on student learning by:

a. making them aware of the potential for useless and inferior information available on the Web;
b. recognizing the distinction between information from refereed scholarly journals, grey literature;
c. un-refereed digital information, misinformation and disinformation;
d. resisting total reliance upon convenient information from the Internet.

iii. Resources and Collection Development : Creation of digital libraries and information portals has made the digital information available easily online. In this context, the Collection development has become an extremely complex process with the need to develop and maintain a collection that balances the various types of print and non-print materials in the library.

iv. Administration and Cooperation : Due to more emphasis on information infrastructure building, the academic libraries are reprioritizing the four main components of information organizations in the information age: software, hardware, human resources and data/information.

v. Budgeting Constraints : In the current situation of increasing costs and budget constraints, academic libraries facing the challenge of mixing traditional and IT based services to users at reduced costs. Few methods have been developed are:

a. consortia,
b. obtaining extracurricular funding for research,
c. tough negotiations to acquire the best price possible,
d. rebuilding collections paying special attention to expensive electronic information, and
e. redirecting and reallocating funds to meet current needs

vi. Staff and Training : In an environment of new technological breakthroughs, staff and staffing is an important step in promoting professional service oriented environment that required continuous human resource development plans and training.

Every aspect discussed above is significant because searching for information is one part of learning about the world of learning, and part of the experience of coming to a college or university. The efficient library environment promotes learning, now and in the future.

Common Services in Academic Libraries

In general to serve the users, the academic library offers quiet, comfortable study space and designs those services that are techniques to access the knowledge and information stored in the library. The college and university libraries offer services on the basis of wide selection of resources (print and electronic services). The libraries offer:

i. information services,
ii. literature searches,
iii. tracing and obtaining materials
iv. advising on the availability of data sources.

The library provides both demanding and anticipatory library services to the users. The services are:

i. Lending service : Books are issued to users. The numbers of books issued are based on the category of the user for specified period of time.

ii. Reference service : Reference service is provided for queries from the available reference sources.

iii. Current awareness service : This service is about the requirement of current information and this service can be provided through the display of new books in new arrivals rack.

iv. Text Book Service and Book Bank Service : Important and prescribed text books are issued for reference against the library membership card. Sometimes a library has Book bank service also.

v. Photocopying service : By photocopying service, the users are given the demanded information of the journal articles and other materials that are not lent out.

vi. Inter library loan service : Books/journal articles that are not available in library can be obtained from other libraries.

vii. CD-ROM service : The libraries provide CD-ROM service. Few libraries provide the copying of CDROMs to users.

viii. Newspaper service : Library subscribes newspapers for the benefit of its users.

ix. Online journals : Library provides online access to electronic/online journals. These journals may be provided under membership of consortium or on subscription basis.

x. Internet/Wi-Fi service : Libraries are connected with internet facility or Wi-Fi enabled and allow the users, accessing the online resources.

The services can be little bit different according to the nature of users and type of college university. For example, the services of University of Texas at Austin library are given as below:

Borrowing : Borrowing, renewing, holding, recalling, returning library materials - Appealing fines - Confidentiality of Library Records - Summer library privileges - TexShare Card Program

Ask a Librarian : Email or Chat with a Librarian - Call or visit a reference desk

Reserves : Finding hard copy and electronic reserve materials - Placing materials on reserve

Interlibrary Services : Interlibrary loan request - Location and hours of services - Research Libraries Cooperative Program - Big 12 Plus Library Consortium - Document Express

Copying/Printing : Copyright restrictions - Copy cards - Copier/ Printer locations - Price list

Study Spaces : Places to study in groups - Places to study alone - Carrels - Lockers

Instruction : Online tutorials - Library Classes & Citation Management workshops to introduce you research resources and services - Faculty services including requesting library instruction for class

Media Services : Collections of Audiovisual materials - Media services for faculty and for visitors

Request a Purchase : Request that the library purchase a book, journal, musical score, CD, DVD or any other material

UT Digital Repository : The UT Digital Repository accepts, archives, and provides access to the scholarly and research works of UT, as well as works that reflect the intellectual and service environment of the campus.

Digital Services : Protecting the intellectual property - Current and past digital projects

Sources: Library Services. http://www.lib.utexas.edu/services/

Finding information in Academic Libraries

There are several reasons why user might want to find an academic library, physically or virtually. An academic library helps the user to:

- find the full text of an article.
- find news coverage of an event from historic times to today
- find content not available free
- find a brief overview or in-depth scholarship about a subject
- look at historic manuscripts, maps, writings, and images or footage, or find audio

Designing of Academic Libraries

The academic libraries are designed keeping following factors in mind:

Space : The library should provide well-planned, secure, and adequate space for users? For this purpose the organizational Functional / Operational--Account for Functional Needs should be taken into consideration.

Building : The building mechanical systems must be properly designed and maintained to control temperature and humidity at recommended levels.

Seating : The perceptions of users regarding the provisions of spaces are important. It includes sufficient number of seats and varied types of seating.

Library Collection : Library should have enough space for the growing collections.

Workspace : There should be enough and sufficient space for the staff. The staff needs sufficient workspace to promote efficient operations.

Coordination : Library should have coordination with the branch libraries.

Ergonomics : The library must provide ergonomic workstations for its users and staff.

Electronic Access : The infrastructure of the library should be in that way that it supports the electronic access and future planning of the library. The electrical and network wiring should be sufficient to meet the needs associated with electronic access.

The planning requires attention due to growing nature of library in terms of collection and users. The libraries continually update the collections. As collections grow, storage/shelving space decreases so the solution lies in compact shelving. Storage of periodicals or government documents in compact shelving has become common practice. Most building programs now include information systems, instructional space, media storage, production facilities, and often the computer services. The main academic libraries are College Libraries and University Libraries. The college and university libraries provide an important environment for the education, research and learning by providing the opportunity:

i. to receive individual and group instruction,
ii. to study alone or in groups,
iii. to obtain assistance with assignments,
iv. to use books and journals,
v. to use computers for accessing databases and web-based resources.

Certain consideration are necessary while the college and university libraries provide facilities:

Building and space : The library building should be easy to find. The library space should be inviting. There should be adequate space for users and collections, including a variety of study spaces for different kind of users.

Library hours : The library hours should be in accordance with the academic institutions' timings and convenient to students and faculty members. They should be arranged in such a way that the users get opportunity to use the library before and after the class and lecture.

Special facilities : The library should accommodate for any disabilities or special needs a user might have.

Multimedia facilities : The multimedia production facilities should be available for uses as per their course or research requirement.

Resources in College and University Libraries

In college and university libraries, electronic information is supplementing the wealth of print and other types of information sources. The college and university library users find important information available in a variety of formats answering to following aspects:

Formats and currency : Is there an adequate collection in a variety of formats? If the collection sufficiently current?

Web based locating the documents : Is there a web-based catalog? Are there electronic tools for locating magazine and journal articles?

Electronic format : Are required readings available electronically? Are resources available electronically in full-text format?

Access : Are library resources available remotely? Will the library readily obtain and provide materials for users that are not owned by the library?

Library services support the college and university experience. These services may range from providing photocopy machines to having librarians available to assist users in locating information from a variety of sources. Therefore, variety of services are offered to enhance the user's chances for academic success.

Availability of sufficient staff to help users : The staff needs to be friendly, helpful, knowledgeable, and available when users need them.

Availability of user education : There are instruction programs to teach users how to use the library and its resources.

Computer and Information Technology : The sufficient number of computer terminals should be available. Easily accessible information technology based services are ***replacing traditional services in libraries.*** The college and university libraries allow users in certain conditions to access the library from their personal computer and also to bring their laptops etc. in the library.

Photocopying : At the reasonable fees the duplication services should be available for the library users.

How University Library is different from College Library?

One of the objectives of setting up a university is to encourage and promote scholarship and conduct research in all field of learning and human endeavour. In the university, to support the teaching and learning process as well as research, the three major infrastructure are:

i. teachers/classrooms,
ii. laboratories and
iii. libraries that contain a rich and balanced collection and equipment

University Libraries have information dissemination as their predominant function. The library has a unique position as a potential educational force. The library can achieve its aims and objectives by catering the services to the changing needs of its users. The University Library is seen as the heart of the University and no other single non-human factor is as closely related to the quality of university education. The philosophy of university library is based on:

i. The concept of service
ii. The provision of relevant materials for users.

The university libraries are busy due to research oriented services to users. Through out the year, the libraries are collecting and organizing printed and other forms of recorded knowledge in other to provide current and retrospective information. It is observed that students' use of books and libraries in academic institutions depend largely on faculty attitudes towards the library, its role in the educational process, and the way faculty promotes and encourages students' use of the library by way of their own examples as well as their teaching methods. Facilities given to users in university libraries commonly are:

- Study without using library material
- Use of library material within the library
- Types of library materials used:
  - Books
  - Journals
  - Newspapers
  - Governments Publications
  - Microforms
  - Electronic resources

To maximize the usage of university library, following measures should be taken:

- The library orientation for freshmen should be revolutionized to enable students conceptualize the use of library. Slides and motion pictures should be used to practicalise the instructions given to them;
- Librarians should work more closely with teaching faculty to make students aware of libraries resources.
- A user education programme should focus on the use of the library, advantages of reference services to students; the role of librarians and their relation to students.
- Librarians should find new ways of eliciting faculty co-operation, whose assistance and support would increase students' use of the libraries.
- Libraries should be pleasant and comfortable. The library environment should be made to be welcoming to the users.

Changing Roles of Academic Libraries

In its placement and prominence, the academic library conveys its integral role in supporting higher education's core missions of research and education.

The iconographic power of a college or university library expresses a purpose not just to collect, but also to organize, preserve, and make knowledge accessible. Today on the campus of virtually every higher education institution the library occupies a central position. Like higher education through recent decades, college and university libraries also have forged pathways to serve faculty and students more effectively due to following factors:

Dwindling between Print and Digital collection : Most university and college libraries find the real tradeoffs between print publications and digital resources. Many college and university libraries devoting more time and resources to negotiating licensing agreements with digital providers, acquiring access to important databases and digital collections, re-profiling approval plans, or implementing new software to provide federated searching.

The WWW is replacing the Real library : At the same time the web accelerates the pace of knowledge dissemination, it gives rise to changing conceptions of knowledge production and use. Data can be copied, pasted, mixed, adapted, recast for evolving purposes and new modes of understanding.

It is argued that the challenge for libraries, their leadership and staff, is to recast their identities in relation to the changing modes of knowledge creation and dissemination, and in relation to the academic communities they serve. Librarians need to reposition the fulcrum and reconceive the kinds of leverage they can provide to faculty and student productivity.

The university and college libraries have the unique potential to provide common space to strengthen academic community and foster new developments in teaching and research within the institution through:

i. Broaden the catalog of resources libraries provide in support of academic inquiry and discovery
ii. Foster the creation of new academic communities on campus.
iii. Support and manage the institution's intellectual capital.
iv. Become more assertive in helping their institutions' strategic purposes.

4

Special Library

INTRODUCTION

The research and action-research based organizations are working. The inter-disciplinary nature of research is creating much competitive environment in the library scenario. The organizations which are working in the perspective of interdisciplinary nature of research and overlapping boundaries of subject require special attention in the libraries. To manage such organization and information, special libraries and thematic, issue-based information centers have developed. We can take examples of research organizations, businesses, governmental agencies, and similar enterprises. These types of organizations have established libraries which are special in their working and service. These libraries provide information services. In 20th century with the development of industrial, technological and scientific advances the concept of special libraries came in to existence. The growing need for specialized information for further development and research came to play a vital role in the expansion of special libraries.

Definitions

According to American Library Association (ALA) glossary of library and information science-SPECIAL LIBRARY is "a library established, supported and administered by a business firm, private corporation, association, government agency, or other special interest group or agency to meet the information needs of its members or staff in pursuing the goals of the organization. Scope of collections and services is limited to the subject interest of the host or parent organization".

A special library is a term given for the libraries comprising government, NGO, health, law, corporate and other libraries that serve departments, institutions or businesses. These libraries offer information services and affiliated to the research units of the concerned organization. Special libraries are said to be "special" in their collection, clientele/users and service. The Special Library is a library maintained by an organization, as a business, association, or government agency, to collect materials and provide information of special relevance to the work of the organization.

Special libraries have been defined by Mount and Massoud as "those information organizations sponsored by private companies, government agencies, not-for-profit organizations, or professional associations." The Special Libraries Special Interest Working Group (SIWG) states that "Special Libraries cater to specific professional or academic groups whose information needs are defined by a particular subject or activity."

Special libraries have the role in:

i. supporting the information needs of its users or clients so that they can achieve the mission and goals of the organisation.

ii. providing a variety of information services to meet the needs of a specialized population, providing staff and researchers with the information they need to carry out their tasks.

As defined by ALIA guidelines (Australian Library and Information Association, 2005), "Special libraries provide a client focused library and information service. Special library staff obtains, organize and provide access to selected relevant, current and authoritative information sources for their organization.

The special libraries are found in a very broad range: agriculture, art, business/corporate, cultural, defence/military, health/medicine, law, mining, music, religion, research, science/technology and other sectors. Such libraries are highly idiosyncratic as far as their collection, users, services; queries and information processing are concerned because:

i. The special library promotes a collaborative and symbiotic relationship between research and information (i.e. between research staff and library professionals).

ii. Special library staff uses information resources and technology to facilitate effective and efficient client access to information that supports the goals and business of the organization.

iii. Special libraries may include those with collections devoted to materials on a single subject or related group of subjects (art libraries, business libraries, law and medical libraries).

iv. The special library contains all the useful things in all aspects of the organization which maintains it, and can obviously contribute to that organization's success.

v. The special library makes success with the strategic alignment with its parent organization.

vi. The special libraries work in a specialized environment.

Why a library is Special?

The special library is special due to following aspects such as:

a. Special Subject/ Field.

b. Special Kind of Documents
c. Special User Types

Special libraries can vary according to:

i. organizational structure,
ii. purpose,
iii. function,
iv. level of support
v. size
vi. parent organizations
vii. either publicly or privately supported

Objectives of Special Libraries

The main objectives of a special library are as follows:

- It disseminates updated and significant information in the concerned field;
- It gives pinpointed information promptly;
- It provides desired information to its users on demand and mostly in anticipation;

Functions of Special Libraries

The development of special libraries has been governed by the services provided; there have been significant changes in their functions. The services offered by special libraries are directly related to the expansion of research and development programs. The user oriented functions of special library specific in nature. These are as following:

- It selects and procures documents and other sources of relevant information.
- It processes the procured information or documents with the help of classification, cataloguing, shelf arrangements etc. to make them easily available for the users.
- It subscribes to a good number of journals related to its area.
- It identifies research done at other organizations to avoid unnecessary duplication.
- It assists users to locate access, store and transform electronic information resources, services and instructions across multiple applications, databases, networks, platforms and systems through special library's information commons.
- It verifies facts for external and internal reports and publications.
- It creates databases for organizations to access their internal information.
- It evaluates and compares information software and sources of data prior to purchase.
- It provides expertise in the use of innovative emerging technologies

to design and develop web- based applications, programmes and services.

- It helps in assessing, evaluating, recommending and testing various methodologies, policies, and standards for utilizing computer software in the process of creating and preserving digital collections and resources.
- It compiles bibliographies, union catalogues, documentation lists, newspaper- clippings, accession lists etc. to save the time of its users.
- It provides inter library loan (ILL) facility to the users.
- It gives user orientation training through personal interaction with users and by library brochure and pamphlets to make the users familiar with the library collection and services.

Services of special libraries

- It provides indexing and abstracting services to the users to save their time
- It provides reference services to the users by telephone, by post or by e-mail
- It gives current awareness service (CAS) regarding new arrivals and latest services to the users
- It provides Selective Dissemination of Information (SDI) service to the users as per their subject interest and requirement
- It also gives document delivery service to its users at their doorstep
- It brings out library bulletins weekly/fortnightly/monthly to keep the users up to date with latest information
- It gives translation services to provide the desired information to the users in their convenient language
- It also provides intranet as well as internet facility to the users in order to access the library collection and catalogues at their desktop
- It responds to the reference queries and make retrospective search of literature as per the users' demand

Special libraries provide *value adding services* also such as:

- building a dynamic collection of information resources based on a deep understanding of clients' information needs
- training and assisting clients to effectively access information and use relevant technology
- gathering evidence to support decision making
- current awareness of emerging technologies and best practice in information and knowledge management
- Competitive intelligence and market research for business development.

Special libraries provide few *auxiliary services* which are related to and supporting primary reference functions. They include:

- Interlibrary loans
- Abstracting
- Publishing
- Translating
- Photo-duplication services

Special libraries are changing dramatically by adopting new means of technology in all activities from print to electronic environment. The special libraries are also providing services such as OPAC system, online accessibility for 24/7, databases, e- journals, and other online services for users. As said "Information and data are essential for evidence, innovation and competitive advantage", the special libraries are playing an important role in the information and knowledge age. World wide, the special library staff is willing to consider new special services as needed. Few of them are listed as below:

Library-to-Library Book Delivery : Library-to-Library Book Delivery is a service for organizational patrons.

Document Delivery : This service is intended for the organizational patrons who may request electronic delivery of journal articles and book chapters owned by the library.

Borrow Direct : This service enables searching the combined library catalogs of concerned institutions, and directly request expedited free delivery of circulating items with some kind of user ID.

Interlibrary Loan : User can request books, newspapers, journals or journal articles that are not owned by the concerned organizational Library without charging fee. This service can be provided as Inter Library Loan.

Study Space : With the permission of the librarian, library visitors are allowed to set aside research materials from day to day in a designated study area.

Distinctive Features of Reference Work in Special Libraries

Reference service has been identified by some as the distinctive characteristic of special libraries:

Librarian as finder of information : The special librarian finds and provides the information. He does not act as a referral person. The special collections serving instructional programs may require a librarian in the role of a teacher.

Greater participation of the special librarian : The special librarian is active in the search process. The special librarian helps a user by understanding his information needs related with the purpose such as a project or experiment.

Emphasis on information : The special librarian is concerned with the information itself. Special librarian supplies the answer to a question rather than provide the sources wherein the answer is contained.

Time framework : The special libraries have the users who always face time constraints due to their nature of work. The services and information products in special libraries are designed in a way that can be provided with in the targeted time frame.

Special and homogenous users : The users of special libraries have specific subject specialization and working experience in a specific environment. The majority of members of a special library are concerned with a specific subject. The variation in the information needs is task-specific, not the subject dependent. In simple words, it can be said that there are not number of subjects (as in an academic or public library) to be served yet the specialization in a particular subject and discipline.

Involvement of subject specialists : Sometimes the libraries invite the individuals with concerned academic backgrounds in subjects to serve as literature searchers, information officers, literature analysts, or technical librarians.

FRAMEWORK OF SPECIAL LIBRARIES

Special libraries are found in various sectors such as private firms, companies, industries, hospitals etc. The special library may be of either pure research type (basic research) or applied research library. Special libraries constitute a vital link in the process of information transfer. Special libraries work in a way to heighten their contribution to the country's scientific and technological progress. The essential elements of the framework within which special libraries work:

i. The nature of their management
ii. Major activity of the parent organization
iii. Subject-specialization of the library's holding
iv. Documentation activity
v. Staff-structure
vi. Budget-provision
vii. Size of library stock, and its growth rate
viii. Weeding-out policy, etc.

Characteristics of a Special Library

The most significant characteristic which distinguishes the special library from other types of libraries, however, is that it is, as Ashworth has clarified, "one which is established to obtain and exploit specialized information for the private advantage of the organization which provides its financial support, whether the parent organization is a government agency, business or industrial company or group of companies, a nonprofit organization, private society or institution, a research association, or a hospital. Other characteristics are:

- The special library tends to be comparatively small-in the size of its collection, in the space occupied and in the size of staff in comparison with academic and public libraries.

- The users of special library are more clearly-defined community in terms of its objectives, in relation to the parent organization and its products and services.
- Special libraries provide services exclusively to their own organizations and individuals only in special conditions.
- The special library serves the users by fulfilling their information needs related to the organization's mission and development, so the special libraries serve their parent organizations.
- Special libraries ensure their continued relevancy by understanding the needs of their users such as demanded resources, types of interaction and information-seeking skill levels, etc.

These libraries usually have a focus on a specific area that may be broadly or narrowly defined. Some special libraries are focused not on a topic but on the needs of the parent organization. Sometimes few other factors characterize the special library, such as:

i. Subject specialization of personnel.
ii. Use of non-book material.
iii. Need for more detailed indexes and other aids.
iv. Characteristics of the literature and the research methodology identified with dominant subject interests.
v. Outside requests for service.

It is important that special libraries should be relevant to their users both today and in the future. Therefore, understanding user requirements is vital for their continued existence.

Special functions of Special Libraries

Though special library works in a way that resembles "traditional" library yet the functions are quite innovative according to the varied nature of requirements of the special clientele. These works are as:

- Information analysis
- Information services
- Research
- Training to users
- Records management
- Social media consultancy
- Web development / web-mastering
- And more.

Any amount of collection or existing information in any organization does not qualify for enough. The vast amount of information is present in the organizations and their libraries due to capturing, acquiring information more quickly than the past before the last two- three decades. The vast generation and synthesis of information is questioning few aspects for special libraries to consider such as:

- What skills do institutions require in order to organize their knowledge?
- How do special libraries advance the mission of their institutions?
- How are organizations embedding the functionality of special libraries into their structures?
- How do special librarians differ from other information professionals?

STATUS OF SPECIAL LIBRARIES IN INDIA

Poor infrastructure facilities, outdated mindsets and lack of exposure among professionals to the latest developments have been bottlenecks against progress in Indian libraries for a long time. Today, with the advent of both information and communication technologies and global competition, the scenario for special libraries in India is changing fast. With the emerging trends and developments taking place in special libraries in India, particularly as a younger generation of library professionals is now actively becoming involved in developing new skills and competencies in order to become more customer-sensitive and customer-centered, the special libraries aim to provide innovative functions and services. In most Indian special libraries, features are common such as :

i. Internet resources and other electronic/digital resources
ii. Subject gateways
iii. Networks
iv. Consortia

New trends in Indian Special Libraries include various activities and services given as following:

i. The development of libraries' own web sites
ii. The sophisticated application of digital technology
iii. More professional marketing of information products and services
iv. Outsourcing
v. Flexi-workforce
vi. Knowledge management and participative management

Special Libraries and Digital Information Services

The availability of digital literature not only helps the local users but provides access to their resources and thus increases the visibility of these libraries globally. The revelation of special libraries to undertake such ventures is not only helpful to establish better information availability and visibility but also to maximize its value and worthiness. Purpose of the digital projects in special libraries is to provide greater access to their collections to promote research activities. There are the open access initiatives adopted by the special libraries in National Capital Region of India and this is the outcome of the various motivating factors of using digital resources

A special library may house physical and digital resources that will be important to its users but is trending more toward the virtual. The ability for users to access materials virtually has led special libraries to use an increasing number of digital resources that can be accessed from any location to meet their users wherever they are. In the past, though the special libraries had hardware, software, and communication facilities to some extent, ICT-based resources and services were not reaching the users to the expected extent. Now with the advent of participative web, special libraries are moving away from being cost centres to being value-added units.

To survive in the twenty-first century, the special libraries must balance traditional services with the services evolving from new technologies. The small steps the special libraries take in shaping the services they deliver today will take their organization into the future. By accepting and adapting to the challenges the special libraries are becoming competent at searching and finding information. By leveraging the capabilities of electronic communication channels, special libraries are reaching to a larger audience not bound by physical space.

New role of Special libraries in present era can be seen as:

Gateways to Information : A Special library has to function as a central gateway for library users to access, locate, transform, and utilize information resources in a variety of printed and electronic formats via applications, databases, networks, platforms and systems.

Learning Centre : A Special library has to provide library users with dynamic equipment, facilities, resources and services to support their learning activities, which covers assignments, presentations, projects, research papers, reports, etc.

Training Centre : A Special library shall provide best supporting and training facilities for designing, developing, integrating and implementation courses, programmes, and workshops.

Change in time and circumstances have really metamorphosis the nature, role and services of special libraries, which calls for new services, should be focused upon such as:

Library 2.0 : The term Library 2.0 was first coined by Michael Casey in 2006 on his blog Library Crunch. The application of concepts and technologies of Web 2.0 applied to the library services and collections is named as "Library 2.0".

Tagging : Tagging is described as the process by which the resources in a collection are assigned tags in the form of words, phrases, codes or other strings of characters. This allows users to add and change the data and metadata and at times give a local flavour to the data and metadata.

Instant Messaging Reference Service : It is real-time electronic consulting and reference offered by academic libraries via specific software running on the Internet platform,

Information Commons : An Information commons is an innovative and evolving collaborative special library service model built on a variety of networked interactive academic learning platforms. Special library information commons integrate existing information resources, services, instructions.

Wiki : A Wiki is a website that uses wiki software, allowing the easy creation and editing of any number of interlinked web pages, by using a simplified markup language. Wikis are often used to create collaborative websites, to power community websites and for note making. Libraries can use wikis as a communication tool and share information, ask and answer questions, and librarians can do the same within a wiki.

Library Blog : Library blogs typical posting include information about fresh arrivals, e- databases, news and services rendered can be flashed for wider effects and it gives a platform to library users to share the information.

Library Digitization : Library digitization is the process of utilizing ICT and web technologies to electronically collect and classify and transform conventional library information resources to be accessed by users.

Undoubtedly, it can be said that Special libraries have to redefine their nature, role and value in changing world to perform its activities, services to provide state of the art services. Special libraries and staff should be the torchbearers to lead versatile information seekers and relinquish their tasks by providing right information to the right users at the right time and if possible with right personal touch.

TRENDS AND CHALLENGES IN SPECIAL LIBRARIES

Beulah Muller discusses about the trends and challenges to be faced by the special libraries. These steps range from the information explosion to the constantly changing technological advances:

i. Exponential growth in the demand for global information : The English language has become the means of global communication. China and India are world players in the world economy. Organizations in the Western world now demand accurate information on doing business in these countries, their business and social cultures and their economic and political stability. Special libraries' willingness to collaborate will streamline access to authoritative global information.

ii. The new era of global systems : In the mid of last decade, global systems have been identified as: international trade, sea transportation, the metric system, global news services, air transportation, GPS systems (e.g. Google Earth) and the Internet. Special libraries are here to play a key role in the development of global systems.

iii. Transformation from a product- to an experience-based economy : The key in this transformation is the client's experience. Not only is it their experience that is changing, the clients themselves are transforming, leading to the new trends.

iv. Transformation of the library from centre of information : With the evolution of the Internet and electronic communication channels, the special libraries become the cultural hub of the organizations.

v. Innovation : Innovation is the key to the success. Special libraries have not really been faced with the challenge to innovate. The skills and competencies demand attention such as incorporating Web 2.0 trends in library environment to reach across the globe without the restrictions of time and place.

vi. The learning organization : The challenge in the learning organization is to be at the fore-front of information provision. The special library in the learning organization must become the "clearinghouse for ideas and organizational connections."

vii. Technology : Communication systems and global network implementations have the consequence that the flow of information will break boundaries. Some examples are: bandwidth to burn, pervasive sensory networks using radio frequency identification devices (RFID), lightweight infrastructure, modular/scalable power and communication grids, and nanotechnology. Issues around stabilizing information storage and retrieval ability are growing.

5
Public Library

INTRODUCTION

Public library is largely regarded as the People's University. A Public Library is a free public library that is accessible by the public and funded through public and private sources. Public libraries are an essential part of having an educated and literate population by providing free access to information. The mission of a public library is to provide resources and services to inform, educate, and inspire. The library works to be a vibrant place that meets the needs of a diverse and growing constituency by providing library and information services. As reflected in down past and present, a public library is distinct from research libraries, school libraries, or other special libraries because it serves the public's information needs generally (rather than serve a particular school, institution, or research population), as well as offering materials for general entertainment and leisure purposes.

The public library primarily focuses on popular materials such as books, magazines, eReaders and movies, as well as educational and nonfiction materials of interest to the general public. Computer and internet access are often offered, as well as online reference, language, early literacy tools, health, and help resources. It is said "A library is not just a building stacked with books and manuals – it is a repository and source of information and ideas, a place for learning and enquiry and generation of thought and creation of new knowledge. Public libraries have the potential to bridge the gap between the 'information poor' and 'information rich' by ensuring that people from all sections of the society have easy access to knowledge they seek." So we can say that a public library is a nonprofit library established for the use of the general public and maintained chiefly by public funds.

According to UNESCO Public Library Manifesto 1949 which was revised in 1972, a public library is-

- established under the "clear mandate of law";
- maintained wholly from "public fund";
- levies no "direct charge" (fees) from its users for any of its services;
- open "for free and equal "use by all members of the community irrespective of race, colour, caste, creed, religion, age, sex, nationality, language, status or level of educational attainments;
- the local gateway to knowledge, provides a basic condition for lifelong learning, independent decision making and cultural development of the individual and social groups;
- an essential agent for the fostering of peace and spiritual welfare through the minds of men and women.

According to Dr. S. R. Ranganathan, public library is "a public institution or establishment charged with the care of collection of books and the duty of making them accessible to those who require the use of them."This definition describes two functions of a library:

- The care of a collection of books means protection and preservation of collection.
- To make them accessible in real sense so that the right person can get right information at the right time.

In other words, a public library is a social institution established by law, financed by public fund, open for all without any discrimination, for general and free diffusion of knowledge and information in the community. It is the obligation of government to establish a public library system throughout the country at national, state and local levels. Besides this, the rural and suburban areas should also be covered by branch and mobile libraries.

FUNCTIONS OF A PUBLIC LIBRARY

A modern public library performs different functions in the society to achieve its objectives and works as:

- Information Dissemination Centre
- Life Long Learning Centre
- Community's Intellectual Centre
- Recreation Centre
- Community's Culture Preservation Centre
- Instrument of Social Change
- Representative of Democracy

PUBLIC LIBRARIES AND LIFELONG LEARNING

In a society of lifelong learning - whether of a formal or informal nature- public libraries will be nodes connecting the local learning setting with the global resources of information and knowledge. Public libraries must therefore be allowed to play a role of fundamental importance in the development of future systems of lifelong learning. The development of the information and communication technology has already laid the basis for the creation of information networks, giving users even of small local public libraries access to the world wide sources of information. The public libraries also offer guidance and training in information search and quality rating of information sources. Thus, public libraries are necessary if not sufficient prerequisites exist for a democratic knowledge society. In this era, public libraries and professional librarians will though have to change and adapt to new demands, professional tasks and working conditions. At the present though, we need more knowledge about how libraries and the professional profiles of librarians should be designed in order to improve their preconditions to meet the new needs and demands directed towards them. Libraries serve at least three roles in learning:

i. Sharing the resources

Physical resources such as books and periodicals, films and videos, software and electronic databases, and specialized tools such as projectors, graphics equipment and cameras are shared by a community of users.

Responsive and Proactive Services

Human resources—librarians (media specialists or information specialists) support instructional programs by responding to the requests of teachers and students (responsive service) and by initiating activities for teachers and students (proactive services). Responsive services include maintaining reserve materials, answering reference questions, providing bibliographic instruction, developing media packages, recommending books or films, and teaching users how to use materials. Proactive services include selective dissemination of information to faculty and students, initiating thematic events, collaborating with instructors to plan instruction, and introducing new instructional methods and tools.

ii. Organization and Preservation

Libraries preserve objects through careful storage procedures, policies of borrowing and use, and repair and maintenance as needed. In addition to preservation, libraries ensure access to materials through indexes, catalogs, and other finding aids that allow learners to locate items appropriate to their needs.

iii. Social and Intellectual responsibility

Libraries allow people with different perspectives to interact in a knowledge space that is both larger and more general than that shared by any single discipline or affinity group. In many respects, libraries serve as centers of interdisciplinarity—places shared by learners from all disciplines. Digital libraries extend such interdisciplinarity by making diverse information resources available beyond the physical space shared by groups of learners. One of the greatest benefits of digital libraries is bringing together people with formal, informal, and professional learning missions.

iv. Informal learning

The public library system that was developed in the U.S. in the late nineteenth century has been called the "free university", since public libraries were created to provide free access to the world's knowledge.

Major Concern for Public Libraries

The user satisfaction is the major concern of public library because it serves people from different walks of life. The satisfaction of library users is concerned with the quality of information product(s) received, the quality of information system and library services provided to access the information product. The accuracy, completeness, precision, and relevance of the information materials obtained from public library by a user are measures of the product performance in the following ways:

i. The public library is established to provide materials, which communicate experience and ideas from one person to another and make them easily and freely available to all people.

ii. The public library is a local centre of information that makes all kinds of knowledge and information readily available to its users.

iii. The public library is established, supported and funded by the community, either through local, regional or national government or through some other form of community organizations.

iv. The public library provides access to knowledge, information and works of imagination through a range of resources and services.

v. People in all works of life use the public library resources, facilities and services. These users include pupils, students, teachers, scholars, scientists, business executives, government officials and even dropouts.

vi. In the perspectives of Information and Communication Technologies (ICTs), a public library can perform well and meet the needs of the users by embracing the use of information and communication technology.

Problems faced by public libraries

The public libraries in western countries are considered as the community centers where people meet and find the information according to their choice and requirement which is neither academic nor special in nature. Though the public libraries in developed countries are strengthened by the proper funding and user oriented services in the light of information technology with an objective to satisfy each class of user yet the performance of public libraries in developing countries has been hindered by:

i. Lack of infrastructure : The basic infrastructure and comfortable environment is foremost requirement of a public library to give the users an ambience of information service. But the lack of space, poor maintenance and lagging behind the IT oriented services are becoming the cause of decline in context with inviting the users.

ii. Lack of adequate finance : Finance is a major resource for organizational effectiveness. Since library is a growing organism, it is always in need of funds. The problem of funding is the major constraint of ICT application in libraries as well as the maintenance of the same.

iii. Unavailability of technical expertise : The changing environments demand the presence of technical expertise in context with the conventional as well as IT based services in libraries. The unavailability of such expertise inside or outside library creates problem in order to restore the system.

Minimum Standards and User Satisfaction

Public library exists to satisfy users. Hence, in recent times, evaluating users' satisfaction with the information resources, facilities and services of public libraries has become a major concern and an integral part of library and information science practitioners. This is because the ultimate aim of all libraries as a service oriented organization is to satisfy the needs of its clients. Thus, users' satisfaction with the information resources, facilities and services provided by libraries whether public or academic has become the melting pot of the present day librarianship and information science. In this regard, the International Federation of Library Association (IFLA) set the minimum standards for information resources, facilities and services to be provided by public libraries (IFLA, 2001): .

i. The information resources : include fiction books, non-fiction books, textbooks, newspaper/magazines, pictures and posters, records and tapes, audio and video, toys, CD-ROM and Braille materials.

ii. The facilities : to be provided include reading tables adequate enough for users, sitting chairs, book shelves, library space, fans, lighting, ventilation, flooring, restaurant, location of exit point, notice board/bulletin, photocopiers, vehicle parking space, computers, carrels, periodical racks, circulation desks and other facilities that would make users comfortable for reading.

iii. The services : include community information services, recreational activities, reference services, storytelling, reading competition, career information, customer care, adult literacy education, mobile library services, and services to prisoners, online internet search, among others.

The public libraries have vital roles to play in information dissemination at the grassroots to meet the information needs of each of these groups. The public libraries must be proactive, vibrant and abreast of the latest developments in information dissemination to maintain relevance and keep up with the multifarious needs and expectations of library users. It is therefore important that the public library should be able to provide the right materials to meet the information needs of users.

PUBLIC LIBRARIES DEVELOPMENT IN INDIA

The public libraries are supporting pillars to help the social, cultural, historical and scientific and technical knowledge in the public at large. Public libraries arose worldwide along with growth in education, literacy, and publications. Every country has its own public library history with influential leaders.

In India, the ancient time has witnessed the patronage extended by emperors, major capitalists, and scholars. Indian emperors and kings were supported scholars and scholarship. There is evidence of well-developed libraries even in the sixth century A.D. The famous Nalanda University in Bihar had its own magnificent library with a massive collection of manuscripts covering the universe of knowledge. Admission to library was restricted to scholars. Other ancient universities, such as Taxila and Vikramashila, also had valuable libraries. Muslim influence in India during the 13th century A.D. marked the dawn of another era of learning and scholarship. The Mughal period gave a further stimulus to the growth of libraries. Mughal rulers attached considerable importance to libraries and appointed scholars as librarians. The Mughal emperors were patrons of art and literature. In the period of Emperor Babur, Humayun, and Akbar many new libraries were established and existing ones further developed. Mughal libraries featured magnificent buildings, rare manuscripts, and scholar librarians. The names of Maharaja Sawai Man Singh of Jaipur and Maharaja Ranjit Singh of Punjab will be remembered with appreciation in the history of library services in India. The Maharaja of Tanjuar started the famous Saraswati Mahal Library in 17th century A.D. It remains a unique institution in its nature of collection and services. The Bengal Royal Asiatic Society set up library in 1784, Bombay Royal Asiatic Society in 1804 and Calcutta Public Library in 1835. Establishment of these libraries enlightened the community and may be regarded as the foundation of the concept of public libraries to the Indian people. The first significant date in the development of public libraries in India is 1808 when the Bombay Government initiated a proposal to register libraries, which were to be given copies of books published from the 'Funds for the Encouragement of Literature'.

This was the beginning of the first phase of public library development in India. During the first half of the 19th century, the three presidency towns of Bombay, Calcutta, and Madras had public libraries. The University of Calcutta was established in 1857 and its library was opened in 1873. Some of the important libraries set up in 19th. Century in India are Andrews Library, Surat in 1850, Gaya Public Library, Gaya in 1855, Long Library, Rajkot in 1856, Connemara Public Library, Madras in 1860, Government Library, Janagarh in 1867, Adyar Library, Adyar in 1886 and Dahi Laxmi Library, Nadiad in 1892. Apart from these, other libraries, like Gujarat Vernacular Society along with a library, in Ahmedabad 1848 and Barton Library, Bhavnagar in 1882 were also established. Some of the Indian states also established public libraries. The establishment of the public library at Calcutta in 1835 was the most significant. This was the library which later developed into the National Library of India. The first three decades of the 20th century can be looked on as the golden age of the Indian library system.

On January 31, 1902, the Imperial Library Act was passed and Lord Curzon transformed the Calcutta Public Library into the Imperial Library in 1906.

Contributions of His Highness the Maharaja Sayajirao III, Gaekwar of Baroda

The contributions of His Highness the Maharaja Sayajirao III, Gaekwar of Baroda towards library movement in India cannot be overlooked. He is remembered today as the Father of Library Movement in India. It can be traced back that public library movement started since 1910 in India. Borden conducted the first formal library-training programme in India at Baroda in 1911. He was instrumental in the foundation of the Baroda Library Club and its journal, "Library Miscellany", published quarterly in three languages between 1912 and 1919. The development of public libraries in Baroda was influenced by William Alson Borden.

Contribution of Dr. S. R. Ranganathan

Ranganathan published his Five Laws of Library Science in 1931, Colon Classification in 1933 and Classified Catalog Code in 1934. He also prepared Model Public Library Bill and drives to legislate library bill in Indian states.

Scholars, educationists founded Calcutta Public Library in 1835 and the same was opened on 21 March 1836 for the public. Other significant development during the period was the organisation of a host of conferences such as:

i. The first conference of library workers and persons interested in the library movement was held at Beswada, Andhra in 1914.
ii. The first All India Library Conference of Librarians was held in 1918 at Lahore.
iii. The first All India Library Conference was held at Calcutta in 1933.
iv. The first All India Public Library Conference was held at Madras in 1934.

Library Development Committee

Another remarkable development was the appointment of the 'Library Development Committee' by the Government of Bombay. A.A.A. Fyzee was its chairman. This Committee recommended a comprehensive library system. It proposed that this system should be implemented in three successive stages but it could not happen due to financial constraints. Only few part of the recommendations were implemented.

After Independence

After independence, the growth of libraries in general has been remarkable, although not as remarkable as that of academic and special libraries. At the time of independence, India was facing a host of challenges. Nevertheless, the public library scene in India improved considerably during the post independence period. Public libraries in India made a tremendous growth after the independence of India in 1947. The central and the state governments took a number of steps forward for the development of the nation from the point of education and considered library as essential part of it. During the 1951 census, there were 2,843 local governments in the urban and rural areas in India. It was found that only about one third of local governments maintained public libraries, (about 950). In addition, there were about 1,500 subscription libraries. At that time, the public libraries primarily were in the form of reading rooms with a few hundred books for reading on the premises. A big step came in the form of Delhi Public Library. The Delhi public library was founded in 1951 as the first UNESCO Public Library Pilot Project under the joint auspices of UNESCO and Government of India. It was a symbol of "Modern Techniques to Indian Conditions" and aimed to serve as a model public library for Asia. The Connemara Public Library in Madras became the State Central Library in 1950under the provision of Madras Public Libraries Act 1948, and became one of the three depository libraries in 1955. In 1954, the Delivery of Book Act was passed to include newspaper. According to this act, every publisher (in India) is obligated to deposit one copy each of its publications to the National Library in Calcutta, the Asiatic Society Library in Bombay, Connemara Public Library in Madras.

Advisory Committee for Libraries

The Government of India appointed a committee in 1957 to report on the status of public library development in the country. It is also called the Sinha Committee, after its chair, the late Dr. A.P. Sinha, who was at that time Director of Public Instruction in Bihar.

The Sinha Committee's charge included:

- Determining present reading needs, how they are met, and what part existing library systems play in meeting the needs;
- Determining reading tastes, what agencies provide suitable literature, and how reading taste can be improved;
- Recommending future library structure in India ;
- Recommending areas of cooperation between libraries and education systems;
- Considering the training of librarians and the conditions of their service;
- Recommending the administrative and financial measures necessary to support public libraries in India.

According to the report, as of March 1954 there were 32,000 libraries in India, with a little more than 7,100,000 books and a total circulation of about 37,700,000. The chief recommendations of the report were:

- Library service should be made free to every citizen of India;
- The hierarchy of public library service in the country should begin with National Library, and proceed to State Central Library, District Library, Block Library, and Panchayat Library;

- An independent Director of Social Education and Libraries should be set up in every state, with a fulltime senior class-1 officer of the rank of Deputy Director of Education to plan, organize, and administer library services;
- An All India Library Advisory Council should be constituted as a central agency to review and assess the work done at the state level;
- Library Associations should actively assist the development of libraries in the country;
- University libraries should cooperate with public library systems by allowing selected public readers to use their collection;
- State governments should accept responsibility for public library services in their states;
- Librarians and social education workers should cooperate to promote literacy;
- A library cess (tax or fee) of six paisa for each rupee of property tax should be levied with the permission of local bodies.
- The Government of India should match the amount collected in the states. State governments should also give matching grants to local bodies over the succeeding 25 years, their contribution should be raised to three times the cess collected.
- State and national governments should enact comprehensive state library laws incorporating the right of every citizen to have free access to libraries. The Government of India should provide necessary financial assistance to the state governments for this purpose.

Library Development under Different Five Year Plans

1951-1956

i. The first five-year plan for educational development included a proposal for "Improvement of Library Service." This proposal envisioned a network of libraries throughout the country, coordinated by National Central Library at New Delhi.

ii. During the first five-year plan, nine state governments, i.e. Assam, Madhya Pradesh, West Bengal, Punjab, PEPSU, Rajasthan, Savarashtra, Bhopal, and Vindhya Pradesh, decided to set up State Central Libraries.

1956-1961

i. The government allocated funds to set up a national network of libraries in its 320 districts.

ii. Most of the states established State Central Libraries and District Libraries as the main distributing centres.

1961-1966

i. The four national libraries were established at Delhi, Calcutta, Bombay, and Madras.

ii. A Working Group on libraries was appointed by the Planning Commission in 1964 to take a stock of library development.

1969-1974

During this five year plan, there was a substantial sum for the social education programme.

1974-1979

i. This plan included measures to strengthen the buildings, collections, and staff of the central and state libraries, as well as strengthening the district, block, and village libraries.
ii. A district-level library system was considered significant to act as a leader for the smaller libraries in the district.

1980-85

i. A network of rural public libraries was planned to sustain literacy and disseminate information to rural areas.
ii. Integrating school and college libraries with the system of public libraries was also emphasized.

1z985-90

i. The Adult Education Programme and the network of libraries were to play a role in the development of literature for neo-literates.
ii. In 1986, adoption of National Literacy Mission emphasised the education of women and the establishment of rural libraries.
iii. The RRRLF set up an Integrated Research Cell-cum-Computer Unit for promoting research in librarianship and database of public libraries in the country.

1992-97

i. The Central Reference Library was reorganized into the National Bibliographical and Documentation Centre.
ii. The Delhi Public Library set up two new libraries to extend its service area.

1997-2002

i. The National Library, Kolkatta, undertook several major initiatives to upgrade and modernize its collection building programme, reader services, and conservation of library material.
ii. Due to computerization at the Central Reference Library, Kolkatta, the publication of the *Indian National Bibliography* has been up to date.

Tenth Five-Year Plan

i. The Planning Commission proposed further modernization of central and public libraries during the Tenth Plan.
ii. The Commission resolved to strengthen public library infrastructure through the RRRLF.

During Eleventh and Twelfth five year plans, a lot of Govt. support has come.

FIVE LIBRARIES OF NATIONAL IMPORTANCE

The following five libraries were regarded as national importance and may be stated in a very brief manner:

1. National Library, Kolkata

The National Library at Kolkata was established in 1836 in the name of Calcutta Public Library. Prince Dwarkanath Tagore was the first proprietor of the Calcutta Public Library. Both the Indian and foreign books, especially from Britain, were purchased for the library. The Calcutta Public Library had a unique position as the first public library in this part of the country. Such a well-organized and efficiently run library was rare even in Europe during the first half of the 19th century. Because of the efforts of the Calcutta Public Library, the National Library has developed rare books and journals in its collection.

The Imperial Library

The Imperial Library was formed in 1891 by combining a number of Secretariat libraries. But the use of the library was restricted to the superior officers of the Government. Lord Curzon, the then Governor General of India, was the person who conceived the idea of opening a library for the use of the public. He noticed both the libraries, Imperial Library and Calcutta Public Library, were under-utilized for the want of facilities or restrictions. So, he decided to amalgamate the rich collection of both of these libraries. He was successful in effecting the amalgamation of Calcutta Public Library with the then Imperial Library under certain terms. The library, called Imperial Library, was formally opened to the public on 30th January 1903 at Metcalf Hall, Kolkata. The aims and objectives of the Imperial Library, well defined in a Notification in the 'Gazette of India' as:

It is intended that it should be a library of reference, a working place for students and a repository of material for the future historians of India, in which, so far as possible, every work written about India, at any time, can be seen and read.

After the independence the Government of India changed the name of the Imperial Library as the National Library, with an enactment of the Imperial Library (change of name) Act 1948 and the collection was shifted from the Esplanade to the present Belvedere Estate. On 1st February 1953 the National Library was opened to the public, inaugurated by Maulana Abul Kalam Azad. Sri B.S. Kesavan was appointed as the first librarian of the National Library.

The reviewing Committee in its report of 1969 suggested that the following should be the basic features of the National Library :

- Acquisition and conservation of all significant printed materials produced in the country to the exclusion of ephemera;
- Collection of printed materials concerning the country wherever published and also acquisition of photographic record of such materials that are not available within the country;

- Acquisition and conservation of manuscripts having national importance;
- Planned acquisition of foreign materials required by the country;
- Rendering of bibliographical and documentation service of retrospective materials, both general and specialized;
- Acting as a referral centre purveying full and accurate knowledge of all sources of bibliographical activities;
- Provision of photocopying and reprographic services; and
- Acting as the centre for international book exchange and international loan.

2. Khuda Bakhsh Oriental Public Library, Patna

Khuda Bakhsh Oriental Public Library, Patna was open for the public in October 1891. It had 4000 Oriental manuscripts. Maulvi Khuda Bakhsh donated his entire collection to the nation by a deed of trust. In the year 1969, Govt. of India declared the Library as Institution of National Importance by an act of Parliament. It has the immense historical and intellectual value of its rich and valued collection. The Library is now fully funded by the Ministry of Culture (Govt. of India).

3. Rampur Raza Library, Rampur

Rampur Raza Library, Rampur was founded by Nawab Faizullah Khan in 1774 AD. Nawab Faizullah Khan who ruled the state of Rampur, from 1774 to 1794, established the library with his personal modest collection kept in the Tosha Khana of his Palace. It was brought under the management of a Trust. Later on the Government of India took over the library on 1 July 1975 under the Act of Parliament, which declared it as an institution of National importance. It contains very rare and valuable collection of manuscripts, historical documents, specimens of Islamic calligraphy, miniature paintings, astronomical instruments and rare illustrated works in Arabic and Persian languages besides 80,000 printed books. The Library occupies the position of an autonomous institution of national importance under Department of Culture, Government of India and is fully funded by Central Government.

4. Thanjavur Maharaja Serfoji's Sarasvati Mahal Library, Thanjavur

Thanjavur Maharaja Serfoji's Sarasvati Mahal Library, Thanjavur contains very rare and valuable collections of manuscripts, books, maps and paintings on all aspects of Art, Culture and Literature. This library is one among a few medieval libraries existing in the world. The Encyclopedia Britannica in its survey of the Libraries of the world mentions this as "the most remarkable Library in India". This library has been conceived and christened as the Royal Palace Library by the Nayak Kings of Thanjavur (1535-1675 AD). This Library was made as a public Library in 1918. A body constituted by the Government and financed by the Central and State Governments now administers the library.

During the reign of Nayaks of Thanjavur (1535-1675 A.D.), "Sarasvati Bhandar" (Collection place of Manuscripts) was formed and developed. The Sarasvati Bhandar was situated within the Palace campus and the Manuscripts used for the purpose of reading by the Royal personages. Among the Maratha Kings, King Serfoji II (1798- 1832), was an eminent scholar in many branches of learning and with great enthusiasm he took special steps for the enrichment of the Library. The Library is named after Serfoji. The Government of Madras in their G.O. Ms. No.1306 Home (Education) dated 5th October 1918, took possession of the Library under the Charitable Endowment Act and framed scheme for the Library management. In 1983, the Library was declared as an Institution of National Importance. The Government of Tamil Nadu made it as a Registered Society as per G.O. 209 (EST) dated 1-2-83 under the Tamil Nadu Registered Societies Act of 1975.

5. Harekrushna Mahtab State Library, Bhubaneswar

Harekrushna Mahtab State Library, Bhubaneswar was conceived during 1st Five Year Plan under the advice of Government of India. It was completed in 1959, enshrined within a beautiful land of 3 acres in a prime location of Capital City of Bhubaneswar. In 1967, it was named as Gandhi Bhawan commemorating birth centenary of Mahatma Gandhi. In 1987 the four storied building was renovated and decided for the functioning of State Library for the entire State of Orissa and another Public Library for Bhubaneswar City. In 1987, Government decided to rename the State Library and the Public Library as Harekrushna Mahtab State Library (in memory of Dr. Harekrushna Mahtab, the builder of modern Orissa) and the Bhubaneswar Public Library respectively. The former is a Reference Library and lending of books is not permitted whereas the latter is a Lending Library for the public of Bhubaneswar City.

MODEL PUBLIC LIBRARIES BILLS

1. Model Public Libraries Act of Dr. S R Ranganathan

The first Model Public Libraries Acts was prepared by Dr. S R Ranganathan in 1930. it was revised in 1957 and 1972. It was discussed at the First All Asia Educational Conference held at Banaras during 26-30 December 1930. It was introduced in West Bengal Legislature in 1931 and in Madras Legislature in 1933. Salient features of final version of this Bill are:

- Establishment of public libraries in city, rural and other areas;
- Constitution of State Library Authority i.e. Minister of Education;
- Constitution of State Library Committee as an advisory body of the State Library authority;
- Constitution of Local Library Authority for each city and one for each district;
- State Library Authority, Government and Local Library Authority may determine library rate in such a manner and may determine

collection of library cess from time to time.

2. Model Public Libraries Bill of Ministry of Education

The Government of India, Ministry of Education appointed an Advisory Committee for Libraries in 1957, under the Chairmanship of Shri K P Sinha. This committee recommended the need for library legislation for each state. Also another Committee was constituted by the Ministry of Education, Government of India under the Chairmanship of Dr. M D Sen. This Committee drafted Model Public Libraries Bill in the year 1963. The salient components of this Bill are:

- Constitution of State Library Authority as an apex body to advise the Government in the matter of library developments;
- Constitution of State Library Directorate for direction and controlling of library services;
- Constitution of District Library Committee in each district;
- Treatment of employees as government servant;
- Collection of library cess at the rate of 6 paise per rupee on house tax and property tax.

3. Model Public Libraries Bill of the Planning Commission

The Planning Commission, Government of India, constituted a 'Working Group on Libraries' in 1964 to plan and advice on the development of Libraries during the Fourth Five Year Plan. The Working Group recommended a Library Development Scheme to be implemented during the Fourth Plan period. The Bill included the following features:

- Establish, maintain, develop and integrate adequate public library service in the state;
- Constitution of Committee of Experts to prescribe the standards of service;
- Constitution of State Library Council to advise the government for the promotion and development of library service;
- Establishment of State Library Directorate to control, direct and supervise library system in the state;
- Establishment of State Central Library, State Regional Libraries and District Libraries;
- Treatment of employees in the system of State Government Servants;
- Government shall be the financial source and shall maintain the public library system in the state.

4. Model Public Libraries Bill of Indian Library Association

The Indian Library Association (ILA) formed in 1933. the ILA has keen interest in library legislation and it discussed library legislation at its various seminars organized in 1964, 1978 and 1981. Consequently, ILA Council at its meeting held on 23 June 1989 resolved to prepare a Model Library Bill. The Central Sectional Committee on Public Libraries of the ILA prepared a Model Public Library Bill. The final product of the Model Public Libraries

Bill was published in 1991. The bill was revised as the Model State Public Library and Information Service Act in 1995. In view of emergence of Information Technology at all levels, the model act was again revised in 2000. The important components of this Bill are:

- State Library and Information Service, based on a State Policy;
- Constitution of State Library Authority at the apex level with Minister of Libraries as Chairman as policy making and executive body;
- Establishment of Directorate of Public Libraries for directing, controlling and supervising;
- Constitution of City, District Library Authority for rendering service from district to village level;
- Provision for network of Public Library and Information Services from state to village level;
- Constitution of State Library and Information Service;
- Collection of Library cess on house tax and property tax, entertainment tax, professional tax, vehicle tax, etc.;
- Constitution of State Boards for education, book production, co-ordination, etc.;
- Accountability of public expenditure and services.

5. Model Union Library Act

Keeping in view the development of libraries in the entire country, the Government of India appointed a committee to explore the possibilities to establish a National Central Library at New Delhi in 1948. Dr. S R Ranganathan drafted a Library Development plan in 1950 with a 30-year programme. He also drafted a Library Bill for the states and Union Public Library Act. This was revised in 1959 and again in 1972. The main features of this model Act are:

- Constitution of a National Library Authority;
- Establishment of national central libraries;
- Constitution of National Library Committee as an advisory body to the National library Authority;
- Constitution of National library fund;
- Amendment to the delivery of Books and Newspaper Act, 1954.

Each and every effort at the national and the state level has been taken keeping the model public libraies in mind. When we go through the IFLA/UNESCO Public Library Manifesto 1994, we come to know that, "The public library is the local center of information, making all kinds of knowledge and information readily available to its users". (IFLA/ UNESCO;1994) Public libraries, to become an enthusiastic source of information and knowledge for the local community, needs certain forms of developments in terms of infrastructure, collection and the trinity of library as well. It cannot survive by the local contributions and dedication alone, but through the support of government. "The pubic library, as a democratic institution operated by the people for the people, should be established and maintained under the clear authority of law; supported wholly or mainly from public funds; open for free use on equal terms to all members of the community regardless of occupation, creed, class or race".

Though the govt. of India has taken a number of initiatives yet a lot is required to be done to make the public libraries as efficient as other public libraries are in the world.

6
National Library

INTRODUCTION

National libraries are libraries that "offer a national service (to the nation's libraries or population)". The national library involves the erection, equipping, stocking, servicing and staffing of branch or affiliated libraries serving communities throughout the country, including one or more of the following: public, school, hospital and prison libraries, and the special libraries serving the legislature and government departments and agencies.

Definitions

A National Library keeps all documents of and about a nation under some legal provision and thus represents publications of and about the whole nation. The national library is considered one of the most important cultural institutions in a country.

For example:

- British Library-London,
- Library of Congress- Washington,
- The Russian State Library-Moscow,
- The Bibliotheque Nationale-Paris.

The UNESCO defines:

Libraries which, irrespective of their title, are responsible for-

i. Acquiring and conserving copies of all significant publications published in the country;
ii. Functioning as a 'depository' library, whether by law or under other arrangements.

And it performs the following functions also:

i. producing a national bibliography;
ii. holding and keeping up to date a large and representative collection of foreign literature, including books about the country;

iii. acting as a national bibliographical information centre;
iv. compiling union catalogues;
v. publishing the retrospective national bibliography.

This definition states that libraries which may be called 'national' but whose functions do not correspond to the above definitions should not be placed in the 'national libraries' category. A national library service can therefore be defined as follows:

National library service: an institution, primarily funded (directly or indirectly) by the state, which is responsible for providing library services of one or more kinds to communities of defined types throughout the country through a network of branch (constituent) or affiliated libraries and service points.

The National Libraries may be categorized as:

- **By comprehensive functions :** National Library of India, Kolkata.
- **By subject :** National Medical Library, Delhi.
- **By special user group served :** National Library for the Blind, U.K.
- **By type of material :** The Saraswati Mahal Manuscript Library, Tanjore.

RESPONSIBILITIES OF A NATIONAL LIBRARY

National libraries have special responsibilities. As discussed in literature, these responsibilities are defined in law of a nation's library and information system. The responsibilities may vary but more or less these responsibilities are inclusive:

i. The collection via legal deposit of the national imprint (both print and electronic) and its cataloguing and preservation
ii. The provision of central services (e.g., reference, bibliography, preservation, lending) to users
iii. The preservation and promotion of the national cultural heritage
iv. Serving as a national forum for international programmes and projects
v. Establishing a close relationship with national governments for the development of national information policies
vi. Serving the information needs of the legislature directly
vii. Acquisition of at least a representative collection of foreign publications
viii. The promotion of national cultural policy
ix. Leadership in national literacy campaigns

Objectives

A National Library works with the following objectives:

i. It procures nation's all literary output under legal provision as well the foreign literature about that nation;

ii. It works as a depository house for the said heritage by preserving it;

iii. It disseminates information about the stored and procured literary wealth through different publications and services;

iv. It works as a national referral and bibliographic exchange centre;

v. It coordinates with the other libraries in a country to develop a national library system.

Functions of National Libraries

The functions of national libraries are governed by the purposes of their establishments such as:

i. Housing the collection : The first role of a national library is to house the collection of the most important works in that country.

ii. National Bibliographic Control : The second purpose of a national library is national bibliographic control. The bibliographic control is done by mandatory or legal deposit laws. The publishers are legally required to submit copies of copyrightable materials to the national library.

iii. International Bibliographic Control : The international bibliographic control facilitates the location and acquisition of information by foreign users.

iv. National referral centre : It works as a national referral centre of authentic information for all literary work of the country and responds to all national and international queries from individuals as well as from private and government organizations.

The other significant functions are as following:

- The National Library acts as the central library of the state.
- The National library protects national heritage preserved in the form of handwritten, printed, electronic, recorded sound and audiovisual documents.
- It also exchanges data and documents at national and international level.
- The primary task of the National Library is to acquire, store and permanently archive the intellectual output of a nation, whether the works of citizens living in nation, the most important foreign works, or publications related to the nation and published abroad.
- It works as an apex body of the national library system and coordinates with other libraries in the country.
- The national Library is also responsible for a number of tasks that are of crucial importance to a nation's culture.
- It serves as the chief archive of national literary output. It freely collects copies of all published material in the country under legal provision or by law.
- It functions as centre of preservation and conservation. It procures and preserves manuscripts.

- It works as a national depository library for all literary work published in the country.
- It also procures foreign publications about the country; and by the authors of state origin living abroad.
- The national library functions as a national bibliographic agency
- It compiles national bibliographies to disseminate information about literary output of the country. It develops and maintains different bibliographic data bases and works as a national bibliographic centre.
- It produces national union catalogues, current, retrospective and subject bibliographies.
- It provides reading, lending, consulting facilities to researchers, writers and other users.
- It also keeps photocopy collection of available documents for national and international library lending.
- It makes provision for practical training of library professionals.

National services

In many countries, library services of national library that are national in scope (e.g. serving the nation at large) are rendered by institutions that are not national libraries. Such services could be primarily targeted at libraries, for example a bibliographic utility, or at particular groups in the population at large, for example books for the blind or the provision of multiple copies of plays for play -reading and drama groups. The importance of traditional national library functions is recognized with the following scope:

- Services to other libraries;
- Leadership in developing, coordinating, and maintaining an integrated national information system;
- Legal depository and national bibliographic centre roles; and
- Responsibility for the promotion of training and continuing education programmes.

LEGISLATION FOR NATIONAL LIBRARY

National libraries are distinguished as a particular type of library yet they differ greatly from one another in respect of their origins, functions and status in their respective countries. It is difficult to determine the common elements which are responsible for defining and categorizing a library as a national library. The requirement of appropriate legislation for national library establishment and services has been considered significant:

Relationship with the state : The relationship with the state is concerned with:

i. Clarifying the aims and functions of the national library vis-à-vis the state.

ii. Aiming for functions and survival to be dependent on mere administrative decisions
iii. Management of the national library for its enacted aim and statutory functions
iv. Stable basis for an adequate and reliable flow of funding.

Authority : Authority is concerned with the national library's relationships with other libraries and institutions. The national library needs statutory recognition which gives it the necessary authority vis-à-vis other libraries for the functions such as:

i. Cooperation with other institutions
ii. Initiating, coordinating national library and information programmes
iii. Encouraging standardization
iv. Carrying out national and international liaison tasks

Autonomy : A greater degree of autonomy for the national library is concerned with its management in:

i. Determining priorities and allocating resources in a flexible way in response to changes taking place in the library's environment.
ii. Establishing political will for adequately support to empower a country's national library.

NATIONAL LIBRARY OF INDIA

The national Library of India has its own magnificent journey. This has been an outcome of efforts at various levels. The website of the National Library of India is rich with the background information of its origin and establishment etc.

Calcutta Public Library (CPL)

Calcutta Public Library was established in 1836. Being a non-government institution, on proprietary basis it was functioning its establishment. The then Governor General, Lord Metcalf transferred 4,675 volumes from the library of the College of Fort William to the Calcutta Public Library. Also both Indian and foreign books, were purchased for the library. The collection augmented by donations received from individuals and from the Government of Bengal and North Western Provinces. Calcutta Public Library had a unique position as the first public library in this part of the country.

The Imperial Library

The Imperial Library was founded in 1891 by combining a number of Secretariat libraries. Of these, the most important and interesting was the library of the Home Department, which contained many books formerly belonging to the libraries of East India College, Fort William, and the East India Board in London.

Amalgamation of CPL and Imperial Library

Lord Curzon, Governor General of India is usually credited with the idea of opening a library in Kolkata for public use. He decided to merge the collection of Calcutta Public Library with that of the Imperial Library, subject to certain terms. The new library, called Imperial Library, was formally opened to the public on 30th January 1903 at Metcalf Hall, Kolkata. The aims and objectives of the Imperial Library were well defined in a Notification in the *Gazette of India*: 'It is intended that it should be a library of reference, a working place for students and a repository of material for the future historians of India, in which, so far as possible, every work written about India, at any time, can be seen and read.

The National Library

After Independence the Government of India changed the name of the Imperial Library to the National Library, with the enactment of the Imperial Library (Change of Name) Act, 1948. On 1 February 1953, the National Library was opened to the public, inaugurated by Maulana Abul Kalam Azad. B. S. Kesavan was appointed the first Librarian of the National Library.

Collection

The collection of national library is vast and categorized as following:

Indian Languages Collection : The National Library receives books and periodicals in almost all Indian languages. These are received under the Delivery of Books and Newspapers (Public Libraries) Act 1954 (D.B. Act). Language divisions acquire, process and provide reading materials in all major Indian languages. The library has separate Indian language divisions for Assamese, Bengali, Gujarati, Hindi, Kannada, Kashmiri, Malayalam, Marathi, Oriya, Punjabi, Sanskrit, Sindhi, Tamil, Telugu and Urdu. Sanskrit language division also collects and processes Pali and Prakrit books. English books published in India are collected under D.B. Act.

Rare Books : In 1973, a separate Rare Books division was established in the library. At present the books published prior to 1860 are considered rare books, along with limited and first editions, books distinguished by their design, illustration or history, and a few other criteria.

Science and Technology Collection : As per the recommendations of the Reviewing Committee (1968), the Science and Technology division was set up in 1972. The basic function of this division is to collect and disseminate the core material in science and technology.

Indian Official Documents : The library owns a rich collection of Indian official documents from the days of the East India Company to the present. The collection also includes the documents published by the Government of Great Britain relating to India. All the publications of Government of India, State Governments, Union Territories, Government Undertakings, Autonomous Bodies are collected, processed and preserved separately in a separate division for this purpose, established in 1972. At present, the division holds around 4, 90,000 documents.

Foreign Official Documents : The National Library is one of the repository libraries for United Nations Organisation and its agencies. The library also receives publications of the governments of the United States of America, Great Britain, Canada, the Commonwealth nations, and the publications of the European Economic Committee.

Newspapers and Periodicals : All the newspapers and periodicals in Indian languages are received and processed in their respective language divisions. But English newspapers and periodicals, both the Indian and foreign, are acquired and processed separately. The library has a rich collection of late 19th and early 20th century newspapers and periodicals.

Manuscripts : National Library has about 3600 rare and historically important manuscripts in different languages. The xylographs presented by H. E. the Dalai Lama are also preserved in this collection.

Services

a. Lending Services

Local Membership : A local member can avail the facility of limited number of books. The Lending division provides the membership facilities. The division also provides reading facilities to the users who wish to consult these items. At present the division has 4700 monographs, 3000 manuscripts and 1500 microfilms.

Outstation Membership : Outstation memberships are also provided. Outstation members can borrow the books through post.

b. Inter Library Loan

Selected libraries of the country and abroad may borrow the books from the National Library through the inter library loan facility. The National Library also borrows books from other libraries on reader's requests, if the book is not available in the library.

c. Bibliographic Services

Bibliographic services are available to research scholars, Government agencies, universities and national level institutions may make use of this facility. On request, selected and special bibliographies are provided. The library provides support to the Central Reference Library, Kolkata, in compiling the Indian National Bibliography.

d. Reprographic Services

Reprographic services are available on payment basis. The photocopies, microfilms and microfilms printout / photocopy are provided within the limits of the International Copyrights Act.

e. Services for Children

The National Library has a separate division for children without a formal membership procedure. Equipped with books in English, Indian and a few foreign languages, the division provides children with reading material for information and fun.

f. Modernization Activities

To modernize the library and its services, the Computer division was established in 1988. At present a Campus Wide Network is being developed with 98 HP Pentium III PCs as nodes.

g. Digitization

The digitization of rare and brittle books and other documents is on progress. English books and documents published before 1900 and Indian publications of pre-1920 are considered for digitization.

7

Five Laws of Library Science

The Five laws of Library Science were given by Dr. S. R. Ranganathan in 1931. These laws provide the very purpose of use of libraries and their place in the state and society. For a number of libraries, these laws functioned as the inspirational and foundational goals. The five laws are as following:

1. Books are for use.
2. Every reader his/her book.
3. Every book its reader.
4. Save the time of the reader.
5. The library is a growing organism.

FIRST LAW: BOOKS ARE FOR USE

The first law has the message of using the books for the readers. Books are to be taken care but not hurting the sentiment of use of them. In the past when books were stored in closed almirahs and the libraries were the custodians with a purpose to preserve them. The first law of library science also puts forth an obvious and elemental principle. But even so, it is a law that is often violated in the practice and use of libraries. Medieval libraries, as an extreme example, were chained libraries. The first law constitutes the basis for the library services. The emphasis should be on use of the books rather storage and preservation. Due to developments in society, and industries world wide, the perception changed from preservation to maximum utilization of books i.e. library resources. Now the policies and services of libraries are designed in a way that books must be available for use of the readers without any hindrance. This first law gives definition both to the concept of an open stack library and to a library that is appointed with tools and furnishings that make the books it contains useful. This law dictates the development of systems that accommodate the use of library materials. For instance, proper and regular shelving of library materials facilitates the use of books. Logical, topical arrangement of materials also facilitates their use. The following aspects are related with the first law:

a) Location of the Library : The library should be located at a possible central place approachable to each and every reader of the library so that the opportunities can be maximized. The other factors such as noise and other disturbances should be avoided. Thus for implication of this law, is the easy accessibility of the library to its users. The first law is forward-thinking in its emphasis on the library's location. Increasingly we are seeing libraries sited, or even relocated, in more accessible locations in order to increase custom.

b) Library Working Hours : The library working hours should be convenient to users and the timings of library hours should be in according to their working and leisure hours so that the users can visit library.

c) Library Building and Furniture : The library building should be designed to be functional. The furniture should also be functional, attractive and comfortable which does not hinder the purpose of first law. The library building should be attracting. The library should be well organized and decoration such a way so that it could fascinate the readers or users. There should be proper lighting and ventilation, neat and clean environment

d) Staff : The staff should be qualified so that they can organize the library efficiently and provide satisfactory services. The qualifications and willingness to serve works in the direction of ensuring the proper use of books. Staff should be congenial towards the readers and should always be ready to help the readers. The staff should be courteous, cheerful and helpful. The libraries serve the users who are considered as customers so the motto *Service with a smile* should be kept in mind.

- **Services, usages and accessibility :** For the greatness of a library not only the collection but also its services, usages and accessibility are important. The Library schedule must be convenient to the reader. Sometimes a library can be opened on holidays.
- **Publicity :** The librarian should give fair publicity about the services offered, as well as new addition to the library so as to inform his/her clientele.
- **Equipment :** The library equipments are also important in the readers' services. The neat and clean equipments are must. The book-racks should not be so high. The chairs and tables should be suitable for continuous reading in the reading hall.
- **Open access :** Access to the library shelf should be unrestricted so that the readers can go to the shelves and pick out the book most suitable.

The first law is concerned with the use of books which is directly related with the access-related issues. The library's location, loan policies, hours and days of operation, as well as library furniture and the quality of staffing play very important role. The implication of first law of library science in marketing library is the emphasis on the optimum use of resources, facilities, and services. Convenient location, effective signage, and longer opening hours; helping hands for using resources and services are all important.

The first law means that books in libraries are meant to be used, not to be shut away from people. In order to ensure the books for use, we normally keep in view, the location of library, library hours, library building and furniture and equipment, qualified and trained staff. Now the books have been replaced by different types of documents in modern forms. In order to ensure the use of these varieties of documents, necessary news and latest equipments have also been developed. A special training is also being given to specifically train the staff to handle these gadgets. Special types of furniture have been evolved, and modular construction of the library building is being emphasized. Even then the basic concepts remain the same. Whatever steps may be taken to ensure the use of these documents, their usage is most important and hence, the First Law still holds good.

The following practices and aspects oppose the first law:

- Maintaining special collections with limited access
- Storing materials off-site; restricting access to libraries based on memberships, fees, or even by selecting materials under contracts that limit use to particular classes of patrons
- Eliminating print resources in favor of an electronic version of the material that is only accessible to certain patrons.

SECOND LAW: EVERY READER HIS OR HER BOOK

The second law : Every reader his/her books says that every reader of the library should get the book he or she wants. This law is concerned with the universality and democratization of library service irrespective of class and creed. This law suggests that every member of the community should be able to obtain materials needed. Dr. Ranganathan felt that all individuals from all social environments were entitled to library service. He opined that the library staff and library collections should meet the special interests of the community. To reach to every reader, the libraries should promote and advertise their services extensively to attract a wide range of readers.

The advent of democracy and other societal changes paved the way for library services becoming a basic right of all citizens without any distinction. A variant form of this law also is Books are for all. One of the library's primary obligations is to acquire a body of literature or research materials that will benefit each of its readers and researchers. A library must formulate policies that ensure that the collection it is building and maintaining is adequate to fulfill the expectations of its community of users.

In other words, the collection must be appropriate to the library's mission. Similarly, policies must be formulated to ensure that the library has an access policy that is appropriate. Any library that limits access in any way must ensure that this restriction does not prevent adequate access to the collection by the people that the library was created to serve. Access policies also have implications for interlibrary loan, cooperative acquisitions, and consortia to which the library may belong. The second law means that we all have diverse interests and that there is a book out there to satisfy each of us. The core need is to fight for the right of users to information of all kinds, the consistent battle against censorship and inequality of access that has governed civilization since its inception. This law has certain obligations on the State, Library Authority, Library Staff and the Readers of the Library.

i. Obligation of the State : The government of the State should develop and maintain a library system. The obligation of state is very supportive so that all the people may get adequate library services. The establishing library legislation in the State provides for the financial support and laying down rules for proper functioning of libraries. The legislation should be so framed that it would serve as an effective means for achieving the goal.

ii. Obligation of Library Authority : There are two main functions of authorities in libraries. The choice of books and the choice of the staff are two concern of obligation of library authority. The selection of books in the view of shrinking budgets and lack of funds becomes very crucial. Ascertaining the readers' choice and demand of books is significant to frame the policy of book selection and acquisition. To serve the readers effectively, an adequate and competent team of staff is essential. The staff helps in organization of books as well as helps in locating books for the readers.

iii. Obligation of the Staff : The adequacy and competencies of library staff support the role of library staff in reference services to the readers. The knowledge of reader's demand and requirement help in reaching to desired books. Reference service given by library staff is effective means of ensuring books of most possible interest to him.

iv. Obligation of the Readers : In order to fulfill the purpose of the second law, there are certain obligation and responsibilities for the readers also. The readers should follow the library rules. The readers should take care of library rules, regulations and do not ever try to misplace books with a view to monopolize their use, or tearing off pages or stealing books.

v. Book for all : Book should be for every type of readers irrespectively of age, sex, race, caste, religion, etc.

vi. Book selection : The second law not only emphasizes selection of books for the normal people but also for the physical handicapped one. Book has also to take care for new-literate.

vii. Inter-Library loan : The entire book resources of a country can be made available through the inter-library co-operation.

viii. Catalogue or analytical entries : Book of composite and complex nature should be explained fully to readers by catalogue or subject analytical entries.

ix. Open access : In open access books should be kept in open shelves so that the user could easily handle the book whenever he needs it.

It is the obligation of the library authority to develop libraries at all levels. Their involvement regarding making available funds for the books, staff and infrastructure is very essential. Resource sharing is another important aspect. Now the reader has been replaced by clientele and the book has been replaced by information. The basic idea is the same that every clientele or user should get his required information. Finally, reference service gains its legitimacy and its purpose from this law. The importance of reference service cannot be overstated. For many patrons, particularly in a law library, it is through the reference department that they gain knowledge of the materials necessary for satisfying their particular information need.

Reference librarians are trained to bring readers to their books either through formal research instruction, informally in a one-on-one "reference interview," or by the production of bibliographies, research guides, exhibits, etc. In a sense, patrons "use" the skill of the reference librarian to find the library materials they need. The implication of the second law in marketing the library is to meet user needs satisfactorily by collecting and interpreting information, understanding the needs of users, and matching the needs with its resources. The library should develop its collection keeping in mind the present and future requirements of its users. The library collection should be a mix of old and rare material as well as of the latest material reflecting advances in various fields.

THIRD LAW: EVERY BOOK ITS READER

In the third law, that every book its reader the emphasis is on the book itself. Each book or document in the library collection has value and purpose for which it has been acquired. Dr. Ranganathan argued that the library could devise many methods to ensure that each item finds it appropriate reader.

i. Open access : The provision of open access facilitates the book to be visible to possible reader and it gives a chance to be picked up. In closed system users have to wait for their book they do not get a chance to browse the books. In the open system the reader himself can handle and pursue the books. Open access of Bookshelves can also help a lot in this respect.

ii. Arrangement of books : The classification used to classify the books (their subjects) should be in a way that it brings the all books of one subject together. The reader does not have to roam entire library to find out a book. Also it should be near to related disciplines so that the reader finds the book of his interest in the nearby subject shelves.

a. ***Absolute position of books*** : Each title of books has its absolute position of book in the entire collection and it should be given appropriate place in the library. It will help the reader to find the desired book.

b. ***Relative position of books*** : As we know that the arrival of interdisciplinary subjects has created much furor in arrangement of books. The subjects have their own position as well as relative position in the library collection. For example, the reader interested in the books of religion may be interested in some aspect of the subject Philosophy or a reader of subject Dynamics may also get useful information in the subject Physics. So the relative position of books gives books a chance to be reached easily and be issued.

iii. Publicity and promotion of books : The books should be displayed in a different manner sometimes. The library can arrange a separate corner or section of a group of books to attract the attention of users. The promotional activities can vary from library to library and be designed keeping the type and tastes of reader community. By promoting books to users offer opportunities for enrichment that other titles do not. Historically, reference work has been identified within the third law. The librarian should take care to draw the attention of the readers to those valuable books which lie unused and uncared for long period. Besides he must give prompt publicity to new arrivals of books. This could be done by inserting a notification in the press or by periodical circulars, notices and display, etc.

iv. Proper cataloguing : Proper cataloguing can also help in the use of books. A classified catalogue with analytical entries for all the hidden subjects in a book will go a long way in this direction.

v. Book selection : Book selection should be for all users. Books which are not likely to be demanded by readers should not be selected for procurement.

Every book can get its user only when the libraries should have open access system. By this arrangement all types of books can find there users. In spite of open access system, list of new additions can be brought out frequently and regularly and can be displayed for catching attention of the readers. Book exhibitions can also be organized to this purpose. All these steps help in emphasizing the Third Law. But in the present age of IT, OPACs, availability of databases for searching opening home page on WWW of the Internet, the application of Third Law has become rather simpler, easier and more relevant indeed.

The implication of the third law in marketing the library is performing activities that take library products and services to the users: publicizing the value and benefits, promotional campaigns, advocacy, public relations, personal communication, etc. The library should use promotional tools to publicize its resources, facilities, and services. It should direct its efforts to attracting new users to the library and reach out to its existing users by providing library services at their doorstep. It should give its users the personal touch and develop a feeling of belonging in the library.

FOURTH LAW: SAVE THE TIME OF THE READER

The concept of the Fourth Law of Library Science by Ranganathan is basically concerned with the saving of the time of the readers. Readers expect from the library exact and quick service. To meet the needs of the library user efficiently, Dr. Ranganathan recommended the use of appropriate tools and techniques to manage the library.

i. Centralized Location : The centralization of the library collection in one location provided distinct advantages. Reader does not have to wander here and there in the library or visit the branch libraries to get the required book.

ii. Excellent Staff : The qualified staff with reference skills and technical skills in cataloging, cross-referencing, ordering, accessioning, and the circulation of materials are the multiplier in saving the time of reader.

iii. Open Access : In libraries where the closed system is practiced, the readers face difficulties in having access to books. The fourth law emphasizes and advocates open access of the books to the readers. The proper arrangement on shelves and no misplacement, save time. Open access is an effective means of saving time of the readers.

iv. Classification of Books : The books should be properly arranged on the shelves with the help of subject classification. The classification based on the subjects is convenient to the readers as most of the readers demand their books by their subject.

v. Catalogue : The readers can find the books only through the catalogue; hence catalogue has great importance in saving the time of the readers. Catalogue provides information about all bibliographical details of the books. They are designed to meet the various approaches of the readers such as title, author and subject etc.

vi. Circulation System : The circulation system is also called charging system. The single register based circulation process is time consuming. Few modern systems of charging (ticket system, photo charging system and computer charging system) have reduced that time.

vii. Union Catalogue : The provision of union catalogue is very helpful in saving of the time of the readers. The union catalogues give information of holdings of a geographic area or a group of libraries. This union catalogue provides information so that readers know the library where their required book is available.

viii. Reference Service : The tools, methods and bibliographical means in a library require a user to be acquainted and trained to use them in their favor to save the time. The library staff helps the readers to use these tools and collections by providing the reference service.

ix. Changing methods : The methods of issuing books and receiving them when returned should be such a way, that reader does not have to spend much time at the changing or discharging counter. Newark or Browne method are widely used in the library.

Policies always must be formulated with the needs of the library user in mind. Hours of operation must be set so as to ensure the most appropriate and convenient access to the patrons who rely on the library for their research and reading needs. The collection must be arranged in an inviting, clear, and obvious way so as not to waste the time of patrons as they search for the materials they need.

Attention also must be given to the variety of formats in which information is provided. When a library subscribes to electronic resources, appropriate access to them must be provided. There are other ways to satisfy this law. Well-planned and executed library handbooks, stack guides, and library tours, or research instruction sessions serve the goal of saving the time of the reader. Adequate staffing of reference, information, and circulation desks, as well as telephone reference, also helps patrons find needed materials quickly. Employing the best available technologies to provide quick access to materials or using an online catalog also saves the time of the reader.

In place of traditional classification according to a scheme of classification and cataloguing according to a code, both of the processing in this age of IT, can be done instantly by using OCLC database or OPAC by scanning the catalogues of other libraries on-line. In addition to it, computerized circulation system has also resulted in saving of time and energy of users as well as the library staff. The complicated procedures have now become very simpler. Thus the Fourth Law strongly advocates use of IT in the libraries.

The entire journey of librarianship is about devising, designing, and developing methods, systems of organization and dissemination of information to provide the best service to their readers in the most efficient, accurate, and effective manner and thus saving the reader's time. For example, libraries provide catalogues, bibliographies, indexes, and abstracts to save the time of readers. Saving the time of the reader also relates to how libraries actually organize information.

The implication of the fourth law in marketing the library is its focus on the user benefits and preferences. Consolidation and repackaging information into an appropriate form, making information available when it is needed, ensuring the quality of services and offerings, are the tasks that take user benefits and preferences into account. The main objective of the library should be that the user who enters in a library for a specific purpose should not leave empty handed. At the same time, it must also be ensuring that the users' valuable time is not wasted in searching for material.

FIFTH LAW: THE LIBRARY IS A GROWING ORGANISM

Dr. Ranganathan's fifth law is library is a growing organism means that library always grows in the size, space, collection, readers and the staff. He argued that libraries should be able to organize and accommodate the growth of its basic components i.e. books or collection, readers, and staff. This involved allowing for growth in the physical building, reading areas, shelving, and in space for the catalogue.

Biological aspects of Growth

Ranganathan has biological growth in mind and he considered the library as an organism and not the organization. He outlined certain characteristics of the library as a living organism. There has been two types of growth in a living organism, one as growth by accretion (the growth of a child is growth by accretion in it apparent growth takes place which is visible) and the other is growth by replacement or renewal (growth of an adult is not visible).

Thus a library is a dynamic growing entity. The basic components of growth of a library are the following in which library grows.

i. Collection : The growth of book collection is the first implication of growth in libraries. The growth in collection impact on the size of the stack room, the catalogue cabinet and the catalogue room and the number of racks for accommodating the books.

ii. Readers : The growth in the number of readers relates to reading space. The bigger number of users requires more space in library.

iii. Staff : The staff of a library also grows. Depending on the nature and interests of readers, the services will require more staff due to the increase in the collection and number of readers and new services.

iv. Classification and Cataloguing : The classification scheme should be able to accommodate the grown types of subjects and it should be hospitable to the subjects. It should be able to facilitate smooth and easy retrieval of books. The library catalogue should be able to interpolate entries.

v. Weeding of Books : The library should have weeding out policy to weed out the obsolete and unwanted books. The weeding of such document allows the inclusion of new books. Weeding out need not necessarily mean the discarding of the books. It only means the removal of those books, which have cleared their relevance.

Libraries grow with the passage of time. Keeping this law in view, the library buildings, stacks, physical form of catalogue, staff strength, readers' area and acquisition policies are planned. Modular buildings are preferred for future expansions vertically as well as horizontally. Rules for weeding out the no more required material are framed. Unnecessary duplication of documents is avoided. Future planning of library buildings, equipments and materials is done accordingly. In this age of IT, compact and adjustable stack system has been devised which requires less space for stacks area. Micro documents and computer readable documents are being preferred for storage. Newer types and forms of documents have revolutionized the very concept of space problem in the libraries. Thus, it is evident that the IT is being used in libraries keeping in view the bearing of Fifth Law.

Due to proliferating book publishing industry, libraries will continue to struggle with space problems. This is reflected in the statistics of information generation and the acquisition of information resources of libraries of any type. Lancaster's dream of a paperless society is not likely to come true in the near future. The sacrifices librarians have to make between space for books shelves and space for computer terminals to deliver this ever- expanding need will continue to be an issue. One can also see the library as a growing organism in terms of staff and skills. As the library grows in services, the skills necessary to deliver these new services will also grow. The fifth law's implication for marketing is adapting the library to future user needs, including mobilizing resources, dealing with uncertainty about future user needs, new services, new customer groups, new environment, etc. The library should also transform its services to keep up with other changes in the world. The library must not lag behind in adapting to new technologies. The library staff must be technology savvy.

Variants of Five Laws

The five laws are universally accepted and have been interpreted with the different accent in the changing environment. The development in the library scenario has been a recipient of various technologies. Librarian Michael Gorman (past president of the American Library Association, 2005–2006), and Walt Crawford recommended the following laws in addition to Ranganathan's five in *Future Libraries: Dreams, Madness, and Realities* (American Library Association, 1995) Gorman later repeated them in his small book, *Our Singular Strengths* (American Library Association, 1998).

1. Libraries serve humanity.
2. Respect all forms by which knowledge is communicated.
3. Use technology intelligently to enhance service.
4. Protect free access to knowledge.
5. Honor the past and create the future.

During last decade, Alireza Noruzi stated "Application of Ranganathan's Laws to the Web" in year 2004, as:

1. Web resources are for use.
2. Every user has his or her web resource.
3. Every web resource its user.
4. Save the time of the user.
5. The Web is a growing organism.

Carol Simps applied Ranganathan's law in 2008 to enhance the media based services in a way that:

1. Media are for use.
2. Every patron his information.
3. Every medium its user.
4. Save the time of the patron.
5. The library is a growing organism.

8

Digital Libraries and Virtual Libraries

INTRODUCTION

Libraries are portals to all of the world's knowledge and with the duty, the librarians ensure the knowledge to be recorded and saved for the future. Though the information-storage devices and formats keep changing the·use to advancement in technology. The libraries, world wide have been in transition due to various factors. Sometimes the reason may be the community oriented service point of view or the industrial impacts after World War II. The advent of information technology also augmented the transition of the traditional print based libraries into digital libraries. The digital libraries arrived with a goal to offer new and improved services. The computer based library and information services were welcomed by each library that were able to afford them.

A library's existence does not depend on the physical form of documents. Its mission is to link the past and the present, and help shape the future by preserving the records of human culture, as well as integrating emerging information technologies. This mission is unlikely to change in the near future. Decades back the libraries were heading toward an environment in which digital information becoming substitute for print-based information. The collection of the conventional library which were print based were began to be replaced by the electronic resources. During last two decades libraries have been much busy in deciding the electronic resources policies and replacing the print versions with the electronic versions. The libraries look eagerly to the new technology as a solution. There have been tremendous changes in the collection development and implementation policies due to the online resources such as electronic journals, e-books etc. The libraries have been smart enough to consider their

IT based collection and services and redesigning their entire functioning. Digital libraries come in many forms. They attempt to provide instant access to digitized information and consist of a variety of information, including multimedia.

There are libraries which spend more than half of acquisitions budget on electronic resources, rather than paper. Meanwhile, many libraries are finding it impossible to maintain their traditional collecting practices within the constraints of their institutional budgets.

Why this transition has arrived? What are the various factors that can be considered responsible for the change which has been witnessed by the libraries world wide? Where the traditional working in libraries had been facing problems in buying material, with increasing costs for buildings and storage, at the same time the problem of the deterioration of the reading material has always before the librarian. When we face the situation of multi campus institutions, the management and maintenance aspect is cumbersome for the librarian as well. The library budget does not indicate in routine about the cost involved with the requirement of more space. To support the libraries and provide a better way to maintain and provide the user services, the electronic means came forward.

Advent of Digital Libraries

When we talk about the digital libraries, it is related to the digital collection and the information services based on the digital collection. The digital documents or resources in a library enhance better access to traditional materials, easier preservation, and extension of library collections. There are options as well as chances of extension of the provided digital materials to the users. The library can initiate with the digitization or subscribing less number of documents and move to large scale digitization and subscription of each and every subject being taught in the institution. The abstracts databases and full-text resources prove beneficial to the users. The variety and availability of formats is supporting in user services. From text to image, sound or streaming media, everything is the medium of information and popular among the users according to their nature of work and research. For example, printed encyclopedias are giving way to CD-ROMs which are smaller, cheaper, and far more effective to use. Rapid advances in information technologies have revolutionized the role of libraries. As a result, libraries face new challenges, competitors, demands, and expectations. Libraries are redesigning services and information products to add value to their services and to satisfy the changing information needs of the user community. Traditional libraries are still handling largely printed materials that are expensive and bulky. Information seekers want to supplement the printed information with more dynamic electronic resources. Demands for digital information are increasing.

Defining a Digital Library

A digital library is a library in which collections are stored in digital formats (as opposed to print, microform, or other media) and accessible by computers. The content may be stored locally, or accessed remotely.

The Digital Library Federation defines digital libraries as:

> *Organizations that provide the resources, including the specialized staff, to select, structure, offer intellectual access to, interpret, distribute, preserve the integrity of, and ensure the persistence over time of collections of digital works so that they are readily available for use by a defined community or set of communities.*

The DELOS Digital Library Reference Model defines a digital library as:

> *An organization, which might be virtual, that comprehensively collects, manages and preserves for the long term rich digital content, and offers to its user communities specialized functionality on that content, of measurable quality and according to codified policies. ("Digital Library")*

There are many definitions of a "digital library." Terms such as "electronic library" and "virtual library" are often used synonymously. Within the library field there is a tendency to refer to the 'virtual' library, the 'digital' library, and the 'electronic' library interchangeably.

A digital library possesses the same functions and goals of the traditional print-based library and that the difference lies in 'the digital part of the term [which] indicates merely that the material is stored and accessed digitally'. A digital library is the one that 'should be a seamless extension of the library that provides scholars with access to information in any format that has been evaluated, organized, and preserved' and that the digital library 'adds value and saves time while extending the hours of access'.

Advantages

- A single electronic copy can be accessed from many locations, and to many simultaneous users within the permissions of copyright.
- The information sources are delivered with unbelievable speed with the possibility of reformatting of the information product to the convenience of the reader.
- Since readers get a screen display of the object, rather than carrying away the physical object, loss rates by theft may be much reduced.
- Fortunately the digital world has different rules and facilities to tackle with the problems of loss or theft. Everything is concerned there with the copyright issues.
- Another important advantage is preservation. Digital information can be copied without error. As a result, preservation in a digital world does not depend on having a permanent object and keeping it under guard, but on the ability to make multiple copies, assuming that at least one will survive.

- Digital storage also permits libraries to expand the range of material they can provide to their users.
- Digital material preserves and permits access to fragile information sources.

Limitations and Risks

- The major risk to digital objects is usually not physical deterioration but technological obsolescence of the devices to read them. A more serious refreshing problem, in reality, is software obsolescence.
- The lifetime of the reading devices is perhaps only about one decade (except for CD-ROM). The expenditure on the hardware part creates problems in the libraries.
- Lack of screening or validation of the information source or the information itself sometimes.
- Lack of preservation of a fixed copy (for the record and for duplicating scientific research)
- Difficulty in knowing and locating everything that is available, and differentiating valuable from useless information.
- Job loss for traditional publishers and librarians who do not wish to embrace the technological developments and the constantly altering user needs.
- Costs are spread and many become hidden. The funding for the preservation and regular refreshing is difficult. Digital preservation will be an ongoing operation, requiring a regular future expense.

Digital libraries offer greater opportunity for users to deposit information as well as use information. For example, Internet access in classrooms blurs distinctions between teaching and learning. The interesting and important information to class discussions leads students and their teachers to new electronic resources and tools.

Comparing Traditional and Digital Libraries

Traditional Libraries	Digital or Electronic Library
Print collection	All resources in digital form.
Stable, with slow evolution	Dynamic and ephemeral
Individual objects not directly linked with each other.	Multi-media and fractal objects
Flat structure with minimal contextual metadata	Scaffolding of data structures and richer contextual metadata.
Scholarly content with validation process	More than scholarly content with various validation processes
Limited access points and centralized management	Unlimited access points, distributed collections and access control
The physical and logical organization correlated.	The physical and logical organization may be virtually
One way interactions	Dynamic realtime dialogue
Free and universal access.	Free as well as fee based.

Characteristics of Digital Libraries

The developments in library technology and practices during last millennium have helped bring some of Lancaster's paperless society to reality. The characteristics and common aspects of digital libraries are as following:

- Digital library collections contain permanent documents; only the access is permitted or denied. The document itself is present somewhere in digital form.
- The digital environment enables quick handling and/or ephemeral information. Digital libraries are based on digital technologies.
- The digital library is not a single entity. The digital library requires technology to link the resources.
- The linkages between the many digital libraries and information services are transparent to the end users.
- Digital library collections are not limited to document surrogates: they extend to digital artifacts that cannot be represented or distributed in printed formats.
- Due to Digital libraries the physical boundaries of data have been eliminated.

Communication and Internet Technologies have paved way for the access. Telecommunication is facilitating the storage, retrieval, use, and exchange of digital resources. The literature shows that the services of digital libraries enhance communication and collaboration between and among educational institutions. The facilitations to users in the form of other characteristics are such as:

- No physical boundary
- Round the clock availability
- Multiple access
- Enhanced information retrieval.
- Preservation for some print material
- Added value
- Universal accessibility

Functions of Digital Library

The functioning of digital library depends on the co-operative efforts in research resource, computing, and communication networks. The objectives of the digital library are the same as those of the conventional or traditional libraries have had in the past. Since the basic elements of providing the services are different so the routine functions of the digital library are not same. The distinguished functions of a digital library are as following:

- Access to large amounts of information to users wherever they are and whenever they need it.
- Access to primary information sources.

- Support multimedia content along with text
- Network accessibility on Intranet and Internet
- User-friendly interface
- Hypertext links for navigation
- Client-server architecture
- Advanced search and retrieval
- Integration with other digital libraries

COMPONENTS OF A DIGITAL LIBRARY

The digital libraries have a different method to expedite the systematic development of procedures to collect, store, and organize, information in digital form. The digital libraries involve such methods that can promote efficient delivery of information, economically to all users. The components of a digital library are:

Infrastructure : The infrastructure is concerned with the hardware, networking equipments, and software technologies involved in providing digital information based services.

Digital Collection : The collection is in digital format. This can be either born digital or digitized later on. The subscription based digital resources can be provided to the users and the library can opt for in-house development of digital collection.

Systems function : To run the system efficiently, the technical management is a big must. The mere presence of infrastructure, technology and collection does not ensure the efficient information services.

Telecommunication facility : The Internet facility is backbone to disseminate the knowledge and communicate the information. The cost of bandwidth, availability of bandwidth is significant.

Human resources : The library staff plays significant role in maintaining and providing digital information service. Every kind of hardware and software needs 'humanware.' The library staff and supporting staff is crucial in successful implementation and efficient services.

Planning for Digital Library

A library is fundamentally an organized set of resources, which include human services as well as the entire spectrum of media (e.g., text, video, hypermedia). Libraries have physical components such as space, equipment, and storage media; intellectual components such as collection policies that determine what materials will be included and organizational schemes that determine how the collection is accessed; and people who manage the physical and intellectual components and interact with users to solve information problems. A single person from a library cannot plan and execute it to develop or make it successful. A digital library committee should be formed to plan for its creation and maintenance. The members from various library departments, subject specialists and technical consultants should be given place in the committee. The right planning allows re-allocating funds from some staff, collection maintenance, and additional books. There are at least two ways of developing a digital library: converting a traditional library into a digital library, and direct development of a digital library. The planning of digital libraries includes:

IT Infrastructure : the first and foremost step is to establish the IT Infrastructure. The IT infrastructure includes the hardware and software components of digital library. The choice is to be made for the types of computer servers, systems, other supporting hardware components. It again compels to decide the go for the contemporary or the most advanced technology. When the choice for the software is to be made, there is a big room for the commercial and open source digital library software.

Digitization : The digitization involves concentration on types of documents, target population of users and the available hardware for the digitization. The technical aspects such as type of document, presentation style, resolution, formats etc. are very significant for user oriented services and facilitating the effective interface.

Access : The access aspect is very important to plan. The options of access depend on the contract and conditions laid with the publisher or vendor of digital resources. Who are permitted and how long are two significant matters in accessing the information resources. The authentication of users is must and decided by the institution subscribing the digital resources with the help of technological security mechanisms. The longevity of access is something that keeps on ticking like clock, for how many (1-5) years or perpetual? Also what about the archives and back files of the e-resource. How about the downloading the resources in certain conditions. The knowledge of fair use, copyright and guidelines for downloading are must for the users.

Staffing : The staffing in right way and amount leads to compact functioning of library specially the digital library section. The staffing is responsible for managing and maintaining the digital library and its services towards users. The staffing requires the presence of technical persons who can handle the day-today functioning and trouble shooting of the system.

Furniture, equipment, and space : The distinct and specialized furniture, highly sophisticated equipments and the always shrinking space require attention during planning. The rush of users always compel the librarian to replay the planning (which is almost impossible) and wish for more popularity of digital resources among users, dwindle the thinking on the library part. The furniture should be comfortable in a way that it leaves some space for movement. The equipments for establishing digital library and the supporting type equipments need to be protected and continuous vigil.

Services : The user related aspect is the services of digital library. The library committee for the digital library and the meetings with the randomly selected users can give hint towards the desired and projected digital library services. The initially planned services may be modified later on. Depending on the increased and enhanced digital ambit, the services and resources can also be extended.

Funding : Funding! Oh! The most important and foremost resource to establish the digital library. The library has to find out the sources of funding i.e. institutional grant, main annual budget of library, some kind of govt. funding meant only for digital library establishment. There are some other matters such as if this grant or funding is only one time. What about the recurring expenses such as salary to staff and also for the maintenance purposes? So the financial planning is above each kind of other plans. There are other aspects if the digital library is being developed under some special project (time bound) or govt. funding (fixed and limited for a period of time), how the future planning of expansion and extension will take place. The future expansion will necessarily require more funds.

What are Digital Resources

The digital resources are found in number of type and formats such as:

Electronic Books and Texts : The digital library provides access to a variety of electronic books. Some of the electronic books and texts are part of large, searchable databases. Usually the electronic books and texts can be searched through the digital library interface page.

Electronic Journals : The journals are in digital formats. The E-Journals are located in database. The electronic journals are easy to search, timely updated and accessed.

E-Reference Sources : The electronic versions of dictionaries, almanacs, encyclopedias, and other reference sources (online full-text) are very popular among the users.

E-Indexes : An index is reference source which provides bibliographic information about journal articles, as well as other types of materials. While indexes have long existed in print, online indexes have expanded the type of work done by researches. Online indexes allow user to look beyond subject, author, or title also to look for keywords or phrases throughout the bibliographic information—including the abstract.

E-statistical Sources : The electronic form of economic data or statistics is easily to locate.

E-Sound files and Recordings : The electronic version of sound and music files is very popular.

Image Databases (Art, Maps, Medical, etc.) : Some subjects require images and graphics for the better imparting of teaching. The image databases include graphics or images, such as photos, paintings or maps.

UNDERSTANDING THE 'VIRTUAL LIBRARY ENVIRONMENT'

The concept of the virtual library is one that has developed with the growth in telecommunication networks, especially the internet. The 'virtual library' emulates a 'real' library, but is understood to be a product of the virtual world of the internet. A Virtual Library is a collection of resources available on one or more computer systems. A virtual library is visible and accessible to user through a single interface or entry point to the collections. The key point is that the location of particular resources is physically unknown to user; the location is "virtual". 'Virtual' is "a place, not a format" and many people spend a lot of time in this virtual place.

The virtual library is not synonymous with the purely digital or electronic library, but rather 'a parallel library which includes a finely balanced mix of print, multimedia and electronic information resources'. The concept of a library which offers seamless access to integrated print, electronic, local and remote resources has sometimes been termed a 'hybrid library'. The virtual library environment encompasses the concept of the digital library but is more than a collection of digitized resources. The virtual library provides access to an integrated collection of print, electronic and multimedia resources delivered seamlessly and transparently to users regardless either of their physical location or the location and ownership of the information.

Virtual libraries are organized collections of digital information. They are constructed collections organized for a particular community of users, and they are designed to support the information needs of that community. Virtual libraries can offer resources from many sources and in many formats, including audio and video. The items in these virtual collections do not have to reside on one server, but they share a common interface to assist the user in accessing the collection. The emphasis in virtual libraries is on organization and access, not on physical collections.

Importance of virtual libraries

No time limits : Physical libraries operate with designated hours, virtual libraries are available any time and anywhere there is an Internet connection.

Access to collection : A paradigm shift takes place from libraries as collectors of items to libraries as facilitators of access to all kinds of information, provided by anybody, located anywhere in the world accessible at any time.

Just-in-time learning : Virtual libraries, especially those with customized collections, facilitate just-in-time learning. Just-in-time learning is a learning needed for a particular task or purpose. Just-in-time learning is independent of time and place.

Wide range of resources : Virtual libraries provide immediate access to a range of resources not available in physical collections.

Update information : The information sources are searched more efficiently and the information is updated more frequently.

Organized methods : Well-designed virtual library collections are organized and managed to increase the productivity and efficiency of the user.

Just-for-me learning : Virtual libraries, which are customized for the learning needs of particular users-either schools, lasses, or individuals-enable just-for-me learning. Just-for-me learning can be tailored to individual learning styles, preferences, and other characteristics of the learner or community of learners.

Removing the physical barrier : Virtual libraries break down the physical barriers between users and information sources.

Integration of various forms and formats of media : Virtual libraries are integrating voice, video, and text for users involved in distance education in remote locations.

Collaboration among the learners : Virtual libraries can be constructed to facilitate collaboration among learners either synchronously (real-time), or asynchronously. They can also incorporate instruction, tutorials, and reference service or assistance by e-mail or in real-time.

Necessity of trained personnel : Virtual libraries still require skilled professionals to organize, maintain, and help students reap the benefits of this virtual learning environment. "The power of Internet resources remains latent to those without the skills to use them" holds true.

Need of searching capacity : Although some virtual libraries are lists of Web sites and require little Inter- net searching ability, others demand knowledge of Boolean logic and advanced searching skills to realize the potential of the database.

Few aspects do exist to concern and desiring attention and consideration in context with the virtual library:

Copyright law : There are some restriction for sharing and copying the scholarly content in the digital and virtual libraries. It is well known that content in public domain or self generated, the permission is needed due to copyright.

Dependency on Internet and maintained Links : For accessibility, the virtual libraries are dependent on Internet connectivity. The hide and seek of hyperlinks, the broken links create much problem and harass the accessibility.

Digital Divide : The Digital Divide is something that always finds an area of immediate concern in developing countries.

Skilled Staff : Skilled professionals are required to organize, maintain and help users; the help is extended to guide students in the selection, evaluation and use of electronic choices. Scaffolding and coaching and finding the librarians is needed in this virtual library for the unskilled researcher. Guidance by the library staff to students in the selection, evaluation, and use of the many digital or virtual collection options is always required.

Information Literacy : The knowledge to use the available knowledge is very important in virtual libraries. The information literacy skills are needed and the basic knowledge of Boolean searching and advanced searching skills is also required. Increased number of resources challenges student selection.

Authority and Quality of digital resources : The customized purchase of online materials for a particular community of learners is must. It is also significant to assess the authority and quality of resources in virtual libraries. The classification of knowledge and information in virtual environment is something not to be taken casually.

- The learning potential of resources available in virtual libraries.
- Storage of digital information: the permanency, or lack thereof, of digital information; archiving digital information
- Tailoring of online periodical databases on a subscription basis and user community basis.
- Need for instruction in use and evaluation of sources does not disappear in a virtual environment.
- The ability to access earlier issues of an electronic subscription.

ADVANTAGES OF DIGITAL AND VIRTUAL LIRBARIES

Immediate access : These libraries are available anytime and they facilitate just-in-time learning.

Most updated information : The digital and virtual libraries provide up-to-date information. The digital environment facilitates easy and timely updating of information.

Seamless and limitless access : People from all over the world can access information as long as there is an Internet connection. The walls of physical location do not exist and no barrier except technological permission can become hindrance in information access. The digital library and virtual library provide a link to any other resources of other digital libraries and seamlessly integrated resource sharing can occur.

User oriented interface : Users can access information in a variety of formats. The information products are tailored to characteristics of the learner or community of learners. The digital libraries and virtual environments provide wide range of resources to meet the information needs of different users.

Customized Information products : Even the collection subscribed by the institution can be customized according to subject groups and faculty requirements.

Information retrieval : These libraries provide user-friendly interfaces, giving clickable access to resources. The user is facilitated use any search term such as word, phrase, title, name, subject to search entire collection.

Storage of information : These libraries have the potential to store much more information that traditional library and they require very little physical space to contain information

DIFFERENTIATING DIGITAL AND VIRTUAL LIBRARIES

When we go through literature and also visit and use a digital library, we find that digital library is a repository of information in digital form, i.e. stored as data files on a computer. It is also the tool-set provided to enable search and retrieval of the repository. The term electronic library has been very popular in the initial and developmental days of IT based libraries. An Electronic Library is the same thing as digital library.

The digital library is an organization including staff, computers, networks, and all other resources necessary to organize, store provide access to, subsidize, preserve, and retrieve selected digital documents where, when, and how needed by users. The term "Digital documents" is used in the widest sense of the word, and includes, but is not limited to one or more computer usable files and can include everything from text, multimedia, database, motion pictures or any other type of digital document.

The virtual library is 'a digital library' which has the look and feel of a traditional physical library with collections of materials. It may have additional features, as well, but it takes advantage of users' intuitive understanding of libraries. There are very few examples today, especially among those libraries that call themselves a virtual library.

The below description gives an outline clearly to distinguish and differentiate the digital and virtual libraries:

i. Digital Library : It's the same thing as Electronic Library. The name DIGITAL means that the collection is on a binary format and stored on an electronic device. So it is a Library whose material (books, journals, reports, thesis, and so on) is stored on electronic format (on CD ROM etc.). They can be read and printed through a computer. It doesn't mind if those publications can be accessed by a standalone computer, a local network, or the Internet. As described above a Digital Library have a staff, and services. One can borrow material, request copies and so on. As it is on any paper based Library, the only change is the storage media. A Digital Library project may include a "Virtual Library".

ii. Virtual Library : It's a collection of links. Those links do not reflect physical Library material. Instead it reflects subjects' categories of sites on Internet. The name virtual means "not real". There is no borrowing anything from a Virtual Library but the accessibility.

A Digital Library implies the existence of some collection of data, that is, computerized information replacing the traditional printed sources, while the virtual library doesn't necessarily requires the existence of local information. The work of the librarian, in the case of a virtual library, is to maintain a logical and useful order of the resources and update links or the links to assure access.

'Virtual library' is a companion term to 'digital library' and that up to 1995 both terms were 'used narrowly to define a quantity of databases available for use at a given time'.

Role of Virtual Librarian

The role of the librarian in the print environment was confined as the person responsible for selecting, acquiring, organising and providing access to relevant information. Due to digital environment, the tasks and responsibilities have become more complex. The librarian is playing significant role in a way:

To provide intellectual access to information in any format : Providing intellectual access to information is a role librarians have filled for a long time. Within the virtual library environment, the choice of format is not the most crucial issue: it is being able to provide information resources to patrons - regardless of format. The development in electronic access to scholarly journals is a key example of the shift from ownership to access. University and research libraries especially, find the option of providing electronic access to journal subscriptions to be a means of dealing with complex multi-campus organisations where the client population comprises an increasing mixture of on- and off-campus students.

While electronic access to journals appears to be a godsend to patrons and researchers, cutting out countless hours of tedious bibliographic detective work, the behind-the-scenes decisions and negotiations conducted by librarians to provide the service are fraught with numerous complex issues. Electronic serials must be evaluated against the relative importance of content.

With printed subscriptions libraries own and may continue to access those issues they purchase during the lifetime of the subscription. With electronic subscriptions, libraries pay for *access* to the journals rather than ownership, and at the end of a subscription a library may no longer have the right to access a title. Some publishers will provide access to a specific number of issues, for example the previous five years rather than offering a cumulative arrangement. The need to negotiate continuing access with publishers is becoming a significant responsibility for librarians.

Electronic reserves provide the ability to digitise a printed document, video, audio, or data, so that many students can access it simultaneously without the limits of attending a library building within opening hours.

The technology to provide digital access to library reserve collections has been available for some time. However the wholesale adoption of this mechanism has been impeded by a lack of clear copyright and intellectual property ownership laws for the digital environment.

To evaluate available sources of information : There is an increasing diversity of information resources from which to choose the most appropriate vehicle, and that librarians must widen their selection processes in order to decide on the right medium for each situation. The objective in the evolving virtual library is 'to develop information systems providing access to a coherent collection of material, more and more of which will be in digital form as time goes on'.

Electronic sources of information are excellent for data which must be timely and is subject to frequent change, such as stock market data, weather reports, and population statistics. It is also valuable for the ease in which information such as full-text articles from newspapers and journals can be delivered. Printed resources may continue for a long time to be the most efficient form of delivering ideas and theories as opposed to data in subject areas such as history, philosophy, and literature.

In evaluating electronic sources of information there is also a distinction to be made between those sources of data which have been digitised for the speed and ease of transportation, and data which is of limited usefulness, volatile and fluid in nature.

There are numerous free resources available on the web, to say nothing of the full-text journals now available. Whether or not to include these in the library catalogue is a challenge facing librarians in the virtual library environment.

To organize and structure information : Traditionally, librarians have organized and managed information resources through classification schemes. The retrieval of information relevant to a user's enquiry has been facilitated by standardized methods of describing resources, such as MARC. It is ironic that organizing vast quantities of information is becoming a demanding issue for those involved in the development of the internet.

Many of the challenges facing those attempting to organize and structure information in the virtual environment is its nature. One significant management problem in the networked environment compared to traditional library management issues, is coping with the nature of the 'information space'.

The organization and structure of information within the virtual library is critical to ensure the easiest path for the library user to access and use resources. Libraries are providing access to web-based resources, either those freely available or for which the library has paid a subscription. It is essential that users can access all of these through a single interface, usually the library's catalogue.

To ensure the preservation of information : The issue of preservation in the virtual library environment is a complex one. Librarians and archivists have long-established standards and guidelines for the preservation and storage of print materials for long-term survival. The preservation of electronic and digital information resources creates new dilemmas for librarians and archivists.

One of the significant issues affecting preservation of digital information resources is the very technology which creates them. These technologies have an increasingly rapid obsolescence and the preservation of digital information is dependent on ensuring that the software and the mediating technology is also preserved.

To provide specialised staff to offer instruction and assistance in interpreting resources and access to resources : Information retrieval is the most obvious skill a librarian demonstrates to the public. The increasing sophistication of search engine design is creating an environment where anyone can, at varying levels of efficiency retrieve information from the internet. Librarians 'teach information discrimination through personalized research assistance, guidance, and instruction'. Librarians working at integrating new technologies to form the virtual library are discovering an increasing demand for their professional skills.

Librarian 'makes a significant contribution, often defining the search, honing the researcher's goals, and helping the researchers to understand their needs'. The virtual library environment provides both an opportunity and a requirement for librarians to develop greater familiarity with IT-type skills. The ability to network resources and provide digital versions of previously printed material provides the opportunity to reduce the costs of some resources and services. More flexible methods of document delivery are one of the key attractions of the virtual library. The concept of just-in-time information delivery, rather than just-in-case where library patrons can identify required material from a workstation, order it, and wait for its delivery back to the workstation.

Yet a view that the technology revolution will provide significant decreases in budget requirements is overly optimistic. The infrastructure needed to support the many technological developments forms a significant component of today's library budget - an item not previously necessary. The cost not only of computers, printers, scanners, and associated cabling, but the physical space in which to provide these workstations, is considerable. The equipments are expensive to install and maintain, and the cost of upgrading or replacing must be anticipated, as the rate of technological change is increasingly rapid.

Issues that are new to librarians in the virtual library environment are related to the new technologies making digital libraries possible, and the techniques necessary to deliver new forms of information resources and services. In providing access to information, the librarian in the virtual library environment must consider the requirements of any digital resources - any hardware or software necessary, the most effective way to refer patrons to the resource, and whether availability is limited to a defined user group. Young (1998) called this the 'knowledge navigator' role. In navigating access to knowledge, librarians in the virtual library are confronted with the repercussions of the shift from 'ownership to access', and the resulting rights to access considerations which must be specified and negotiated in contracts and licenses.

9

Library Classification

INTRODUCTION

If we watch carefully, we find the classification is pervasive in many areas of our life. According to Richardson, "Classification is putting together like things." In general, by classification we understand the grouping together of alike things according to common qualities or characteristics and segregating the 'alike' things. In the library scenario, the library classification is a system to arrange the library collection. It has aim to enable patrons to find the desired books or other information its materials quickly and easily, as explained in Encyclopedia Britannica. While cataloging provides information on the physical and topical nature of the book (or other item), classification, through assignment of a call number (consisting of class designation and author representation), locates the item in its library setting and, ideally, in the realm of knowledge. Arranging similar things in some order according to some principle unites and controls information from various sources. We can say that library classification is a system of coding and organizing library materials (books, serials, audiovisual materials, computer files, maps, manuscripts) according to their subject and allocating a call number to that information resource. The library classification systems, group entities together that are similar, typically arranged in a hierarchical tree structure.

Further the classification can be distinguished by types:

(1) natural, or fundamental: *e.g.*, books by subject,

(2) accidental: *e.g.*, chronological or geographic, and

(3) artificial: *e.g.*, by alphabet, linguistic base, form, size, or numerical order.

Definitions

According to Margaret Mann, "Classification is the act of arranging things according to their likeness and unlikeness. She further says, It is a sorting or grouping of things."

According to W. Sayers, "The arrangement of books on shelves or description of them in the manner which is most helpful to those who read".

According to Ranganathan, "It is the translation of the name of the subject of a book into preferred artificial language of ordinal numbers, and the individualisation of several books dealing with the same specific subject by means of a further set of original numbers which represent some features of the book other than their thought content."

New Encyclopaedia Britannica defines library classification as a system of arrangement adopted by a library to enable patrons to find its material quickly and easily.

From the above definitions it becomes clear that the arrangement of documents in a systematic way is called classification. In library classification we deal with documents with the sole purpose of arranging them in the most helpful and permanent sequence. Library classification provides a method of putting works about the same subject in roughly the same place on the shelf. The library classification helps in finding the books which are on related topics.

Functions of Library Classification

The functions of library classification can be summarised as follows:

1. Library classification arranges documents in a systematic and most convenient order to the readers and the library staff.
2. It brings related subjects in close contact, called collocation.
3. It helps in identifying and locating the document on a given subject wanted by a reader. Documents can be quickly retrieved from and replaced to their original positions.
4. It helps in organising documents into organised groups like pigeon holes; and when a new document is added to the collection, classification finds an appropriate place for the newly added document among the other documents on the same subject.
5. It helps in organising book displays and exhibitions. It facilitates withdrawal of certain documents from the main collection for special purpose and occasions such as book talks, seminars, symposia, conferences and special exhibitions, on a given topic.
6. It helps in maintaining daily records of issues of documents on various subjects at the circulation counter of a library. It also facilitates compilation of statistics on issues which reflect the pattern of use and demand of documents on different subjects. The feedback helps in the allocation of funds to various subjects and guides the book selection policy of the library. The statistics so collected can be included in the annual report of the library.
7. It facilitates efficient and thorough stock verification of the collection

of the library through the medium of shelf list.

8. It helps in the compilation of bibliographies and union catalogues of books and other reading materials.
9. It assists in the classification pieces of information and suggestions, received from the readers and the reference queries attended to in the reference section. It facilitates proper analysis of the reference queries on various aspects and indirectly helps in efficient reference service.
10. It assists in systematically deriving subject entries. It also aids the cataloguer to use the alphabetical list of subject headings for deriving specific subject headings through class numbers.
11. Non-book materials, such as films, slides, maps, microforms, photographs and correspondence can also be classified and filed systematically.
12. It helps the library staff, especially the classifier, to be aware of and comprehend the complexities in the developments of the universe of knowledge which is the basis for a systematic arrangement of documents in libraries.
13. It is the basis to organize the knowledge embodied in documents for maximum use.
14. It is also the basis for efficient bibliographic control and retrieval of documents.

ROLE OF LIBRARY CLASSIFICATION

Classification has essential part to play especially in assisting in the search process. By classifying books and other kind of documents into different categories, the retrieval of documents is easier. The need of classification in libraries is due to following reasons:

- To search and find a book or document on a certain subject or topic
- To secure an order for searching the books etc.

Need of library classification is explained by following aspects:

a. Helpful Sequence

The basic purpose of any library classification is to arrange the documents in a method most convenient to the users and to the library staff. The books are arranged in classes. The arrangement shows the mutual relations between the books. This kind of sequencing brings together closely related classes. We can say that the related books are grouped in close proximity. It supports the basic idea being of like classes are brought together and unlike classes are separated.

b. Correct shelving and Replacement

The library classification enables the staff and users to shelve and replace the books in proper manner due to class numbers.

c. Mechanized Arrangement:

Once the library classification is decided and implemented in the library, the change or frequent altering will disturb the very goal of the classification. The sequence and re-determining the sequence of documents again will create problem for the returned books. The sequencing is related with the interpolation of new documents in their correct places. The notation allocation expressing order paves the way to easily insert or reinsert the various documents in their correct places. The entire method makes the library classification mechanizing the arrangement.

d. Addition of New Documents

Library classification helps in finding the most helpful place for each of these among the existing collection of the library. The new books are inserted on the basis of already provided subject in the scheme of library classification. There is another way (not existing in the existing scheme), to use the inbuilt qualities of classification scheme. Such in built facilities allow the fixing the position of the newly emerging subjects amidst another subject having literary warrant.

e. Withdrawal of Documents from Stock

In the condition of withdrawal of books, the library classification has arrangements for withdrawal.

Purposes of Library classification

Library Classification has the following purposes:

Classification of pieces information: The classification should be able to classify even small pieces of information

Classification of reference queries : The classification also helps the reference librarian to arrange the queries in a classified order, which makes their redressal quite fast and easy.

- Filing of non book materials such as correspondences, photographs, films and so on.
- Class number is needed in the preparation of catalogue. It assists the user of a catalogue to refer to the location of the documents on the shelf and also helps in arranging the catalogue cards in a classified sequence; and
- Assist the library staff to prepare a subject wise list of documents for to cater to the demand of different departments associated with the library or for maintaining records of documents transferred to branch library or lending centre from the stock of the central library.

The need and purpose of the library classification can be summarized as follows:

Library collections are classified for facilitating the easy access to library collection. The classification helps in locating the document where it is kept. It also fixes the position of the document where it can always be found if it is in the library. Since classification brings similar topics together, user can find related other material also. This also helps in shelving the items.

Goals of library classification

- To serve as a key.
- To facilitate the location of a particular document among the thousands of documents available in huge library collection.
- To ensure optimum usage of books
- To save the time of library staff and users.
- To overthrow burden from the minds of library staff by grouping together the identical documents at one place.

How we locate a document?

The process of classification is applied to the materials being placed in the library collection. A numerical or alphanumerical notation is given to each item in the collection. The notation indicates the subject matter of the item being cataloged. This notation is called as class number. In addition to the notation, an author indicator (letters or letters and numbers that indicate the author's last name) is also given. Sometimes, a title indicator, date of publication, and/or a copy number is added. Combination of notation (class number) and author indicator forms Call Number. The call number provides the address for an item in the library. This address is used to shelve the item and locate and find there. The call number for each item in the library can have only have one address.

Importance of Library Classification

The books are the base of libraries and the base of libraries is classification. Hence classification has special value in libraries. Why classification in libraries is needed and what is its importance? Following are the points for answering these questions.

1. Rearrangement of Returned Books : The books which are returned from the readers systematically may be rearranged on the shelves with the help of classification only. This method rearranges the books, which have come back from the readers, very quickly and is also useful and important method for keeping systematic order of the books on the shelves.

2. Subjectwise Approaches : Most of the readers required their books by their subjects, and classification gathered all of the books of a subject at one place. Therefore the users who demand books by their subject can very best utilize the books.

3. Preparation of Catalogue and Bibliographies : The catalogue of the libraries cannot be prepared without library classification, as class number of books is written on catalogue cards. In the same way classification is also used in compiling various kinds of bibliographies.

4. Estimate of Library Collection : The estimate of total library collection may be on the basis of classification only and it also helps in representative equal collection of each subject in the library.

5. Symbiosis with Cataloguing : Classification has great importance for cataloguing also and it played also a very important role in making cataloguing functional. It also helps in analysing the books and presenting the classified entries in the catalogue.

6. Stock Verification : The annual stock verification of the books can be possible by classification only through shelf-list.

CLASSIFICATION SYSTEMS

The formation and implementation of a classification system may be done keeping in view the type of access and control that a particular library and its clientele's need. It is found that many special and research libraries devise their own unique systems. There may be major divisions and subdivision or any other criterion followed by the libraries.

It is observed that most popular classification systems are:

i. Dewey Decimal Classification,
ii. Library of Congress Classification
iii. Bliss Classification
iv. Colon Classification

Library classification systems are one of the tools used to facilitate subject access.

Library classification is for the following steps:

Aboutness : The "aboutness" of the material is ascertained.

Calling the book : Call number is a book's address. Call number based on the classification system in used at the particular library is assigned to the work using the notation of the system.

Shelving purposes : A book can have only one physical place. In library classification systems, each work can only be placed in one class with the reason:

Role of Classification systems

The use and purpose of library classification system depends on the size of the library collection, sometimes for location of resources sometimes kept in wide classes. Classification systems in libraries usually play following roles:

- The classification system facilitates subject access by allowing the user to find out what works or documents the library has on a certain subject.
- The fixed class number provides a known location for the information source to be located (e.g. where it is shelved).

Types of Library Classification

There are many standard systems of library classification in use. The drawbacks of one type of classification system led the development of another type of classification scheme. Some classification schemes are having qualities and methods of more than one type of basic type. However in general, classification systems can be divided into following types:

Enumerative : In the enumerative classification scheme, the subject headings are listed alphabetically and they are arranged with numbers assigned to each heading in alphabetical order.

Hierarchical : In the hierarchical type of classification schemes, the subjects are divided hierarchically, following a pattern and arrangement. Usually the arrangement of the subject headings or entries is from most general to most specific.

Faceted or analytico-synthetic : In this type of scheme, the subjects are divided into mutually exclusive orthogonal facets. The class numbers are formed on the basis of analysis and systhesis.

It is observed that most classification systems are a blend of two functioning types of schemes. For example, LCC and DDC, are essentially enumerative, though with some hierarchical and faceted elements (more so for DDC), especially at the broadest and most general level. The Colon classification is example of first true faceted system. The examples other faceted systems are as following:

- Bliss bibliographic classification
- Cutter Expansive Classification
- Universal Decimal Classification

The following aspects are considered while comparing and differentiating the classification systems:

Type of Notation

Notation can be pure (consisting of only numerals) or mixed (consisting of letters and numerals, or letters, numerals, and other symbols).

Expressiveness

This is the degree to which the notation can express relationship between concepts or structure.

Hospitality

The degree to which the system is able to accommodate new subjects.

Brevity

The length of the notation to express the same concept.

Speed of updates and degree of support

The better classification systems are frequently being reviewed and improved.

- Consistency
- Simplicity
- Usability

Few major Library classification Schemes

Dewey Decimal Classification

This classification scheme was designed by Melvil Dewey in 1876. Dewey Decimal Classification system divides knowledge into ten main classes. These main classes are h further divided into subdivisions which are accompanied by decimal notation. This notation repeats patterns, develops subjects with parallel construction, and repeats standard subdivisions so that it is easy to browse the shelves in a logical manner. This system is explained in separate chapter.

Library of Congress Classification

The Library of Congress Classification system (LC) is developed and used at the Library of Congress since 1897. This classification system divides the field of knowledge into twenty classes with an additional class on general works. The notation in LC allows more combinations and greater specificity without long notations. With the developments in information technology, LC has made its records available electronically; more libraries have adopted LC for both shelving and cataloging. Due to its special notation system, the LC allows for greater precision in most fields and more room for expansion. Each Library of Congress classification is represented by a set of capital letters and numbers. The first letter in the set indicates one of 21 major areas of knowledge.

A — General Works
B — Philosophy, psychology, and religion
C — History: Auxiliary Sciences
D — History: General and Old World
E — History: America and U.S., general
F — History: America and U.S., local
G — Geography, anthropology, folklore, etc.
H — Social sciences, economics, business, sociology
J — Political Sciences
K — Law
L — Education
M — Music
N — Fine arts
P — Philology, linguistics, language, and literature
Q — Science
R — Medicine
S — Agriculture
T — Technology
U — Military Science
V — Naval science
Z — Bibliography and library science
I, O, X, and Y are not used

WEB BASED CLASSIFICATION SYSTEM

Web-based library classification schemes play an exclusive role on web. Web-based editions have many additional features over the print version and allow multiple searching by terms and numbers and have user friendly browsing option. The innovative web-based services are provided to the users. There are three topmost web-based library classification schemes

- WebDewey 2.0 (DDC 23rd Ed.)
- UDC online (UDC)
- Classification web (LCC)

Electronic versions of the DDC, UDC and LCC make it possible to realize the potential of Library Classification to improve subject retrieval. It creates renewed interest in classification as an organizing and retrieval device for information resources has been sparked by the growth in usage of the Internet and World Wide Web (WWW).

Advantages of web-based library classification schemes

- Easy access of related terms by using different keyword indexes
- Online retrieval of class numbers
- Simply, universal classification schemes are available online
- Uses online retrieval subject heading list, dictionaries and glossaries
- Access through hyperlinks
- Most updated and advanced than print editions
- Facilitates OPAC
- Boolean searching

Disadvantages of web-based library classification schemes

- Technological barriers
- Language barriers (Use standard dictionary)

10

Dewey Decimal Classification

INTRODUCTION

The Dewey Decimal Classification (DDC) system was conceived by Melvil Dewey in 1873 and first published in 1876. This was first published in the United States. The Dewey Decimal Classification is the most widely used classification system in the world.

Libraries in more than 138 countries use the DDC to organize and provide access to their collections, and DDC numbers are featured in the national bibliographies of more than sixty countries. It has been revised and expanded through 23 major editions. Initially it was a four-page pamphlet in 1876 with fewer than one thousand classes and now appears in a four volume set. The four-volume unabridged edition is published approximately every six years, the most recent edition (DDC 23) in mid-2011. For smaller libraries it is available in an abridged version. "Abridged 15" was published in early 2012. It is currently maintained by the Online Computer Library Center (OCLC), a library research center. OCLC licenses access to an online version, WebDewey, for catalogers, and has an experimental linked data version on the Web with open access. The first electronic version of Dewey was created in 1993. Dewey is also used for other purposes, e.g., as a browsing mechanism for resources on the web. There are several convenient formats of DDC:

Print edition : The four-volume print edition includes thousands of updates added to the system over the past seven years.

The electronic version 'WebDewey' : It enhances the print updates with online delivery that is updated continuously.

Abridged Edition 15 : It is a simplified version perfect for smaller collections. It is available in print as well as electronic format and can be subscribed in both versions.

SALIENT FEATURES OF DDC

i. Enumerative Scheme : Enumeration is the most important feature of DDC. It makes by enumeration not only basic subjects, but also many compound subjects, where enumeration means the listing of subjects of the past, present and foreseeable future with their ready made notations.

ii. Ten main classes : The DDC attempts to organize all knowledge into ten main classes. The ten main classes are each further subdivided into ten divisions, and each division into ten sections, giving ten main classes, 100 divisions and 1000 sections.

iii. Use of Decimal : The use of decimals allows it to be purely numerical and facilitates the infinite hierarchy. Dewey used decimal among the class numbers to show hierarchy of subjects and to expand the notation without disturbing any other topic in future. Hence he used the word Decimal in naming his classification scheme as Decimal Classification.

iv. Supporting shelf arrangement : It supports shelf arrangement as the books are placed on the shelf in increasing numerical order of the decimal number, e.g. 145, 320, 321.3, 890.331.

v. Multiple class numbers : An important feature of the scheme is the ability to assign multiple class numbers to a bibliographical item and use of one of them for shelving.

vi. Relative location and relative index : The Decimal Classification introduced the concepts of *relative location* and *relative index* which allow new books to be added to a library in their appropriate location based on subject. Libraries previously had given books permanent shelf locations that were related to the order of acquisition rather than topic. Index is always an important part of any classification scheme and is also a key to the schedule. The index of DDC is relative index, which not only arranges the concepts and their terms in an alphabetical sequence but also shows the relation between the terms and the contexts in which the subjects appear in the schedule. Its index also makes an independent approach to classification. Its index helps the classifier also in finding a given topic in the schedules.

vii. Notation : DDC uses pure notation only which contains only one kind or set of symbols, i.e.. Indo-Arabic Numerals. DDC used only Indo-Arabic numerals (0,1, 2,3, 4, ———9), this is said to be the use of pure notations. Dewey divides knowledge into ten main classes with further subdivisions accompanied by decimal notation. This notation repeats patterns, develops subjects with parallel construction, and repeats standard subdivisions so that it is easy to browse the shelves in a logical manner. The classification's notation makes use of three-digit Arabic numerals for main classes, with fractional decimals allowing expansion for further detail. Arabic numerals are used to represent each class in the DDC. A decimal point follows the third digit in a class number, after which division by ten continues to the specific degree of classification needed.

viii. Well-defined categories and hierarchies : The structure presents network of relationships among topics as the basic classes are organized by disciplines or fields of study.

ix. Auxiliary Tables and Common Isolates : In order to provide synthetic features in the scheme and to meet the challenges posed by the developments in the universe of subjects, seven auxiliary tables have been provided. The common isolates have undergone several changes in both nomenclature and presentation. They were designated by different names different editions of DDC. In last editions they are called Standard Subdivision.

x. Phase Relation : DDC being an enumerative scheme, has very limited provision for the explicit use of phase relations. However sometimes it is seen in complex subjects.

xi. Mapping of universe of subjects : DDC treated entire knowledge as unity and divide it in 10 mutually exclusive main classes denoted by decimal numbers 0 to 9. Strictly and mathematically speaking these numbers denoting main classes should have been written as follows:

0.	Generalities	→ 0.0	Generalities	→	000
1.	Philosophy	→ 0.1	Philosophy	→	100
2.	Religion	→ 0.2	Religion	→	200
3.	Social Sciences	→ 0.3	Social Sciences	→	300
4.	languages	→ 0.4	Languages	→	400
5.	Pure sciences	→ 0.5	Pure sciences	→	500
6.	Technology	→ 0.6	Technology	→	600
7.	The arts	→ 0.7	The arts	→	700
8.	Literature	→ 0.8	Literature	→	800
9.	Geography/ history	→ 0.9 0.9	Geography and History	→	900

Advantages

Simple numerical notation : The Dewey Decimal System uses numerical notation opposed to words or letters which is helpful universally even in different alphabet/language environments.

Easy Narrowing Search : Topics are listed and classified by subject. This arrangement fulfills the goal of the classification system to help user in finding book quickly.

Helpful Shelving : The hierarchical system makes shelving books and locating books within a library very simple.

Disadvantages

More than one subject area : A book may fall to different subject areas, therefore, troubling the user in locating in shelves.

No direct relation of Numbers : The numbers do not have a direct correlation with the subject they represent; therefore, unfamiliar with the system may be difficult for the user to use.

Innovative features of DDC

Dewey introduced the following innovative features in subject arrangement:

Relative Location : Earlier to Dewey, fixed location (Fixed arrangement) was in practice and it was problematic. This system did not provide subject wise arrangement in library. Dewey introduced the principle of relative location comprised of ordered subjects in a sequence, assigned a notation to them and marked books, and not shelves, with this notation.

Decimal Notation : The decimal notation refers to the principle of dividing each class into ten subdivisions and each of these sub-divisions into yet another ten sub-divisions and so on. This system gives tremendous capacity for expansion to accommodate minute sub-divisions without the necessary relocation.

Relative Index : Looking for a book is concerned with the classified catalogue and Dewey introduced the relative index. The relative index paved a way to find a given topic. It also supports to find out the relative aspects of a subject.

UNDERLYING PRINCIPLES IN DDC

Classification by Discipline : DDC has the division of classes and subclasses based on disciplines or fields of study. This approach is known as classification by discipline.

Revision Process : Revisions usually take the following forms:

- ***Expansion*** : Expansion is undertaken in order to accommodate new subjects as well as to provide more minute and specific sub-divisions under the existing subjects.
- ***Reduction*** : Reduction consists of discontinuing very rarely used existing sub-divisions. Such topics are, then, classed with the more general topic.
- ***Relocation*** : Relocation of a number of existing subjects takes. Place in every new edition.

Phoenix Schedules : The bringing out the Phoenix Schedules is a piecemeal approach to bring DDC up-to-date. Certain schedules, which are out of date and require drastic changes, are destroyed and new schedules are completely recast and their arrangement is remoulded in each of the recent editions of DDC since the sixteenth edition. These new schedules rising out of the ashes of the destroyed old schedules are called phoenix schedules.

Synthetic Devices : The synthetic devices provide the facility of accommodating minute and broad aspects of a discipline. The enumeration helps in the process of synthesis. The synthesis is achieved though the use of the seven Tables. In addition, there is another device, called add to instructions which facilitates detailed specification with economy of presentation.

Add to Device : There are following kinds of 'add to device':

- ***Add from tables*** **:** Notations from table 2-7 may be added to certain numbers in the schedules to make them more specific.
- ***Add from schedules*** **:** Certain numbers in the schedules may be made more specific by adding appropriate numbers from other places in the schedules.
- ***Add from both tables and schedules*** **:** Sometimes numbers are derived by adding first from a schedule and then from a table, or in the reverse order.

Special Topics of General Applicability : The principle of special topics of general applicability refers to the sub-division of a subject according to a characteristics having general applicability to its (subject's) sub-divisions, which are based on different characteristics.

Mnemonic Features : The DDC achieves mnemonics in notation with the use of synthetic devices like tables and add to instructions.

Optional Provisions : Library classification, being a pre-coordinate system, has a fixed citation order for the various facets in a number. Due to the circumstances and the interests of the majority of users, to overcome the problem, DDC provides for optional provisions. Certain topics are given two (or more) placements.

Transparent Facet Structure : The completely revised schedules not only incorporate new subjects with details but also provide opportunity to rectify the order of classes and the facet structure to reflect modern thinking in the profession. In DDC-21 the new schedules have transparent facet structure. It means that the topic of a particular discipline can be collocated by more features.

Dewey for Windows (DfW) : Dewey for Windows (DfW) is a Microsoft Windows based LAN compatible version of the Electronic Dewey with DDC-21 database.

Principle of Hierarchy : Hierarchy in the DDC is expressed through structure and notation.

- ***Structural hierarchy*** **:** Structural hierarchy means that all topics (aside from the ten main classes) are part of all the broader topics above them. It gives the idea that the corollary is also true (whatever is true of the whole is true of the parts). This important concept is called hierarchical force.
- ***Notational hierarchy*** **:** Notational hierarchy is expressed by length of notation. Numbers at any given level are usually subordinate to a class whose notation is one digit shorter; coordinate with a class whose notation has the same number of significant digits; and superordinate to a class with numbers one or more digits longer.

SIGNIFICANT PRINCIPLES TO DETERMINE SUBJECT, DISCIPLINE AND WORK

Determining the Subject of a Work

Classifying a work properly depends first upon determining the subject of the work in hand on the basis and supports of the following:

i. The title
ii. The table of contents
iii. The preface or introduction
iv. Text of the book.
v. Bibliographical references and index entries
vi. Cataloging copy from centralized cataloging services

Determining the Discipline of a Work

After determining the subject, the classifier must then select the proper discipline, or field of study, of the work. The discipline of the work based on the direction in which it is intended.

More Than One Subject in the Same Discipline

What if a work is including multiple subjects treated separately or in relation to one another from the viewpoint of a single discipline? The following guidelines are helpful:

i. Rule of application : A work is classed dealing with interrelated subjects with the subject that is being acted upon. This is called the rule of application, and takes precedence over any other rule.

ii. First-of-two rule : If two subjects receive equal treatment, and are not used to introduce or explain one another, the work is classed with the subject whose number comes first in the DDC schedules.

iii. Rule of three : A work is classed on three or more subjects that are all subdivisions of a broader subject in the first higher number that includes them all (unless one subject is treated more fully than the others).

iv. Rule of zero : Subdivisions beginning with zero should be avoided if there is a choice between 0 and 1–9 at the same point in the hierarchy of the notation. Similarly, subdivisions beginning with 00 should be avoided when there is a choice between 00 and 0.

Table of last resort

When several numbers have been found for the work in hand, and each seems as good as the next, the following table of last resort (in order of preference) may be used as a guideline in the absence of any other rule:

i. Kinds of things
ii. Parts of things
iii. Materials from which things, kinds, or parts are made
iv. Properties of things, kinds, parts, or materials
v. Processes within things, kinds, parts, or materials
vi. Operations upon things, kinds, parts, or materials

vii. Instrumentalities for performing such operations

This table is helpful when there is no clarity of the author's intention and emphasis.

ARRANGEMENT OF THE VARIOUS EDITIONS OF DDC

a. Arrangement of the DDC 21

The print version of Edition 21 is composed of nine major parts in four volumes as follows:

Volume 1

(A) *New Features*: A brief explanation of the special features and changes in Edition 21

(B) *Introduction*: A description of the DDC and how to use it

(C) *Glossary*: Short definitions of terms used in the DDC

(D) Index to the Introduction and Glossary

(E) *Tables*: Seven numbered tables of notation that can be added to class numbers to provide greater specificity:

- T1 Standard Subdivisions
- T2 Geographic Areas, Historical Periods, Persons
- T3 Subdivisions for the Arts, for Individual Literatures, for Specific Literary Forms
  - T3-A Subdivisions for Works by or about Individual Authors
  - T3-B Subdivisions for Works by or about More than One Author
  - T3-C Notation to Be Added Where Instructed in Table 3-B, 700.4, 791.4, 808–809
- T4 Subdivisions of Individual Languages and Language Families
- T5 Racial, Ethnic, National Groups
- T6 Languages
- T7 Groups of Persons

(F) *Lists that compare the previous edition with the new edition*: Relocations and Reductions; Comparative and Equivalence Tables; Reused Numbers.

Volumes 2 and 3

(G) *Schedules*: The organization of knowledge from 000–999

Volume 4

(H) *Relative Index*: An alphabetical list of subjects with the disciplines in which they are treated subarranged alphabetically under each entry.

(I) *Manual*: A guide to classifying in difficult areas, information on new schedules, and an explanation of the policies and practices of the Decimal Classification Division at the Library of Congress. Information in the Manual is arranged by the numbers in the tables and schedule.

b. Arrangement of DDC 22

DDC, Edition 22 is composed of the following major parts in four volumes:

Volume 1

i. *New Features in Edition 22*: A brief explanation of the special features and changes in DDC 22
ii. *Introduction*: A description of the DDC and how to use it
iii. *Glossary*: Short definitions of terms used in the DDC
iv. Index to the Introduction and Glossary
v. *Manual*: A guide to the use of the DDC that is made up primarily of extended discussions of problem areas in the application of the DDC. Information in the manual is arranged by the numbers in the tables and schedules Tables: Six numbered tables of notation that can be added to class numbers to provide greater specificity
vi. Lists that compare Editions 21 and 22: Relocations and Discontinuations; Reused Numbers

Volume 2

i. *DDC Summaries*: The top three levels of the DDC
ii. *Schedules*: The organization of knowledge from 000–599

Volume 3

Schedules: The organization of knowledge from 600–999

Volume 4

Relative Index: An alphabetical list of subjects with the disciplines in which they are treated subarranged alphabetically under each entry.

Entries

i. Entries in the schedules and tables are composed of a DDC number in the number column (the column at the left margin).
ii. A heading describing the class that the number represents, and often one or more notes.
iii. All entries (numbers, headings, and notes) should be read in the context of the hierarchy.

Special features

- The first three digits of schedule numbers (main classes, divisions, sections) appear only once in the number column, when first used.
- Subordinate numbers appear in the number column, beginning with a decimal point, with the initial three digits understood.
- Some numbers in the schedules and tables are enclosed in parentheses or square brackets. Numbers and notes in parentheses provide options to standard practice. Numbers in square brackets are never used. Square brackets represent topics that have been relocated or discontinued, or are unassigned.
- Square brackets are also used for standard subdivision concepts that are represented in another location.

c. Arrangement in DDC 23

DDC 23 is composed of the following major parts in four volumes:

Volume 1

i. *New Features in Edition 23*: A brief explanation of the special features and changes in DDC 23.
ii. *Introduction*: A description of the DDC and how to use it.
iii. *Glossary*: Short definitions of terms used in the DDC.
iv. Index to the Introduction and Glossary.
v. *Manual*: A guide to the use of the DDC that is made up primarily of extended discussions of problem areas in the application of the DDC. Information in the Manual is arranged by the numbers in the tables and schedules.
vi. *Tables*: Six numbered tables of notation that can be added to class numbers to provide greater specificity.
vii. *Lists that compare Editions 22 and 23*: Relocations and Discontinuations.
viii. Comparative and Equivalence Tables; Reused Numbers.

Volume 2

i. *DDC Summaries*: The top three levels of the DDC
ii. *Schedules*: The organization of knowledge from 000–599

Volume 3

(i) Schedules: The organization of knowledge from 600–999

Volume 4

Relative Index: An alphabetical list of subjects with the disciplines in which they are treated subarranged alphabetically under each entry.

Special features

- New provisions in 004–006 Computer science and elsewhere to reflect changes in technology
- Updates to provisions for the Orthodox Church and Islam in 200 Religion
- Improved provisions in 340 Law for legal systems based on civil law
- Updated provisions for food and clothing
- Updates to 740 Graphic arts and decorative arts
- A new location and expanded development for cinematography and videography at 777
- Significant expansions throughout 796 Athletic and outdoor sports and games
- Significant expansions in Table 2, with parallel provisions in 930–990, for the ancient world, Italy, Switzerland, Sweden, Finland, Turkey, Indonesia, Vietnam and Canada
- Updated historical periods throughout 930–990.

ROLE OF LIBRARY OF CONGRESS AND EFFORTS OF OCLC

One of Dewey's great strengths is that the system is developed and maintained in a national bibliographic agency, the Library of Congress. Due to this provision and arrangement, the trends are detected in the literature that must be incorporated into the Classification. Proposed schedule revisions and expansions forwarded to the Decimal Classification Editorial Policy Committee (EPC) for review and recommended action. EPC is composed of professionals from various national, public, special, and academic libraries, and from library schools which helps in understanding the current requirements and future oriented revisions.

OCLC states that Dewey Decimal Classification (DDC) system is the world's most widely used library classification system. The 23rd edition of the DDC enhances the efficiency and accuracy of the classification work. In the year 2011, WebDewey 2.0 installed DDC 23. WebDewey and Abridged WebDewey, correspond to the unabridged and abridged print editions. The Web versions also offer additional electronic functionality not available in the print editions to make the classification work more efficient. There are sources and platforms which continuously provide information and updates on DDC developments. On requirement, news about DDC developments in several ways can be found on OCLC web site. The site also provides a semiannual DDC newsletter, DDC conferences and workshops, OCLC Newsletter articles and case studies for updating the self knowledge.

11

Colon Classification

INTRODUCTION

Colon classification (CC) is a library classification system which was developed by Dr. S. R. Ranganathan. It is a faceted or analytico-synthetic type of classification system. The first edition of Colon Classification was published in 1933. As stated in Britannica, this classification system is general rather than specific in nature, and it can create complex or new categories through the use of facets, or colons. Its name "colon classification" comes from the use of colons to separate facets in class numbers. In Colon Classification main classes has been increased from 33 to 108. There are 10 generalized classes (broadly divided between the humanities and sciences). The colon Classification uses mixed notation of Arabic numerals and roman and Greek letters. Ranganathan's main contribution to *classification* was the notion of these fundamental facets, or categories. Each main class comprises five fundamental facets, or groups: personality, matter, energy, space, and time. Different from Dewey or Library of Congress systems, the book number is an integral part of the call number according to this system. The remarkable feature is that each main class has its appropriate facets and focuses. In addition, there are four tables that correspond to subdivisions—*e.g.*, form, geography, time, and language.

Emergence of Colon Classification

The limitation of Enumerative Schemes : An Enumerative Classification scheme tries to enumerate classification numbers for each and every subject known to the designer. It suggests numbers for some anticipated subjects which may come up in the future.

Succession of semantically rich digits : The enumerated class numbers are built of a succession of semantically rich digits. These numbers (notations) are, not broken into meaningful facts by semantically poor digits.

Difficulty in filiatory positioning : The accommodation of new subjects or documents is difficult in the filiatory position vis-a-vis existing subjects. Placing appropriately new subjects according to the relation with the broader or narrower subject is difficult and a cumbersome job.

Lengthy enumerative schemes : The enumerative classification schemes provide a lengthy schedule of subjects.

The 'facet and isolate' concepts of Colon Classification came further to overcome the limitations of enumerative classification schemes. The emergence of new subjects at the rapid pace necessitated the conceiving of faceted Classification scheme. It was Ranganathan who felt that classification schemes must not be enumerative in nature and he was trying to design a schedule consisting of facets.

HISTORY AND GENESIS OF COLON CLASSIFICATION

Shiyali Ramamrita Ranganathan was a mathematician. Later on he turned to Library Science and due to his efforts and contributions in this field; he was named as father of library science in India. S.R. Ranganathan was well aware that a scheme of classification should be able to meet the challenge of ever growing universe of knowledge. He was thinking of the classification system that can accommodate, at an appropriate place, any new subject without disturbing the arrays already formed. He introduced one of his greatest contributions to the field, the Colon Classification scheme, in 1933. This was published in two slim volumes. One volume held the rules of using the scheme and the other held the schedules needed to use it. Ranganathan, a mathematician by education, first thought of the scheme while studying in London, soon after his appointment as the first official Librarian at the Madras University Library in 1924. He studied at the London School for Librarianship and was greatly influenced by W.C. Berwick Sayers, a professor there.

He felt that the schemes contained flaws because they were developed in order to organize existing collections. He felt there was a need to create a scheme that would be able to reflect forthcoming titles with different subject matter than had been seen in the libraries and to expand to new areas of knowledge over time. His Colon Classification scheme was developed to fill this need. As Ranganathan traveled back to India after his studies, he worked on the scheme that would eventually become Colon Classification. He tested it on the ship's library. He then tested it on the Madras University Library and determined that it was ready to be published. The name comes from the use of the colon as the character to differentiate the pieces of the Class Number, which is comparable to a Dewey number. Colon Classification includes an additional guide for creating what it calls a Book Number. The Class Number and Book Number work together to give individual volumes a place on the shelf.

The first edition of CC came in 1933 Subsequent editions appeared in 1939, 1950, 1952, 1957, 1960 and 1989.Ranganathan was working on the

7th edition of the Colon Classification system when he died. This was finally published in 1987. The seventh edition of CC has succeeded to a large extent in fulfilling this objective.

Two basic strategies for number building in CC are:

Subject analysis : The analysis of a given subject results in the facetisation of subject, as treated in the document, on the basis of the five fundamental categories and their manifestation in it. Synthesis consists of bringing together the facets manifest in a subject to represent, as completely as possible, the description of that subject.

Synthesis : Synthesis has also other connotation. It consists of connecting to the core subject those other aspects, which it shares with other subjects. CC is known as an analytico-synthetic Scheme.

In the fourth edition of Colon Classification, the introduction of separate connecting digits for personality, matter and energy facets created many provisions for classifying any number of subjects. This development led the Colon Classification to be a freely faceted scheme.

Mapping of Universe of knowledge in Colon Classification

Colon Classification scheme is different from the DDC due to its two predominant features: facet analysis and synthesis. Ranganathan mapped out the universe of knowledge by broadly dividing it, at the first instance, on the basis of traditional divisions of knowledge, viz., Natural sciences, Humanities and Social sciences, which he called Partial Comprehensions. Secondly each broad division is further divided into a set of main classes. Thirdly each main class is divided into facets by the application of different trains of characteristics. Fourthly, each facet is further divided into isolates. Fifthly, each isolate is further divided into sub-isolates.

VARIOUS EDITIONS OF COLON CLASSIFICATION

The features of Colon Classification are given according to the emergence and development of different editions:

Edition 1 : The Ranganathan was continuously busy in designing Colon Classification research from 1924 to 1932. The First edition of CC appeared in 1933. This first version was guided by six general laws, and Five Laws of Library Science.

Edition 2 : Ranganathan formulated 'general theory of classification' which provided some guiding principles to rectify some inconsistencies found in the use of the first edition. The first draft of this theory was published as 'Prolegomena to Library Classification' (1st ed. 1937). This theory guided the formulation of 2nd edition of CC (1939).

Editioin 3 : The third edition of CC was published in 1950. This edition was influenced by the developments in the classification theory this edition incorporated new terms such as foci, facet and phase. Also the phase relations were introduced.

Edition 4 : CC edition 4 incorporated the further developments in the theory of classification presented in 'Philosophy of Library Classification (1951)'. This edition was published in 1952. This edition witnessed few new aspects and changes such as:

- The capacity of notation for depth classification,
- The order of facets in Library science and Chemistry was changed from (Problem; Personality) to Personality; problem).
- The concept of five fundamental categories with new connecting symbols took a concrete change.

Edition 5 : The phase after the edition 4 was devoted to continued research in the Theory of Classification, ('Classification and Communication'). The research paved the way of edition 5 which was published in 1959. This edition had following developments:

- A brief alternative schedule of divisions of India was given.
- A new schedule giving details of phase and inter-facet relations was designed.
- The canonical divisions of 'N fine Arts' were revised.

Edition 6 : The 6th edition of CC published in 1960. It gave a selection from the schedules for second levels of time and space facets, and common evergy isolates. A short energy schedule was added to Nuclear Physics and Nuclear Engineering. The connecting symbol for time was changed from a dot to a single inverted comma and octave to sector.

Edition 7 : CC7 introduces many new ideas, e.g. the more complex facet formulas now found. The single volume so far published consists of five parts as:

- Part A is the introduction, giving a history of the development of the scheme and its underlying theory.
- Part B is a short section of 'Guidance to the beginner', Part BB deals with 'how to classify a simple subject', while BC explains 'how to classify a complicated subject'.
- Part C is a lengthy section on general rules, which explains the general principles on which the scheme is constructed.
- Part D covers General divisions and common isolates. The common facets listed are those for language; time, place; common energy isolates; common forms and subjects; and phase relations. The section concludes with a list of the facet indicators used, and a table showing the changes in the facet structure from CC6 to CC7.
- Part F contains the index; Part G the schedule of classics; and Part H the index to Part G. Part E contains the schedules, with the rules for each class immediately following class a much more helpful arrangement than their separation in CC6.

NATURE AND CHARACTERISTICS OF COLON CLASSIFICATION

i. Colon Classification scheme is based on the concept of facet analysis.

ii. Any concept could be built by using a term from a basic class to start the concept at a very broad level and then adding terms that corresponded to facets of that basic class in order to arrive at the very specific topic.

iii. A Class Number was made up of a Basic Class number and as many additional facets (Isolates) that the cataloger needed to add.

iv. The Basic Class number is sometimes referred to as the Basic Subject or the Basic Facet.

FIVE FACETS AND THEIR IDENTIFICATION

The Personality, Energy, and Matter values vary according to subject. The Time and Space values are much more regular across all subject areas. Also, Ranganathan named in 1933 a small number of common subdivisions such as Bibliography, Maps and charts, Biography, History, Statistics, etc. which are used across all subject areas.

The five facets always are placed in a fixed order. The five types of facets are associated with different punctuation. The punctuation indicates what type of facet would follow:

, (comma) = Personality
; (semi-colon) = Matter
: (colon) = Energy
. (period) = Space
' (apostrophe) = Time

Identification of the Facets

Personality facet : The Personality facet indicates the base and core point of the subject at hand. It is the most "elusive" of the five, as Ranganathan himself admitted in the 4th edition. In fact, he stated that if a concept could not easily fit into the other four categories then it is probably a Personality facet. The Personality element is most difficult sometimes to understand because the personality facet relates to the subject. In many cases the Personality element is indicated by a Basic Class number only.

Matter facet : The Matter facet typically deals with some concrete object, typically inanimate. This includes basic elements/materials as well as finished products. This category also includes adjectives to describe inanimate objects.

Energy Facet : Energy indicates action and interaction. This could be persons, objects, or any entity acting alone or with another. This could include conceptual or intellectual entities as well.

Space and Time : These facets are the easiest of the five to understand. However, it is important to note that these are meant to be facets of some other concept, when they are the main focus of a work in themselves, then they are considered to be Personality elements of the work's Class Number.

SALIENT FEATURES OF COLON CLASSIFICATION

Colon Classification (CC) is a classification scheme devised by Dr. S.R. Ranganathan. The first edition of the scheme was brought out in 1933. The features are as following:

i. **Naming of Colon Classification :** Ranganathan gave the name Colon Classification to the scheme, he used colon (:) as connecting symbol for joining facets of a subject to provide the class number to the book.

ii. **Structure :** The scheme has been divided into following three parts.

Part 1	:	Rules
Part 2	:	Schedules
Part 3	:	Classics and sacred books

An index is given at the end of Part-2.

iii. **Basic Principle of PMEST :** Ranganathan postulated the concept of Five Fundamental Categories viz. Personality [PI, Matter (M), Energy IE], Space [SI and Time [T], called PMEST.

iv. **Notation :** CC uses mixed notations of Indo-Arabic numerals, Roman capitals, Roman smalls and some indicator digits, which are as follows:

Indo-Arabic Numerals (1-9)	9
Roman alphabets (Capitals A, B, C,- -Z)	26
Roman alphabets (Smalls a-z excluding i, 1, o)	23
Greek letters (A Delta and I Sigma)	02

and so many other indicator digits.

v. **Analytico-Synthetic feature :** The schedule of CC consists of certain standard unit schedules. Two basic operations involved in number building in CC viz. subject analysis on the basis of five fundamental categories and synthesis. The former results in the facilitations of the subject and synthesis consist in bringing together the facets manifest in the subject to represent as completely as possible the description of that subject. Because of the operations of analysis and synthesis CC is called an analytico-synthetic scheme.

VARIOUS POSTULATES OF RANGANATHAN

Postulate is not a law but it lays down few principles. Various postulates have been discussed in Ranganathan's Prolegomena as follows:

a) Postulate of Fully Faceted Classification Scheme.

b) Postulate of Basic Subject.

c) Postulate of Fundamental Category.

d) Postulate of Facet Sequence.

e) Postulate of Rounds and Levels of Fundamental Categories.

f) Postulate of Systems and Specials.

The most widely used postulates are explained as following:

Postulates of Rounds and Levels

Dr. Ranganathan identified five fundamental categories in a subject. Some of the categories manifest themselves more than once in a subject. Ranganathan called this situation as Rounds and Levels. A type of repetition of any of the categories is called Round and Levels of Fundamental Category.

(a) Postulate of Rounds

There is no problematic situation before classifier if the facet terms of a document identified and selected are only five, each of them being regarded as the manifestation of one or the other of the five fundamental categories P M, E, S and T. Their analysis and synthesis are not difficult. But, if any facet manifests more than once, the facet sequence has to be obtained with a few more additional postulates. Only [P], [E] and [M] facets can manifest more than once in a subject. Their manifestation is shown in the following table:

Fundamental Category	First Round	Second Round	Third Round
[P] Personality	[PI	[2P]	[3P1
[M] Matter	[M]	[2M[	[3M[*
[E] Energy	[El	[2E1	[3E[*

* The use of [3M| and [3E]- can be done in depth classification if needed. There is (It* founds in [S] Space and [T] Time facets.

i) Rounds in Personality: Fundamental category [P] can be occurred second, third time and fourth round of manifestation. These manifestations are respectively called Second Round Personality [2P], Third Round Personality [3P] and Fourth Round Personality [4P] so on.

ii) Rounds in Matter: Fundamental category [M] can be occurred second, third time fourth rounds of manifestations. These manifestations are called Second Round Matter [2M], Third Round Matter [3M] and so on. Rounds of Matter occur only in the classes Physics, Biology, Botany, Zoology and Medicine. The use of [M] after the [E] [2P] called the Second Round of Matter.

iii) Rounds in Energy: Fundamental category [E] can be occurred second, third and so on rounds of manifestations. These manifestations are called Second Round of Energy [2E], Third Round of Energy [3E] etc. In the main classes of Agriculture, Medicine, and Sociology, Energy facet occurs more than once.

(b) Postulates of Levels

The concept of Levels denotes recurrence of one and the same fundamental category within a round. The first manifestation of the fundamental category within a round is known as level-1 and a similar second manifestation within rounds as Level-2. The fundamental categories

[PI, [S] and [T] can manifest at more than one levels.

(i) **Levels in Personality :** Personality has been manifested in 4 levels in the main classes Literature, Linguistics, General Bibliography and Law. The second, third, fourth manifestation of Personality are called respectively Second, Third and Fourth Level Personality such as [P2], [P3] and [P4].

(ii) **Levels in Space and Time :** The Fundamental categories [S] and [T] occur in the last round only. Both of these two categories can manifest themselves in two levels in the last round.

Postulates of Systems and Specials

In some of the traditional main classes of knowledge, some Specials and Systems are prevalent, which may be given the form of the main classes and plentiful reading materials is also available on these main classes in view of the bibliographic requirements. So they have the right of getting their place in the form of main classes, but their basic subject can be only their basic class. This kind of concepts is called School of Thought, but in 1952 Ranganathan called them Specials and Systems.

(a) Postulate of Systems

System refers to exposition of a basic subject according to some special school of thought. Thus system denotes divisions of a main class expounded after a school of thoughts, which is a group or succession of persons devoted to some cause or philosophy. The class number for a system is derived by the Chronological Device (CD), i.e. by using the year of origin of the system as the epoch.

L Medicine	X Economics	S Psychology	C Physics
LB Ayurveda	XB War economics	SM Experimental	CK Gravitation
LCSiddha	XM Cooperative	SN Gestalt	CM Kinetic
LDUnani	XM2 Socialism	SN1 Behaviouristic	CN Relativity
LL Homeopathy	XN Communism	SN2 Typological	CN1 Quantum
LM Naturopathy	XN 19 Technocracy	SN8 Field	CN2Wave

Systems are treated as the Basic Classes. The facet formula for the main class to which the system belongs is also applicable to the System Basic Class. But, in case of System Basic Class, the personality isolate should always be preceded by a comma, even if the facet formula does not provide comma after the main class.

(b) Postulates of Specials

Specials refer to specific areas of a subject. It means specialization in a particular aspect which deals with the entire subject. Specials facets are enumerated at the end of some of the main classes, such as Physics, Chemistry, Biology, Agriculture, Medicine and Economics.

L Medicine	C Physics	G Biology	X Economics
L9A Specials	C9A Specials	G9A Specials	X9A Specials
L9C Child	C9B2Atom	G9B Embryo	X9B Small scale
L9E01dage	C9B3 Nucleus	G9C Child	X9D Large scale

L9F Female	C9B5 Electron	G9D Adolescent	X9S Private
L9X Industrial	C9D1 Low Temp.	G9E01dage	X9W Public

Specials are also treated as the Basic Class. The rules for joining the special facets are the same as rules for system facets.

3. Systems and Specials : If a title has both system as well as special facets in it, the sequence of these facets, according to the rules remains as follows:

System, Special, Personality

PHASE RELATIONS

The classification of a complex subject requires understanding of Phase Relations. Complex subjects are those in which two subjects are interrelated and have two phases of either Basic or Compound subjects. The constituent classes of a complex subject are called its phases. The relation between constituent classes is known as Phase Relation. The related aspects are such as:

i. Phase relation is a device to represent interconnected subjects by their correct class numbers.

ii. A phase relation may occur between two or more main classes, within one and the same facet of a main class or within one and the same array in isolates.

iii. The relation notice in inter-disciplinary subjects is known as Phase Relation.

Phase relations have been identified in CC explicitly and classified into their types and kinds also. Their three types of phase relations are Inter Subject, Intra-facet and Intra-array. Each of these has been categorized into 6 kinds of relations (6th edition).

Phase Relation	Intra-Subject	Intra-Facet	Intra-Array
1. General	0a	0j	Ot
2. Bias	Ob	Ok	Ou
3. Comparison	Oc	Om	Ov
4. Difference	Od	On	Ow
5. Tool	Oe	Op	Ox
6. Influencing	0g	Or	Oy

Inter-Subject Phase Relations : When the relation is indicated between two or more subjects.

Intra-Facet Phase Relations : When the relation is indicated between two isolates within one and the same facet.

Colon Classification 7th Edition

The 6th edition was published in the year 1964 and the 7th edition has been published in 1987 with substantial changes from the earlier editions. The whole details of the 7th edition have already been published in brief in the journal "Library Science with a slant of Documentation". The modifications may be regarded as the features or characteristics of the 7th edition:

1. In two parts : The 6th edition was published in 3 parts but the 7th edition is published into 2 parts only.

2. Based Pattern : The 6th edition of the scheme was almost faceted but the 7th edition is likely to be freely faceted due to its analytico-synthetic quality.

3. Number of Subjects and Increased Main Classes : Nearly 5000 subjects have been given place in 7th edition, out of them 32 are those which are being represented by a single digit and they are main subjects. 84 are represented by two digits. Three digits for class numbers are also used, but they are very few. Since it has more subjects, the number of main classes in it has been increased from 47 to 105.

4. Connecting Symbols : In 7th edition, some more connecting symbols exist for use. The connecting symbol & (Ampersand) has replaced of 0 (zero) in the phase relation. One new connecting symbol Double Inverted Comma is introduced.

5. Increase in Energy Isolates : A large number of energy isolates have been newly created which fall under different main classes like - Petrology, Economics, Geology, Botany, Zoology, Medicine, Agriculture and Animal Husbandry.

6. Matter Category divided : The fundamental category [M] Matter has been put into 3 kinds, such as (a) Material, (b) Method, (c) Property.

7. First Facet Indicator : The first indicator Full stop (.) was not necessary to put for isolate number after basic class in 6th edition but in 7th edition the putting of the same will be necessary.

8. Other changes : The use of semicolon (;) is possible at so many places in 7th edition in place of colon (:). In the same way hyphen (-) is to be used in place of full stop (.)

THE LIMITATIONS OF COLON CLASSIFICATION

The gradual developments and frequent changes made this scheme not that much popular, it could be. The few aspects are as following:

- This scheme is better suited for classification of academic libraries than public or general-interest libraries as some critics say.
- Due to major changes from one edition to the next, this added a burden of retrofitting to the libraries that used the scheme.
- The rapid changes gave the international community the impression that Colon Classification was a work in progress rather than a fully functioning scheme.
- The Colon Classification notation and code numbers are simply too complex to gain acceptance from average library patrons.

12

Library Cataloguing

INTRODUCTION

Different types of libraries collect information sources to serve the users. The library serves different types of users who might face difficulty in searching and finding the desired document from the library collection. The libraries organize to give easy access to library collection with the help of classification but locating the specific document is somehow cumbersome. Cataloguing and classification are basic processes in organizing information resources and services to support user needs. Here cataloguing is the process that describes documents. The information present in the catalogue helps in identification of the documents. The library catalogue is an index or a key to the collection. The catalogue not only identifies but also inform about the location of a book in the library.

Why cataloguing?

The introductory information in the beginning of this chapter states about the description, identification and location of a book or document in the library. This is important because library collections house a wide variety of materials on many different topics and in many different formats. The bigger the library, the bigger the challenge is in making the books and other documents available for the use of library users. To present what is available in the library collection, the need of library cataloguing was emerged long ago. The library catalogue considered as an index has been for a book. The index informs about the contents contained in a book without having to read every page. The library catalogue tells availability and presence of a book according to his or her requirement. The catalogue provides the approaches and access points by which a user can search and find the book in a library. These approaches and access points are in the form of author name (s), titile and subjects. Other points of access were additional authors, names of series, illustrators, and sometimes the titles of contents.

What is Library Catalogue?

As defined in literature, a library catalogue is a list of books, maps, sound recordings, or materials in other medium that represents a collection arranged alphabetically by authors, titles, number, or subjects. The main purpose of library catalogue is to record, describe, and index the holding of a collection. Thus we can say that a catalogue is a list of things (Documents) exhibited in a library, usually with description (access points) and often illustration (notes). A library catalogue serves the purpose by filing of records for a library's collection. It informs about the materials owned by the library, listing what the library possesses by a certain author, on a given subject, and with a certain title, and enabling library materials to be located easily.

Very earlier, Ranganathan has defined a library catalogue as "a list of document in a library or in a collection forming a portion of it". A "list" refers to some kind of arrangement based on a set plan and a "document" constitutes embodied thought, which is a 'record of work on paper or other material fit for physical handling, transport across space and preservation through time'. This means that document includes all types of records in which information can be stored or presented.

According to Ruth French Strout, a catalogue may be considered "a work in which contents are arranged in a reasonable way, according to a set plan or merely word by word".

In more technical sense we can say that a library catalogue is a register of all bibliographic items found in a library or group of libraries, such as a network of libraries at several locations. A bibliographic item can be any information entity (e.g., books, computer files, graphics, cartographic materials, etc.) that is considered library material.

Various types of library catalogues are as following:

Author catalogue : This catalogue is arranged alphabetically according to the authors' or editors' names of the entries.

Title catalogue : this type of catalogue is arranged alphabetically according to the article of the entries.

Dictionary catalogue : In dictionary catalogue, all entries (author, title, subject, series) are interfiled in a single alphabetical order.

Keyword catalogue : a subject catalogue, sorted alphabetically according to some system of keywords.

Classified Catalogue : this is called Systematic Catalogue also. It is basically a subject catalogue. These catalogues are arranged subdivision of subjects.

Shelf list catalogue : This type of catalogue has the order of bibliographic items are shelved.

It is well said that the catalogue is one of the oldest and most important means by which humans have sought to control information. The modern library catalogue serves both the inventory (listing) and retrieval (finding) function.

Comparing the Library Catalogue with a Database

The Library Catalogue is a database comprised of Library material description. The library catalogue is a big *database and* a database is considered a collection of *records.* Each record represents an item in the library.

This catalogue database reflects the material owned by the library such as:

- Books
- Reference Books
- Titles of Periodicals (magazines, newspapers and journals) etc.

Using a catalogue saves the time by accessing the online catalogue. While being present in the library, the user can check the catalogue itself and know the location.

BIBLIOGRAPHIC CONTROL AND GOALS OF LIBRARY CATALOGUE

In 1876, Charles Ammi Cutter discussed about the objectives of a bibliographic system in his *Rules for a Printed Dictionary Catalog.* According to Cutter, those objectives were:

1. To enable a person to find a book of which either
    - the author
    - the title
    - the subject
    - the category

    is known.
2. To show what the library has
    - by a given author
    - on a given subject
    - in a given kind of literature
3. To assist in the choice of a book
    - as to its edition (bibliographically)
    - as to its character (literary or topical)

Thus the objectives talked by Cutter are of the three identical nature of the library catalogue:

1. Identifying objective
2. Collocating objective
3. Evaluating objective

In this context, "if it is the interest in the subject which takes him to the library, his wants will be better served if the catalogue can spread before him a full connected panorama of all materials on his specific subject, all its subdivisions and all broader subject of which it is itself a subdivision," as pointed by Ranganathan. Also Ranganathan in the light of the five laws of library & information science expressed the objectives of a catalogue as the following:

i. Disclose to every reader his or her document;
ii. Secure for every document its reader;
iii. Save the time of the reader and with this save the time of the staff.

The theories of bibliographic control state that the library catalogue allows users to find, collocate, identify, select, and obtain materials in a library. So bibliographic control functions of the library catalogue are such as :

i. find
ii. collocate
iii. identify
iv. Select
v. obtain materials

Catalogue functions to remember the items available in a library. In a library, each entry in the catalogue is the representation of a bibliographic record at a particular point in the catalogue. It is a bibliographic records transcription of the complete cataloguing information for any item. The purpose of a bibliographic record is:

i. to provide all the information to describe an item both physically and intellectually in order to distinguish it form other item.
ii. to provide its location in the collection. .

Objectives and Functions of Library Catalogue

The objectives of a library catalogue are to enable a user to find a book when one of the author, or title, or subject is known; to show what the library has by a given author, on a given subject, in a given kind of literature; and to assist in the choice of a material as to the edition or as to its characteristic.

The main functions of a library catalogue are to enable the library users to determine:

a. whether the library has a certain item
b. which works by a particular author are in the collection
c. which editions of a particular work the library has, and
d. what materials the library has on a particular subject.

VARIOUS PHYSICAL FORMS OF LIBRARY CATALOGUE

The various physical forms of a library catalogue are book catalogues, card catalogues, microform catalogue and online catalogue. The library catalogue should have following features to be useful to the users:

i. flexible and up-to-date to the changing of library collection
ii. easy to use

iii. easy to produce in multiple copies
iv. adding or removing of entries.

Looking back in the history of catalogue emergence and development, the printed book or book catalogue is the oldest type of catalogue which was commonly used in American libraries. This type of catalogue was expensive to produce and quickly became out of date or inflexible in changing of the collection. Due to problems of being expensive and hard to update, it was replaced by card catalogues. The size of card catalogue is a standard 7.5 x 12.5 cm. card. The entries are filed in alphabetically order by author, subject, title, or call number in the drawers to provide access to the collection. The card catalogue is very flexible; it can be easily added or removed whenever necessary. Due to advent of computer-output microform (COM), COM catalogues have been produced in microfilm or microfiche. The online catalogue replaced the COM and the bibliographic records are displayed on computer screen. The Online catalogues are most popular due to being most flexible.

CATALOGUING ENTRIES AND METHODS

The basic work of cataloguing is to prepare various types of entries. We can say that an entry is a certain amount of information that is recorded for a specific purpose. The entry displays the information which has been entered into a kind of record. The recording of the information about the document in the catalogue is called an entry. It means that we are preparing an entry for the document.

Definitions

Entry is a ultimate unit record in a catalogue or a documentation list. —*Ranganathan*

An entry in a catalogue is the record of a book. —*ALA Rules*

A record of a bibliographical entry in a catalogue. —*AACR*

The need and importance of Catalogue entries

Library catalogue is a record of the documents available in a library as well as a search tool. It helps the users in finding their documents. The user could have different approaches to the document-author, title, subject or series. The library catalogues provide various types of entries. Thus entries record the information about documents and help the users by describing an item. Entries are also helpful sometimes to find out the documents that are inter-related.

Classification of Entries

Entries can be classified according to AACR-2 and CCC codes as follows:

AACR-2	CCC
1. Main Entry	1. Main Entry
2. Added Entries	2. Added Entries
(a) Joint Author Entry	(a) Class Index Entry
(b) Title Entry	(b) Book Index Entry
(c) Subject Entry	(c) Cross Reference Index Entries
(d) Series Entry	(d) Cross Reference Entries
3. Reference Entry	
4. Analytical Entry	

Main Entry

Main entry is prepared under the access point which is considered prime, important and main. The main entry is the basic and most important entry of the book. In the main entry, all the essential information is provided. It provides the useful and relevant information for the identification of a document. It fulfills the purpose of satisfying the different approaches of the library users. It displays the bibliographical details and it carries maximum information about the book. It functions as a key to all the added entries.

Definitions

The complete catalogue record of an item, presented in the form by which the entry is to be uniformly identified and cited. —*AACR-2*

Main entry is the entry which gives maximum information about a document. All other entries relating to the document are usually derived from the main entry. —*CCC*

Added (Additional) Entries

There are few more entries other than main entry, which are called as added or additional entries. The added entries are intended to help the user to find a document by different approaches which are different from the main entry. The additional entries provide access points other than the main access point. Added entries function as supplementary entries.

Definition

An added entry is an entry, additional to the main entry by which an item is represented in a catalogue; a secondary entry. —*AACR-2*

An Added entry is an entry other than main entry. —*CCC*

CATALOGUING AUTHORITY CONTROL

Authority control is the process of establishing a single preferred form of a heading, which can then be used consistently, uniquely and unambiguously to refer to a single entity or concept. Authority records may also provide references from equivalent headings, as well as references to related headings (former and later names; broader, narrower and related subjects). It has following purposes:

- To assist the catalogue user in locating items of interest. The reference structure of the authority record guides catalogue users to the form of heading under which all relevant works are collocated.
- To improve the efficiency of cataloguing processes and maximizing resources.
- To record decisions made about the choice of a heading and information gathered in the course of cataloguing, which avoid the need to repeat this work when another item by the same author, or concerning the same topic, is catalogued?

13
Cataloguing Codes

Various Standards for Cataloguing are being used in the library and information world. In the past when the concept of cataloguing was arising, there was considered the need of certain rules, some provisions to be followed so that uniformity and consistency could be achieved in cataloguing and its presentation. The libraries were in need of guidelines which could be meant to be purposeful for the cataloguer as well as users. The cataloguing codes emerged but after gradual developments. The authority and guidance provided by these catalogue codes has been impactful. The codes and their standards have been base for the cataloguing scenario world wide. The libraries recognize the importance of adhering to common codes and standards in the creation of catalogue data according to following cataloguing codes, standards and supporting sources for cataloguing:

- Anglo-American Cataloging Rules 2nd ed. Rev. (AACR2R)
- Library of Congress Rule Interpretations (LCRIs)
- Classified Catalogue Code
- Library of Congress's Subject Headings Manual
- Library of Congress' Descriptive Cataloging Manual : Z1 : Name and series authority records, MARC 21 Format for Authority Data
- The Australian National Bibliographic Database (ANBD) authorities and headings

The present chapter introduces two main cataloguing codes and their features.

History and Beginning of Cataloguing Codes

The codification of library cataloging rules stared with the *Rules for a Dictionary Catalogue* published in 1876 by Charles Cutter. The international applicability of Cutter's rules was further reinforced with the arrival in 1908 "Joint Code of 1908." This code was largely based on the Library of Congress' adaptations of Cutter's rules. The revisions were published in 1941 and 1949 by Library of Congress. In October 1961, at a convention of the International Federation of Library Agencies and Institutions (IFLA), the twelve "Paris Principles" were drafted at the International Conference on Cataloguing Principles in Paris. These principles provided the foundation for the first edition of the *Anglo-American Cataloguing Rules* which was published in 1967. The first edition of AACR appeared in 1967, a cooperative effort of catalogers in the U.S., U.K., and Canada. The first edition of AACR was published in 1967 in somewhat distinct North American and British texts. In 1971, IFLA published the first preliminary version of its International Standard Bibliographic Description (ISBD). The ISBD was applied only to books. Later on, more ISBDs were developed for other formats, including cartographic materials, non-book materials, printed music, antiquarian books, monographs, and serials. The *General International Standard Bibliographic Description (ISBD(G))* was introduced in 1977 and it is "intended to provide the maximum amount of descriptive information in a range of different bibliographic activities." It distributes elements into eight areas:

i. Title and statement of responsibility;
ii. Edition;
iii. Material (or type of publication) specific data;
iv. Publication, distribution data (including place and date of publication);
v. Physical description;
vi. Series;
vii. Notes; and
viii. Standard number and terms of availability.

The ISBDs are meant to provide a "common basis for the construction of national and multinational cataloguing codes." The *Anglo-American Cataloguing Rules* are based on ISBD(G).

Anglo-American Cataloguing Rules-2 (AACR 2)

The second edition of *AACR* was published in 1978. The Joint Steering Committee for Revision of AACR was constituted of representatives from the U.S., U.K., and Canada, Australia for the review and maintenance process for *AACR*. The Anglo-American Cataloguing Rules, Second Edition was published jointly by the American Library Association, the Canadian Library Association, and the Chartered Institute of Library and Information Professionals in the UK.

Again the substantial revision appeared in 1988. This revision contained an explanation of the history, structure, and working methods of the international group of catalogers who are responsible for maintaining and revising the rules. The AACR 2 was unified the two sets of rules (adopting the British spelling 'cataloguing') and brought them in line with the International Standard Bibliographic Description. The second edition had a substantial change in the form of headings for corporate bodies.

The revision of second edition was developed by the Joint Steering Committee for Revision of AACR, Michael Gorman and Paul Winkler, editors. The American Library Association's Committee on Cataloging: Description and Access (CC:DA) is the U.S. representative to the Joint Steering Committee and the body responsible for making recommendations on rule revision and maintenance in the U.S. The Society of American Archivists appoints a liaison to CC:DA.

Versions of AACR 2

AACR2 exists in various print versions, as well as an online version. There are AACR2 revisions including a concise edition. The online version is available from the Library of Congress. For the ease of use, various translations are also available from other sources. Over the years AACR2 has been updated by occasional amendments, and was significantly revised in 1988 (2nd edition, 1988 revision) and 2002 (2nd edition, 2002 revision). The 2002 revision included substantial changes to sections for non-book materials. A schedule of annual updates began in 2003 and ceased with 2005.

Scope and structure

Rules for descriptive cataloging of all types of materials are likely to be found in general library collections. AACR2 is meant for the cataloguing in libraries of various types and sizes. The AACR 2 provides rules for the description, access points.

The Individual chapters cover:

i. books, pamphlets, and printed sheets;
ii. cartographic materials;
iii. manuscripts;
iv. music;
v. sound recordings;
vi. motion pictures and videorecordings;
vii. graphic materials;
viii. computer files;
ix. three-dimensional artifacts and realia;
x. microforms; and serials.

These rules provide guidance for the catalogers in:

i. constructing descriptions to identify and represent bibliographic works in catalogs; and
ii. constructing uniform headings (for persons, corporate bodies, geographic places, and titles) to be used as access points in catalogs. They do not cover subject cataloging.

Related standards

The implementation of AACR-2 was begun by Library of Congress in 1981. This was the time when there were rapid developments taking place by emergence of many new fronts of items in the libraries. Thus the rules were found inadequate in dealing with these new forms of library materials. Therefore attempts were made to classify, expand or alter rules in necessary cases. Hence the revised edition of this code AACR- 2 came out with 3 sets of revisions, which were issued in 1982, 1984 and 1986. The revised code was given the name AACR-2R where R means revised edition. This revision did not result either in the change of basic concepts, principles or structure.

- AACR 2 is based on the twelve "Paris Principles" developed by the International Conference on Cataloguing Principles in October 1961 and on ISBD(G).
- The Library of Congress Name Authority File is a data value standard containing authorized name headings formulated according to AACR 2. These are formulated by the Library of Congress and institutions participating in the Name Authority Cooperative (NACO) project.
- Library of Congress Rule Interpretations are interpretive guidelines for U.S. users of *AACR 2*.

Features

i. AACR 2, Chapter 4, "Manuscripts," focuses on description of individual manuscript items, particularly literary manuscripts and letters.
ii. For archives that sometimes catalogue books, pamphlets, and nontextual materials, other AACR 2 chapters offer guidance.
iii. AACR 2 has additional rules on choice or form of entries.

How AACR- 2 helps in Cataloguing?

Anglo-American Cataloguing Rules-2 is very important and useful code for cataloguing of emerging new types of reading items along with books and periodicals.

This code has been very important and useful for cataloguing purposes. Its first edition (AACR-I) was published in 1967 after a great discussion about cataloguing rules in conference held in 1961. This was an effort to bring uniformity and similarity in cataloguing systems. This code was devised in three parts and was seen as a better code in terms of its more logical grouping of the rules with emphasis on conditions of authorship rather than on classes of authors and kinds of publications. The expanding cooperation between the cataloguing agencies in UK, USA and other countries as well as the increase in the use of UKMARC and LCMARC, brought about agreement for a single unified text of code, the ambiguities and differences resolved, and as a result, the second edition of AACR was published in 1978 (AACR-2). The rules in this code were based on ISBDs and it also presented descriptive rules also. In description the code permitted alternative rules and options to suit the needs of the libraries and cataloguing agencies. This code also standardized punctuation to conform to the pattern established in ISBDs. AACR-2 code is divided into two parts. 4 Appendices are also given and an index is also presented at the end of the code. Some features of AACR- 2 code are as following:

Structure: AACR-2 has been divided into following two parts:

Part-1: Description

a) In this part, rules for standard description of all kinds of materials are given, which are of general applicability. These rules are given in 13 chapters and provide data elements for preparing entries for the books.

b) Rules are also given for recording descriptions of specific types of items.

c) It also provides the use of ISBDs for descriptions cataloguing developed and determined by 1FLA.

d) Rules have also been provided for other so many types of documents.

e) The various areas/items to be included in the description are : (a) Title and statement of responsibility: (b) Edition; (c) Materials or type of publication; (d) Publication, distribution; (e) Physical description; (f) Series; (g) Notes; (h) Standard number; (i) Tracing.

Part-2: Determination of Headings or Access Points .

In this part, the rules for determination of choice of entries and form of headings are provided. These rules are applicable to all library materials irrespective of the medium. In this way the rules are provided extensively in this part as follows:

a) Rules are also given for rendering of headings for preparing main as well as added entries.

b) Rules are also given for preparing entries for various types of inner forms of the catalogue according to unit card system.

2. Levels of Description : The catalogue entries vary from library to library on the basis of description of the items. The description is categorised into levels on the basis of amount of information to be included. The code has recommended that all descriptive elements may not be useful to all the libraries. The inclusion of these descriptive elements is of 3 levels as follows:

a) *First level* : The first level of description provides minimum information which is necessary to identify a given document. This level is used in small libraries. Example-

Agrawal, Rajat
Textbook of Botany.-Agra: Jeevan Publications, 1967.
344p.;35 cm.

b) **Second level :** This level can be called a standard description. It provides all the data which are considered necessary for description of document. This level of description is used for medium to large sized libraries. This serves the requirement of most of the users. Example - The same book under second level of description will be as follows:

Agrawal, Rajat
Textbook of Botany /by Rajat Agrawal. - Agra : Jeevan Publications, 1967.
344p.;35 cm.- (Botany series, no. 2).

c) *Third level*: This level provides description of the documents covering every possible elements of description included in the code. This level is used in large and special libraries. For this level, include all elements set out in the rules that are applicable to the item being described. This applies in very rare cases.

3. Appendices: After the Part-1 of the structure, four appendices have also been presented, in which—

a) Directions are given for the use of numerals, abbreviations, capital and small letters of English alphabets.
b) A glossary has also been provided in the appendix, which represents various cataloguing terms which are useful in catalogue.
c) The technical terms are presented in the context of the rules.

4. Index: In the end of all, an index has also been provided which is complete itself but it is brief.

LATER DEVELOPMENTS AND AACR

Principles of AACR include cataloguing from the item 'in hand'. It is based on the concept of the 'chief source of information'. AACR2 has been succeeded by Resource Description and Access (commonly referred to as RDA), which was released in June 2010. This new code is informed by the Functional Requirements for Bibliographic Records and was conceived to be a framework more flexible and suitable for use in a digital environment. In the fall of 2010, the Library of Congress, National Library of Medicine, National Agricultural Library, and several other institutions and national libraries of other English-speaking countries performed a formal test of RDA, the results of which were released in June 2011.

CLASSIFIED CATALOGUE CODE

Ranganathan published the Classified Catalogue Code in 1934. Before Ranganathan, in India, there was no bibliographic/cataloguing tradition. Since Ranganathan was educated in England so he was aware of the western thought and practice. This awareness and exposure definitely provided the needed background to work out independently. As we know that the function of a catalogue is to itemize works so they can be found by author, title, series, and so forth. It is also implied that it must also allow readers to review the selection of works on a given subject. Ranganathan maintained, however, that a catalogue should consist of two components:

- One part should be classified by subject, reflecting the library's classification system, with class number entries.
- The other should be a dictionary catalog, including author, title, series, and similar identifiers, as well as alphabetized subject entries.

Various Editions of Classified Catalogue Code

Ranganathan (Shiyali Ramamrita) (1892-1972). Classified Catalogue Code with Additional Rules for Dictionary Catalogue Code. Ed 5. Assisted by A Neelameghan.

Ranganathan's Classified Catalogue code (CCC) is prominent code of the cataloguing pracice. Like Cutter's rules and Vatican code, the CCC is the only other code which covers all the cataloguing procedures and to provide rules for entry, description, subject cataloguing/indexing and filing.

First edition : The first edition appeared in 1934 and was continued through five editions, the last (i.e., the 5th edition) coming in 1964. Each later edition was an improvement on the earlier one, the revision, addition or improvement made on the basis of practical application and critical examination supported by teaching and reasoning. This empirical, analytical and critical approach shaped the code progressively.

Second edition : The second edition (1945) had following features:

i. The symbiotic relationship between classification and cataloging and evolved chain procedure for subject cataloguing/indexing.
ii. Rules for style of writing and alphabetisation correlating the two through Gestalt theory of alphabetisation were other added features of this edition.
iii. Ranganathan's comparative study of classified and dictionary, catalogues and evaluation of Cutter's rules helped him publish his Dictionary Catalogue Code in 1945.

Third edition : The third edition (1951) had following features:

i. Rules for compiling union catalogue of periodical publications, abstracting periodical and incorporating
ii. Glossary of English-Sanskrit terms to be helpful for developing cognate terminology in other Indian languages.

Fourth edition : The fourth edition (1955), as a result of his comparative study of five codes (Heading and Canons published in 1955) made necessary further corrections and alterations which eliminated the need for a separate dictionary catalogue code. It had following features:

i. The lay-out for a catalogue code (in the light of Heading and Canons),
ii. Supplementary rules for national bibliography,
iii. Rearrangement of the rules for determination of authorship, choice of heading and rendering the heading.
iv. Additional rules for style of writing effecting corresponding changes in the rules for alphabetisation.

Fifth edition : The fifth edition (1964) had following features:

i. New chapters on Law of parsimony, physical form, centralized cataloguing, homonyms in class index entries and feature headings, and non-conventional documents.
ii. Correction of typographical and other simple errors.

While the codes for alphabetical, author and dictionary catalogues are quite large in number, the codes oriented to classified catalogue are few in number.

Structurally, it is a well laid code. The code can be divided into three units.

- The first 9 parts/ chapters (A to H and D form the approach. Many basic issues, more importantly, canons and normative principles; parts and physical forms of catalogue, centralized cataloguing; recording, style, language and script, arrangement of entries; conflict of authorship and resolution (determination of authorship); name of person, (i.e., structure, element, etc.) are dealt with.
- Chapters (K to N, P to V) constitute the substantial part, i.e., rules for rendering names (persons, corporate bodies, geographical entities); preparation of class Index entries; main and book index entries for different categories of books and periodicals; additional rules for compilation of union catalogues of books and periodical publications; National bibliography; indexing periodical; abstracting periodical; and cataloguing of incunabula and non-book materials.
- The last part (W) constitutes end matter (glossary of terms, bibliographic references and index).
- The rules are marked for their simplicity, clarity and brevity. The code draws a distinction between a library catalogue and a bibliography. Elaborated description is a necessity in bibliography and not in a library catalogue. Therefore, CCC does not prescribe recording of imprint, collation, many details in notes, statement of responsibility in the title section, etc. The rules for determining authorship are based on a set of problems explained as conflicts of authorship.

The rules relating to rendering of names/headings for persons, corporate bodies and geographic entities are based on language, nationality and cultural preferences which are postulated through principles. The empirical approach and application of normative principles in drafting and arranging the rules have CCC a model code. The fact that it does not cover the entire range of various types of material makes it a less comprehensive code. No code can be perfect in all details. CCC is no exception. It needs revision and rethinking so as to capture and respond to the many changes that have come about after its publication in 1964.

Various Kinds of Entries in CCC

The classified catalogue code is an important cataloguing code. It is based on the normative principles and canons of cataloguing. According to

Ranganathan, the classified catalogue has two parts: the classified part and the alphabetical part.

The classified part contains main as well as cross reference entries, these are prepared by call number and class number respectively. These entries are called as number entries also. The arrangement of the entries in this part is logical and based on the call numbers and class numbers. The entries serve as a systematic classified subject catalogue.

The alphabetical part is comprised of word entries and they are arranged in alphabetical manner as in dictionary. This part functions well as alphabetical index to the classified component. Several index entries such as Book index entries, Class Index entries, and Cross Reference index entries are prepared.

The types of entries according to CCC are as following:

i. Main entry

ii. Added entry

a. Class Index Entries

b. Book Index Entries

i. Author Entry

ii. Joint Author Entry

iii. Collaborator Entry

iv. Title Entry

v. Series Entry

c. Cross Reference Index Entries

i. Alternative name Entry

ii. Variant Form of Word Entry

iii. Pseudo-Real Name Entry

iv. Editor of Series Entry

d. Cross Reference Entries

14

Forms and Types of Library Catalogues

The forms of catalogue are related with the internal arrangement as well as external format and presentation. This chapter describes the forms and types of catalogues.

INNER FORMS OF LIBRARY CATALOGUE

Inner form of library catalogue is related with the order of arrangement of entries in the catalogue. Inner forms are concerned with the mode of arrangement of entries. It is observed, "Catalogues like sentences or grammar, are of three kinds: simple, compound and complex." Inner forms of library catalogue deal with the organization and arrangement of bibliographic data in a catalogue entry and the systematic and logical arrangement of the resultant entries for storage and retrieval. This recognized order of arrangement determines the inner forms i.e. types of library catalogue. There are a number of ways of arranging catalogue entries to fall into a helpful order. The most popular of them, are to arrange the entries in an alphabetical order or to arrange them in a classified order on the basis of the classification scheme. A simple catalogue may be either an author, title or subject catalogue, a compound catalogue is a combination of two simple entries (author and title, for instance, or author and subject); and a complex catalogue is one containing subjects, titles and series in subordination to the principle (author) entry. The inner forms are categorized on the basis of mode or order of arrangement of entries, as following:

1. Alphabetical catalogue
2. Classified catalogue
3. Alphabetico-classed catalogue

Alphabetical catalogue

If the entries of the books arranged alphabetically in a catalogue, the catalogue is called alphabetical catalogue. Alphabetical catalogue can be arranged in several ways, some of which are by authors, by name of persons, by title or by specific subject of the book. In the Alphabetical catalogue, the entries are arranged in the alphabetical manner. It has only one part in which entries for author title, subject and cross reference entries are arranged in one alphabetical sequence according to the words or letters forming the headings. Alphabetical catalogue are categorized as following:

- Author catalogue
- Name catalogue
- Title catalogue
- Subject catalogue

Since it follows alphabetical arrangement, readers can get information about their book of interest by looking into the catalogue once only. It follows alphabetical arrangement so entries for related subjects are normally placed far from each other. The sufficient number of cross reference entries are provided. As a consequence of alphabetical arrangement, filiatory sequence among subjects cannot be maintained is arranging entries.

Classified catalogue

Classified catalogue is a subject catalogue. It is arranged on the basis of notation (class number). A classified catalogue is a form of subject catalogue in which the entries are arranged by the class number of the books given by a classification scheme. A classified catalogue can be defined as a catalogue in which some entries are number entries and some are word entries. In other words we can say that it arranges its entries in a systematic order of subjects, the order usually being that of the classification scheme used for arrangement of books on the shelves.

The arrangement by notation or class number fulfills the subject approach only. What if a user searches through the author approaches.

Definitions

a) A catalogue in which some entries are number entries and some are word entries. —***Ranganathan***

b) A classified catalogue is a subject catalogue in which the entries are arranged by some recognised system of classification. —***M. Mann***

c) A classified catalogue arranges its entries in a systematic order of subject order usually being that of the classification scheme used for the arrangement books on the shelves. —***Henry Sharp***

As Ranganathan defined classified catalogue as a catalogue in which some entries are number entries and some are word entries, the classified catalogue has two parts:

i. classified part

ii. alphabetical part

The Classified part : The Classified part is the main part and alphabetical part is index or secondary part. Classified part contains number entries i.e. subject entries and cross reference entries. These are arranged according to the call numbers assigned according to the scheme of classification used. In this part of the classified catalogue, entries of documents are arranged by their class number. It maps out the subordinate and coordinate subject divisions and puts them in a logical sequence. The classified part is not very helpful for users who have no knowledge of the classification scheme for the library.

The alphabetical or index part : The alphabetical or index part contains index or added entries. The entries are arranged alphabetically. Alphabetical index in classified catalogue is meant to support the classified part of the catalogue. It consists of author, title, subject entries and other entries for collaborators, series, editor of series, and a host of cross references. Thus it fulfils all the functions of a dictionary catalogue, i.e. collect the works of an author together, bring all the different editions of a title, provide cross references for subjects etc

The classified part is to be supported by an alphabetical index which comprises entries, whereas classified part has class number entries. The classified catalogue will never be able to fulfill the functions of a library catalogue without an alphabetical index. Hence Ranganathan's definition and the two parts of the classified catalogue bifurcated by him are most suitable features of classified catalogue.

Features of Classified Catalogue

i. Due to classified order, the entries for related subjects are found in a logical and filiatory order.

ii. In Classified catalogue, entries are arranged as the books are kept in shelves.

iii. Classified catalogue brings together in one place all the entries relevant to a particular subject with all its related subjects. The arrangement of entries reflects the rearrangement of documents on the shelves of the library.

iv. The printed version of the catalogue can be brought out in parts by subjects without inconvenience.

v. It facilitates compilation of reading lists and subject bibliographies for special purposes.

vi. The reader is not shunted from one end to the other of the catalogue for finding the books of his interest from the catalogues.

vii. The classified catalogue reveals the strength and weakness of the collection on a subject.

viii. Classified catalogue serve as subject bibliographies and book selection tools for smaller entries.

Limitations of Classified Catalogue

1. Time consuming : Process of search longer and time consuming because the user is not aware of the classification system used for arranging the entries.

2. Dependency on classification Scheme : The shortcomings of classification scheme may affect the classified catalogue less effective.

Alphabetico-Classed Library Catalogue

It is a form of subject catalogue. This kind of catalogue combines the attributes of alphabetical catalogue and classified catalogue both. Alphabetical catalogue is popular due to:

i. Easy arrangement of entries.
ii. Easy in use for readers.

Classified catalogue is helpful because:

i. It brings like subject together.
ii. It arranges subjects in filiatory order.

Alphabetico-classed catalogue has group of these above noted qualities of both types of catalogues; i.e.,

i. It arranges its entries in alphabetical order, and
ii. In addition to bringing related subjects together, it brings specific subjects under their broader subjects.

The quality and popularity of method of Alphabetico- classed catalogue depends upon:

i. The classification scheme/method is selected.
ii. Subject headings are derived from headings used by the scheme of classification for class numbers including main class and important classes.
iii. Subject headings for specific subjects are placed under their broad classes in alphabetical sequence.

OUTER OR PHYSICAL FORMS OF CATALOGUES

The outer or physical form of the catalogue is that by which it appears before users. By physical form of library catalogue is meant its outer appearance. In other words outer appearance or format determines physical form of library catalogue. There are various types of physical forms of library catalogue, having advantages and disadvantage of their own.

A suitable account of physical description is as following:

Printed Catalogue : The printed catalogue is also known as or bound book catalogue. Sometimes used synonymously for Page catalogue and 'Book form catalogue'. In book catalogue, entries for books in the collection of a library are printed and bound in book form. One page of the catalogue contains more than one entry. This arrangement and format makes it easy to consult for the user. The flexibility of printing blank leaves facilitates new additions.

Advantages of Printed catalogue are as following:

i. It is easily transportable.

ii. It occupies too less space.

iii. It supports the concepts of centralized and cooperative cataloguing,

The limitations of printed or dictionary catalogue are as following:

i. Updating and production.

ii. Interpolating new entries and maintaining correct sequence.

iii. Printed book catalogue does not reflect the actual and up-to-date picture of the collection of a library. It has one more major demerit as it uses comparatively thin quality of paper and therefore, is less durable. Most of the library tries to avoid this form of library catalogue.

Guard Book Catalogue : It is a variation of book catalogue. This type of catalogue is also known as paste down catalogue. More than one entry is normally pasted on one sheet and sufficient vacant spaces are left to accommodate new entries. In this, additional new entries can be pasted in and also new pages can be inserted. It is sometimes used in conjunction with a printed catalogue and used prior to its production, bringing a new edition or in producing a supplement for making addition, deletion, amendment and so on. It has better qualities of being updated and is more flexible than book catalogue. Though the work and process of updating it is time consuming and complicated. It occupies more sheets in appropriate order.

Sheaf Catalogue : Also known as loose leaf book form catalogue, this catalogue contains about six entries on a single paper slip with holes or slots at one edge. These entries are fastened into binders. It has a mechanism to allow the insertion of new entries.

Card Catalogue : The Card catalogue is of 125 mm X 75 mm. The cards are arranged in specific trays and held in their relative position by a rod passing through holes near their bottom edge in a Catalogue card cabinet.

Online Public Access Catalog (OPAC) : The computerized form of catalogue changed the way of using a catalogue. The online public access catalogue has transformed the form, purpose and function of a library catalogue. The OPAC has been together with more advanced form i.e. the Web OPAC. Though libraries have card catalogue till yet, the OPAC is more popular among users.

Shelf catalogue or shelf form : It is a variation of Guard Book catalogue.

Other Forms : There may be many more physical forms of library catalogue such as in the form of magnetic tape, microfilm, computerized form etc., but the above mentioned four forms are most popular and traditional.

CARD CATALOGUE

A library catalogue can be explained as a searchable collection of records of every item in that library. Libraries also use catalogues to record what is available. What a library owns on a desired topic, the catalog card points to:

i. the location of a particular source, or
ii. group of sources,

Why a user can find a book of choice? The card catalogue makes us reach to books as well as journals and many other kinds of documents in the library. A scene in a library routine helped by use of the Card Catalogue:

- to find out what items the library owns on a topic
- to find where a specific item is located in the library
- to find out what issues of a periodical the library owns or provides access
- to place a hold, recall or paging request

The card catalogue is widely used and has been popular among different kind of libraries. Card catalogues are used to locate the available books. The most widely used types of catalogue cards (entries) are by subject, title and author. A catalog card is an individual record in a library catalog. In a physical catalog the record fills one small card, which is placed in order in the catalog drawer depending on the type of record.

The card catalogucs arc categorized accordingly they are grouped or arranged based on one of the following basis:

Subject : With this type of card catalog, the cards are grouped by subject area.

Title : In a title system, the books will be arranged alphabetically by title. Information about the book's subject and author will then be listed underneath on the card.

Author : In an author catalog, the books are listed alphabetically based on the author's last name. Cards for all books written by that author will then appear, and will be grouped alphabetically by either subject or title.

Format of Card Catalogue

The standard size of catalogue card is 12.5 cm x 7.5 cm. or 5" x 7". The catalogue cards, after preparing entries, are placed in predefined order in a catalogue cabinet. This order is meant for the easy access as well as uniformity in arrangement of catalogue cards through out the extent. One entry is prepared on one card. Therefore, each card is a unit i.e. on one card only one entry is prepared. Due to the structure of card cabinet, each card can be accommodated at and placed or removed from any place. The torn or distorted cards can be replaced without much trouble. There can be variation in the outlook of the card, plain or ruled. There are twɔ vertical lines present in the card. These lines are known as first and second indention's respectively.

The card is punched (one hold) half inch above the bottom. Through this hole a thin rod of iron is passed in the catalogue cabinet so that the card is not scattered in the cabinet. This type of arrangement does not allow leaving the card its place.

Qualities of Card Catalogue

Card catalogue is the most popular form of library catalogue. The card catalogue has the following qualities:

Up-to-dateness and flexibility : The card catalogue can be kept completely up-to-date and is fully flexible. Card catalogue has immense capacity of being up-to-dated because:

- Each card is an independent unit in itself.
- New entries can be accommodated at appropriate place without disturbing the existing arrangement
- The obsolete or unused cards or entries can be taken out of it without any inconvenience.

Durability and Economy : Card catalogue is inexpensive in comparison with other physical forms of catalogue. It is economical in preparation and maintenance.

Expansibility : Card catalogue is fully expansible as new catalogue cards (entries) can be prepared and accommodated in the existing system due to collection development in the library. It can grow in size without any inconvenience with the growth of the collection of the library. Due to limited capacity of being multiplied, the accessibility is limited in it.

Utility with grouped cataloguing : This form of catalogue is suitable for centralized and cooperative cataloguing due to its economical and durable nature.

Drawbacks of Card Catalogue

1. Occupying space : The biggest drawback of Card catalogue is occupying much space in library. Placing of Card Cabinets and provision of additional space for users, required during consultation is much enough to create lack of space for other activities.

2. Difficult to transport : Card Catalogue when alone is small and light but the entire collection of the library is bulky and cumbersome to shift or move.

3. Not long lasting : Card catalogue can be removed easily and be torn. Also much use and touch distorts the very purpose of card catalogue.

WAYS OF CATALOGUING

Cataloguing can be grouped into the following types:

(i) Individual Cataloguing : This type of cataloguing is most usual kind of cataloguing method adopted by libraries. Cataloguing is done by individual libraries, institution, people to serve their own need and purpose or for their own sake.

(ii) Cooperative Cataloguing : In Cooperative cataloguing, a small number of independent libraries share the work of producing a catalogue for their mutual benefit. In general, two or more libraries come forward for the benefit of each participant. Depending upon the policies decided the benefits may or may not be made available to other libraries. The example of cooperative cataloguing is Union catalogue.

(iii) Centralized Cataloguing : Centralized cataloguing is defined as the cataloguing of documents by some central organization for the benefit of other libraries. Sometimes centralized cataloguing is done by another agency. Some of the forms of centralized cataloguing services are Card or shelf service, Cataloguing in source, Cataloguing in publication, and Prenatal cataloguing.

(iv) Prenatal cataloguing : Dr. S.R. Ranganathan used the term "Prenatal cataloguing". He assumed that this process can save 79% in the technical manpower. In this process the cataloguing work has been done by the National Central Library of a country on each book before its release by the publisher. This is done with the help of a copy of the form proof of each book sent by each publisher. The catalogue cards are later made available for distribution to libraries on order along with the release of books themselves. The back of the title pages are supplied Call numbers.

Cooperative Cataloguing

Cooperative cataloguing emerged by the early 18th century, when William Desborough Cooley thought in 1850 about universal catalogue. Cooperative cataloguing was introduced by the outcome as the LC Printed Cards in 1901. On the basis of library cooperation, the work and process of cataloguing of documents can also be performed cooperatively. This cataloguing is known as cooperative cataloguing, which refers to a situation where a number of independent libraries share the work of producing a catalogue for their mutual benefits. Cooperation is adopted among libraries as libraries have many things in common. Due to similarity in the processes and practices, several libraries are finding the cooperation beneficial to their performance. Thus, when two or more libraries come together to work with each other with mutual cooperation, it is called library cooperation. The cooperation among a group of libraries is to work together for a single objective. Library cooperation is adopted within a group of libraries as well as within the main library and its branch libraries of the same library system. In the case of cooperation, there can be a central coordinating library or coordinating body which monitors and overseas these activities. Sometimes the libraries themselves may agree to cooperate with each other following certain broad guidelines and principles, without any type of coordinating bodies.

Definitions

A situation where a number of independent libraries share the work of producing a catalogue for their mutual benefit. —*Needham*

One simple form of cooperative cataloguing may be said to exist when a number of libraries take a share in the cost or work of providing and maintaining a centralized cataloguing bureau and reap the benefits acquiring from it. —*Henry A. Sharp*

Objective of Cooperative Cataloging : The following ate the basic objectives of cooperative cataloguing:

(a) The basic objective is to affect economy in the cost of cataloguing which the cooperative libraries share to obviate the wasteful duplication of cataloguing processes of the participating libraries.

(b) The most important objective is to reveal the total resources of a region which enables the users to select the desired materials.

Benefits of Cooperative Cataloguing : Cooperative cataloguing provides the following advantages:

- ***Better use of resources :*** The cooperative cataloguing provides a channel to use the available resources in an efficient manner. The plenty of one library may be useful for the scarcity found in another library.
- ***Standardization of practices:*** The cooperative cataloguing maintains the adherence to the common and standardized practices. When libraries follow certain standards and the guidelines to prepare catalogues, the uniformity is the outcome. The uniformity is desirable as well as mandatory. It gives ease to library users when they search catalogues of group of libraries.
- ***Economy in expenses :*** The economy is also felt by the cooperating libraries due to sharing of resources. The shared burden leads to economy in expenses for the individual libraries.
- ***Improvement in quality of services :*** The cooperation paves way for improvements in quality of cataloguing services. The availability of resources as well as guidance is very much helpful for the infrastructure-lacking libraries.
- ***Preparation of union catalogue :*** The cooperation leads to a fruitful venture in the form of Union Catalogue. The shared information of libraries' holdings and their collection advise the formation of union catalogue.

Centralized Cataloguing

The centralized cataloguing means the provision of cataloguing process from a central point to several clients. It is one of the forms of cooperative cataloguing. Both of these two terms sometimes are used interchangeable. They seem to be synonymous, but not so in their functioning. Though they are very closely related yet a remarkable difference is found in between them. We can understand its basic characteristics:

i. Centralized cataloguing is a cataloguing carried out by a central library or organization so that all libraries may make use of cataloguing.

ii. It intends to avoid duplication of work.

iii. Centralized cataloguing may be carried out at different levels such as national or local levels.

iv. It may range from a simple cataloguing to complete cataloguing with the preparation of catalogue cards ready to be inserted into the clients catalogues.

Definitions

Centralized cataloguing is the cataloguing of documents by some central organization. —*C.D.Needham*

Centralized cataloguing is a cataloging carried out by a central library or organization so that all libraries may take use of cataloguing, thereby avoiding duplication of work. —*M.Norris*

The cataloguing of a large library system is often centralized, but it is not cooperative, except in very insulator sense. —*H.A. Sharp*

The centralized cataloguing is usually conducted in library system which consists of numerous branches or sections. In the central place the entire cataloguing processes are done and the catalogue cards are supplied to the branches. The British National Bibliography (BNB) is a good example of centralized cataloguing in Great Britain.

Advantages : The following are the advantages of centralized cataloguing:

1. It eliminates duplication of cataloguing work.
2. This system reduces the cost of cataloguing in individual libraries.
3. Higher standard of work done by the central place or library.
4. The centralized cataloguing system brings greater uniformity in cataloguing.
5. It provides more time to the staff for other important readers' services.

UNION CATALOGUE

The foundation of the union catalogue was laid in USA in 1901, when the Library of Congress authorized an exchange of catalogue cards with card producing libraries. The LC (Library of Congress) has been publishing since 1956 the National Union Catalogue comprising a cumulative author list. This list includes entries of LC printed cards and also entries in cards representing titles reported to the National Union Catalogue by other libraries of North America. The union catalogue is symbol of economy and advantages in cataloguing besides cooperative and centralized cataloguing is. The union catalogue is brought out when different libraries in a region or in a country are combined. The aim of the union catalogue is:

i. to identify, locate and retrieve materials stocked in different libraries of the particular area.

ii. to provide a guide to the holdings of the libraries of the concerned area.

Definition

The union catalogue may be defined as follows—

A catalogue listing in one sequence of the documents of two or more libraries. —*K. Larson*

List of all documents of two or more libraries, giving the names of all the libraries where copies of each document can be found. —*S.R. Ranganathan*

The union catalogues can have any of the structure and arrangement for their compilation. The arrangement of entries may be in dictionary pattern, classified sequence with alphabetical index and dictionary pattern with subject index and place index.

Advantages : The users of the libraries can get the following advantages from the use of union catalogues.

1. ***Myriad information at one place :*** Union catalogues make available the information about the total resources of the books stocked in the libraries of that particular area in which the system is adhered.
2. ***Tools for books selection :*** Union catalogues can be consulted more quickly than separate catalogues of the individual libraries. These provide guidance in selection of books and periodicals.
3. ***Nation's output:*** If union catalogues have been compiled at national level, then National Union Catalogues provide information about the total resources of books of the country as well as their availability.
4. ***Locating the Book/document:*** Union catalogues provide the location of the required book, where the book is available.
5. ***Inter Library Loan:*** Inter library loan service may only be possible with the help of union catalogues.
6. ***Saving time and resources:*** Union catalogues help in avoiding the duplication in acquisition of books or periodicals.
7. ***Bibliographical tools:*** In this way union catalogues are the best bibliographical tools which provide bibliographical details about the books stocked in the library or in other participating libraries.

15
Online Public Access Catalogue

INTRODUCTION

The Online Public Access Catalogue (OPAC) is the modern and flexible form of the catalogue. It gives easy and sophisticated access to the recorded information in a computer. OPAC contains all the bibliographic information of an information centre. User can search for information via OPAC. The provision of Keyword searching and Boolean operators have made this searching easier to find relevant information according to user's needs.

Definitions

ALA Glossary defines OPAC as, "A Computer based and supported library catalog (bibliographic database) designed to be accessed via terminals so that library users may directly and effectively search for and retrieve bibliographic records within the assistance of a human intermediary such as a specially trained member of the library staff."

Online Dictionary for Library and Information Science (ODLIS) defines OPAC as, "An acronym for online public access catalog, a database composed of bibliographic records describing the books and other materials owned by a library or library system, accessible via public terminals or workstations usually concentrated near the reference desk to make it easy for users to request the assistance of a trained reference librarian. Most online catalogs are searchable by author, title, subject, and keywords and allow users to print, download, or export records to an e-mail account."

SIRSI : Glossary of terms defines OPAC as, "A computer workstation used to search a library's catalogue. OPAC can refer to either the actual workstation in the library, or to the interface provided by the library that is accessible from anywhere"

Why and how OPAC emerged?

The access was limited due to limitations of printed catalogs. Due to advent of microforms and the advanced information technologies and internet, the access has come out from locally available libraries catalogue to remotely reaching libraries catalogue but in electronic form.

The cross-references on a topic through different subject-headings typed on index cards was always time consuming and cumbersome on the user's end. The libraries had to take utmost care in facilitating access to information. Information technology changed the entire environment of the library including resources, techniques, services, etc. in the OPAC system, data is spread within computer and easy to access. The data is not scattered like card system. It functions as a gateway to information centre's collection. Why the changes could be brought in favour of users' services, the reasons are listed below:

- Online public access catalogues are edited and updated easily and quickly Searching is easier with flexibility. The OPAC searching interface allows the user to use Keywords as well as various approaches and access points. The access does not depend on physical locations. The OPAC is accessible from computers located outside the library depending on its availability on some network.
- Online public access catalogues show the current status of each item (i.e., "available" or "checked out"). The time is not wasted in searching the document, later on finding it not available in library.

Characteristics of OPAC

The characteristics are as following:

1. The catalogues which are available for searching online are known as OPAC.
2. The interlinked fields and elements in the OPAC allow the user to choose author, title, keyword, or systematic order dynamically. The searching for any word in a title or other field enhances the ways to find a record.
3. Physical storage space is saved for new collection and updates are significantly more efficient.

GENERATIONS OF OPAC

The development of OPAC has been categorized into following generations:

First Generation OPAC : First generation OPAC has been derived from traditional catalogues or computerized circulation system. First-generation online catalogues were in fact computerized card catalogues with almost the same traditional features. These new library catalogues provided limited author, title and controlled vocabulary subject heading access points. The first generation OPACs are also referred to as phase – indexed or pre-coordinated OPACs and it demands exact matching between the search term and pre-coordinate phrase. The number of access keys was limited and they were similar to that of manual catalogue i.e. author, title, class number and possibly subject heading. For this reason, first-generation online catalogues have been criticized as having no advantages over the card catalogue.

Second Generation OPAC : The second-generation online catalogues are characterized as being powerful tools for the searching of bibliographic information. Due to origin from common bibliographic information retrieval system, it reflected the similarity between second generation OPAC and traditional information retrieval system. This generation OPAC provided key word searching that is post coordinate searching together with phrase searching or pre-coordinate subject heading. The features of second-generation online catalogues have been keyword search, Boolean keyword search, cross index search and increasing or reducing of search results.

There have been few factors to improve the structure and content of bibliographic records:

i. The design of database management software
ii. Incorporation of full records
iii. Links to full electronic texts
iv. Considerable increase in the length of fields

The major development in the screen interface was also seen. The interaction between the user and the catalogue became more flexible due to help screens, error messages and suggestive prompts. There was ease of use and user-friendliness. The interfaces were of two kinds:

i. Menu-driven
ii. Command-driven

Third-generation online catalogues : The third-generation online catalogues were full of enhanced features such as free text search, enriched database search and simultaneous journal citation searching. The emphasis was on the retrieval facilities. User preference was given much importance by providing:

i. The adaptive dialogue
ii. Tailored bibliographic format
iii. Provision of automatic and context-based correction

Fourth-generation online catalogues : The fourth generation OPAC came into existence during the last few years of 1980s. The fourth generation began with the provision of easy access to bibliographic information by using graphical user interfaces (GUIs). The traditional menu-type interfaces were replaced by client server and graphical user interface. The concept of WIMP (windows, icons, mouse and pointers) came into existence. The post-Boolean searching allowed to interpret users' search requests in order to present matches of greater or lesser interest to the user Leading to 'relevance ranking'. To include new data elements, the access has been enhanced by text retrieval qualifiers such as 'language', 'date' and 'form' of the text. Integral or add-on text retrieval modules were effective in:

i. range searching
ii. related term searching
iii. wild card features
iv. adjacency and proximity

COMPONENTS OF OPAC

There are three main components of OPAC. They are:

i. Computer and Terminal : The hardware requirement for OPAC i.e. computer terminal and server from which databases can be accessed.

ii. Software Enabling Networking : The network enabling software which will be able to manage the entire database.

iii. Database : The database of books, serial, dissertation, etc can be generated by two different ways. One is developing database by direct entry and the other is developing database through retrospective conversion process.

HISTORY AND DEVELOPMENTS OF ONLINE CATALOGUES

After the Second World War, due to significant growth in scientific and technological information and expansion in library collections, manual systems were not responding effectively. The manual systems were incapable in handling the ever-growing information needs of various strata of society. The card catalogue was ineffective in retrieval of bibliographic information. The advancing of computer began during 1950s and 1960s in house-keeping function rather than the public access of catalogue. The MARC (Machine-Readable Cataloging) project was initiated in 1060s towards the development of automated catalogues. The Library of Congress initiated and augmented the supply of MARC magnetic tapes mainly for automated cataloguing in the standard form. MARC services in cataloguing led to more developments in automated catalogues such as:

i. Centralised cataloguing services gave way to the establishment of bibliographic utilities in the early 1970s.
ii. The Online Computer Library Center (OCLC, formerly the Ohio College Library Center) was established in 1971. The OCLC proliferated MARC-based cataloguing. This stage recognized the importance of uniform, standardised bibliographic description. MARC bibliographic information was taken to circulation systems in an online mode during 1980s. The use of MARC in circulation operation gave a platform for public enquiry.
iii. The public enquiry led towards the development of online public access catalogue (OPAC).

OPAC Vs Card Catalogue

The differences between OPAC and card catalogue are represented in the following table.

Characteristic	Card Catalogue	OPAC
Time spending in searching	More time consuming.	OPAC allows fast retrieval.
Access point	Access is limited.	It provides multiple access to the database and helpful for Boolean searches
Indexing techniques	Only pre-coordinate searching is possible.	It support both pre-coordinate and post coordinate searching.
Current Status	It does not provide current status of the document. Ways nothing about the reservation or availability.	OPAC informs whether a document is on the shelves, on loan, on reservation or at binders or the document is lost.
Union Catalogue	Due to decentralized arrangement, resources sharing through card catalogue is very difficult.	It helps to develop centralized database and resource sharing among different libraries.

There are many big differences between the OPAC and the card catalogue:

i. Users have more access points with the OPAC in comparison to the card catalog, e.g., standard numbers like ISBN and ISSN; keywords, etc.

ii. Almost every single part of the bibliographic record is accessible through keyword searching.

iii. There are few other access points, e.g., government document numbers, music numbers, reserved book lists by courses or by instructors, etc.

iv. Use of Boolean operators

v. OR, AND, and NOT in the OPACs broaden up or narrow down the search.

DISTINGUISHING FEATURES OF ONLINE CATALOGUES

Structure and content of bibliographic records : The bibliographic description consisting of data elements is arranged and presented in a given order in card catalogue formats as well as MARC formats. With the advent and further development of online catalogues it has become possible to assign a larger number of access points to bibliographic records.

MARC format and categorization of data elements : MARC has significantly contributed to the growth of library automation and to the development of online catalogues. It has been very supporting in identifying, storing and communicating of cataloguing information. The MARC record has been flexible enough to store bibliographic information in more detailed fields and subfields due to the requirements of automated systems for separate identification of data elements.

Bibliographic standardization : The online environment gives much more emphasis to the concept of standardization in:

i. Choice and form of data elements to be included in a bibliographic record,
ii. Conformity to standards

The cataloguing codes such as ISBDs and MARC formats have been providing guidelines for uniformity and consistency.

Structure and content of the catalogue : The advent of the online catalogue has given new dimensions to the catalogue's structure i.e. built up, the kinds and content of files and indexes constituting it and the relationships of these files and indexes to one another. Access to various kinds of information became possible through the development of the contents and structure of the catalogue.

Integration of the catalogue : Since different parts of the library automated system are integrated through the use and manipulation of the same record as the basis for different library operations, the integration of online catalogue was inevitable. In integration, a single master bibliographic record is tagged and used for different library operations and it facilitates more access to bibliographic information.

Authority control : Authority control ensures the consistent use of names, series and subjects and verifiability of bibliographic records against the approved authority file. The authority control in an online catalogue is must to maintain cataloguing operations in context with revisions to name and subject headings.

Filing rules and problems : The arrangement of access points has been governed by filing rules such as the *ALA Filing Rules*, the *Library of Congress Filing Rules.* The use of the computer has influenced filing practices and it is generally agreed that the principle of file as is. The filing is affected by:

i. Format of bibliographic information
ii. Software specifications
iii. Logical arrangement of data elements

SEARCHING AND RETRIEVAL IN OPAC

Online catalogues are capable of greater number of access points searching facilities. In addition to controlled-vocabulary searches by author, title and subject headings bibliographic records are searched through access points such as other title information, series, standard numbers and any other significant data through the following types of searching:

Keyword searching : Keyword access is a very powerful search tool. The keyword searching is also known as Post Coordinate Searching. In this type of searching, a query is formulated using Boolean expression in fields such as author, title, subject, or cross index. Along with the keyword searching, the subject access and keyword searching of abstracts and entire text of a document (i.e., full-text searching) is being facilitated to users.

Boolean searching : Abstracting and Indexing services have affected the use of Boolean operators, such as AND, OR, NOT as Boolean Searching. The Boolean searching allows defining subsets of the desired subject or concept when two or more sets are combined.

Phrase Searching : Phrase searching is done on pre-coordinate subject heading. It is also very popular.

Browse searching : When the information needs are not precisely defined, the user can browse and determine the exact forms of entry of a subject heading or author name. Since the desired results are not precisely known in advance, "browse searching is the most useful and preferred approach". The browsing helps in providing the correct terms for representing the user's query are not known at the outset.

Hypertext searching : The hypertext searching or 'hypersearch is found in non linear, associative hypertext systems. The search approach attempts to mimic human thought processes. It is stated that hypertext overcame the static nature of the then existing catalogues. The hypertext facility helped users to navigate throughout the catalogue to find possible related works.

Author-title search : This is the example of execution of known-item searches. This type of search happens when user searches a known item through the author's surname combined with any keyword from the title.

ID numbers : Various identification numbers helps in searching the information given the option available in the OPAC. These numbers are such as call number; International Standard Book Number (ISBN); International Standard Serial Number (ISSN); document number; computer system number.

Search options in OPAC: an example of Libsys

OPAC gives essential information about informational entity i.e. the book or any other document. The search of books in OPAC is facilitated through the various fields such as author, title, place of publication, name of publisher, year of publication, edition, editorship, pagination, illustration, etc. Here is an example, as OPAC in Libsys software provides three kinds of searches:

1. Simple Search : In the simple search, the options available for the user are in the form of fields:

- Database.
- Field Enter word(s) or phrase

- Connector
- Specify Year(s) of Publication
- A simple search can be made on any field, title-wise, author-wise or subject-wise.

2. Advance Search : Advance Search facilitates the user to refine a search using a combination of search fields. The advance search options has the following data fields:

- Database
- Field Enter word(s) or phrase
- Connector
- Specify Year(s) of Publication

3. Additional Search : In the additional search facility, the data fields are:

- Database
- Field Connector Specify Year(s) of Publication

There are few other kinds of searches facilitated by the OPAC such as:

- Search by ISBN
- Search by accession number
- New arrivals

WEB OPAC

Web OPAC is an OPAC, which is provided on the web and with the help of internet anybody can access it from anywhere. Web-based online public access catalogues (OPACs) began to appear in the late 1990s and many libraries are currently considering implementation.

Definitions

According to Washington University in St.Louis, "A Web OPAC interfaces, which uses the World Wide Web protocol to act as an OPAC."

According to ODLIS, "An Online Public Access Catalogue (OPAC) that uses a graphical user interface (GUI) accessible via the World Wide Web, as opposed to a text based interface accessible via telnet."

The characteristics of web OPAC are as following:

i. Web OPAC is an OPAC provided on the web.
ii. The access is not without internet.
iii. Web OPAC interfaces use the World Wide Web protocol.
iv. Remote access.
v. Integration of many document types and sources via a single interface.

While understanding Web OPAC, we say that web-OPAC is connected via internet and we are not confined locally within library premises to search or browse the library collection.

The web based OPAC allows:

- Request for borrowing
- Request for reservation
- Making automatic reservations

Web OPAC is a simple yet sophisticated searching platform that provides access to library's Online Public Access Catalog over the Internet. The following types of search facilities are available in web OPAC:

Simple Search : This search allows searching for any keyword or phrase and the results are displayed by relevancy order.

Browse Search : Browse Search allows searching by a specific category such as 'Author', 'Title', 'Subject', etc. Search results appear in alphabetical order beginning with the nearest field matching the information entered.

Power Search : Power Search gives the advantage of combining different categories such as 'Author' AND 'Title' OR 'Subject' enabling user to search multiple terms simultaneously.

My Searches : These searches are composed and saved under the user's own web page ID. Cross Library Search. Cross Library Search allows Z39.50 searching.

Differentiating OPAC and Web OPAC

OPAC and Web OPAC are same in some aspects like searching and browsing in both the cases provides pre-coordinated as well as post-coordinated phrases options. They differ from each other in some aspects such as:

OPAC : (LAN/Intranet) usage is limited. Users are bound to follow the program of the particular OPAC software in that library.

Web OPAC : The usage is global. In Web OPAC, html files are used supported by hyperlinks to navigate the subject areas or disciplines.

16

Information Sources: Concept and Types

There are various types of information sources in libraries, available in printed and other forms. Due to ease and convenience, the printed sources are popular among masses. There are other different kinds of information sources which are neither printed nor systematically presented or compiled in a form that is suitable for reading. On the basis of very physical nature, use and arrangement, the information sources have been divided into two following categories:

i. Documentary Sources : The information sources available mainly in printed form, are called as documentary sources. They are also called printed sources of information. Printed, i.e. documentary sources are rich in their content and style. Due to recent advances in technology, many of the documentary sources are also available On CD-ROMs and online too. These sources are categorized into three main classes such as:

- Primary Sources
- Secondary Sources
- Tertiary Sources

ii. Non-documentary Sources : Besides the traditional documentary sources, there are other information sources which are known as non-documentary sources. The problems and impediment created by the documentary sources paved the way for generation and development of these non-documentary sources. Due to various features associated with these non-documentary sources, these are quite useful and popular among readers. These types of sources have features such as reduction in study-searching age an easy searching of information. The high cost and use of sophisticated equipments sometimes hinder their usage yet easy handling and availability made them very popular with a wide variety of users.

Thus we can say that the information sources but are not generally printed or published in the documentary form, are known as non-documentary sources. These documents are in a vague form and also not easily available, yet they contain important information. These types of sources can be grouped into formal and informal categories. Formal sources are not published and so are beyond the access of general readers. They include pamphlets, reprints, prints, newspapers clippings, manuscripts, dissertations etc.

Non-Documentary Sources of Information

Various types of sources of information are around us. A library provides different documentary and non-documenatry information sources. The documentary sources provide information in a more systematic manner but the importance of non-documentary sources is also acknowledged. The various types of non-documentary sources are as following:

1. **Human sources :** Human sources of information are those in which any individual serves as a source of information such as experts, fellows, specialists, family members.

2. **Institutional sources :** The information sought directly from the research organizations is the institutional source of information. The specialized information centres, referral centres, clearing houses, trade promotion councils, learned societies and associations, universities, etc. can be referred as institutional sources of information.

3. **Mass Media :** Mass Media is a means of communication of information through broadcasting and telecasting or a combination of these two for the masses. It provides information in many new ways. Hence mass media channels are playing better role in providing information to the masses.

INFORMAL SOURCES OF INFORMATION

The information sources but are not generally printed or published in the documentary form, are known as non-documentary sources. Formal sources are not published and so are beyond the access of general readers. They include pamphlets, reprints, prints, newspapers clippings, manuscripts, dissertations etc. Another important type of non-documentary information sources is the informal sources. Although, these sources are outside the purview of the librarian, yet he should acquaint with these sources, for providing effective service. These sources are as follows:

1. **Conferences and seminars :** Conferences and seminars strengthen the informal communications throughout the world because they provide a platform for discussions to scholars and professionals.

2. **Technological Gatekeepers :** T.J. Allen conceptualized and emphasized upon research and development laboratories as technological gatekeepers. The technological gatekeepers are persons working in an

organization who can provide some technical discussion and consultation. These persons are other than the scientists.

3. Unpublished Works : The unpublished documents also contain information. These types of documents are called unpublished works. These documents may be of great use to users in a subject field, as they contain solutions to problems, study or new innovations. These types of documents include dissertations, theses, research reports etc. If they are available in published form, may be of great use and importance.

4. Conversation and correspondence : Another way of gathering information is through the conversations between colleagues and to the visitors. People exchange information via their interaction with their colleagues or visitors. The information generated by telephone talk or by correspondence has become a very convenient form of information source these days.

5. Reprints and Progress reports : The reprints of the manuscripts to be presented in the seminar help to understand the on-going discussions, effectively. Also the progress of any research work (progress report) gives the information of the progress in work and other details.

PRIMARY SOURCES OF INFORMATION

Primary source contains information that someone creates himself. Primary sources of information are the sources that contain original information. These sources convey new ideas, discoveries, or information. These sources originate from the time period under study. We can say that a primary source of information is a firsthand or eyewitness account of an event. It is also raw data or facts which were gathered at an event. A Primary Source of Information is actual evidence presented without any analysis or interpretation. The primary sources of information are direct sources of information.

Primary sources include diaries, letters, newspaper articles reported from an event, public documents, laws, court records, speeches, statistics, surveys, logs, journals, family bibles, etc.

Features of Primary Sources of information

Original manuscript, documents or records used in preparing a published or unpublished work are all primary sources of information. The features of primary sources are as following:

- Primary sources are created by witnesses or recorders who experienced the events or conditions being documented.
- A primary source is a document or physical object which was written or created during the time under study.
- Often primary sources are created at the time when the events or conditions are occurring.
- Primary sources provide direct or firsthand evidence about an event, object, person, or work of art.

- Primary sources provide the original materials on which other research is based and enable students and other researchers to get as close as possible to what actually happened during a particular event or time period.
- Primary sources reflect the individual viewpoint of a participant or observer. Primary sources can be written or non-written (sound, pictures, artifacts, etc.).
- They are usually the first formal appearance of results in physical, print or electronic format. They present original thinking, report a discovery, or share new information.
- In scientific research, primary sources present original thinking, report on discoveries, or share new information.

Examples of Primary Sources

- Autobiographies and memoirs, first-person accounts, case studies
- Original documents such as diaries, personal letters, and correspondence, emails, manuscripts, lab data/notes
- Diaries, Interviews, surveys, and fieldwork
- Internet communications on email, blogs, listservs, and newsgroups
- Photographs, drawings, and posters
- Works of art and literature
- Books, magazine and newspaper articles from the time period under study
- Public opinion polls
- Speeches and oral histories
- Original documents (birth certificates, property deeds, trial transcripts)
- Research data, such as census statistics
- Official and unofficial records of organizations and government agencies
- Artifacts of all kinds, such as tools, coins, clothing, furniture, etc.
- Archival material such as official documents, minutes recorded by government agencies and organizations, photographs, coins, fossils, natural specimens
- Speeches;
- Survey Research (e.g., market surveys, public opinion polls);
- Audio recordings, DVDs, and video recordings, sound clips, video clips
- Government documents (reports, bills, proclamations, hearings, etc.)
- Patents, technical reports
- Scientific journal articles reporting experimental research results; original research studies (often in the form of journal articles in peer-reviewed publications), also called empirical studies

- Information collected through interviews, questionnaires
- Web site

The above examples reflect that primary sources are original materials. The time period involved is categorizing factor. The primary sources are not been filtered through interpretation or evaluation. Primary sources are original materials on which other research is based.

Role of Primary Sources

For the progress and development of a country, the primary literature is very important. The role and importance of primary sources as follows:

Original, current and up-to-date information : The information published in the primary information sources is new, recent, current, primary, full and up-to-date to all other investigators working in the same field. In this way primary sources have special importance for other researchers. These sources are the means of transfer, dissemination and communication of original research. Therefore these sources play a very important role in communicating the information contained in them.

Quick Subject Reports : The primary sources are published only after the publication of research or investigation. The current and new information is found in these sources.

Avoidance of Duplication in research : Information published in primary sources is of original nature, the doubling and duplication in the research cannot be possible.

Compilation of other sources : Information contained in the primary sources is original and it provides base and content to the compilation and publication of the other secondary and tertiary sources of information.

SECONDARY SOURCES OF INFORMATION

A Secondary Source of information is something which comes after the fact. Information that has been produced by somebody else is known as a secondary source. The secondary sources are the outcome of analysis, interpretation, relation or evaluation of a primary source or other primary sources. For example, textbooks, encyclopedias, dictionaries, any book or article which is an interpretation of events or of primary sources are considered secondary sources. In other words we can say that a secondary source interprets and analyzes primary sources. These sources are one or more steps removed from the event. Secondary sources may have pictures, quotes or graphics of primary sources in them. The secondary sources of information present the organized information by collecting data from a number of different primary sources so new ideas and insights into an event may be found. Secondary sources of information include for example:

- directories, books and maps
- DVDs and websites

Thus the secondary sources are less easily defined than primary sources. Generally, the secondary sources are interpretations and evaluations of primary sources. Secondary sources are not evidence, rather commentary on and discussion of evidence. However, what some define as a secondary source, others define as a tertiary source. Context is everything.

Examples of secondary sources

- Bibliographies
- Biographical works
- Reference books, including dictionaries, encyclopedias, and atlases
- Magazine and newspaper articles (this distinction varies by discipline);
- Literature reviews and review articles (e.g., book reviews)
- History books and other popular or scholarly books
- Works of criticism and interpretation
- Commentaries and treatises
- Indexes and abstracts
- Journal articles (depending on the discipline can be primary)
- Monographs, other than fiction and autobiography
- Textbooks (also considered tertiary)
- Web site (also considered primary).

The Nature of Secondary Sources of Information

- Secondary sources describe, discuss, interpret, comment upon, analyze, evaluate, summarize, and process the primary sources.
- A secondary source is generally one or more steps removed from the event or time period and are written or produced after the fact with the benefit of hindsight.
- Secondary sources lack the freshness and immediacy of the original material.

Features of Secondary sources

- Secondary sources collect, organize, and repackage primary source information to increase usability and speed of delivery.
- Secondary sources involve generalization, analysis, synthesis, interpretation, or evaluation of the original information.
- Secondary sources use primary data to solve research problems, written for scholarly and professional audiences.
- Like primary sources, secondary materials can be written or non-written.

VARIOUS SECONDARY SOURCES

In the present time, as secondary sources of information, reference books are authoritative carefully designed to fit into a defined scope and to be accurate, objective and readable in treatment of information. These are logically arranged, appealing in format and useful in their special features.

These reference books help the libraries and librarians. In other words, we can say that secondary sources are the sound base for any reference enquiry in a library. In libraries, generally following types of reference sources in book form are stored in their reference sections.

Dictionaries : Dictionaries are the main reference sources in a library. These explain the words of a language arranged in some definite order, usually in alphabetical order. The words are listed with explanation of their meanings and usages. Dictionaries also provide the pronunciation, sage and meaning of each word. There are four types of dictionaries:

a. Abridged
b. Unabridged
c. Bilingual
d. Multilingual dictionaries.

Examples :

a. Oxford English Dictionary, 1933.
b. Collins Pocket German Dictionary.

Enyclopaedias : An encyclopaedia is a systematic summary of the knowledge. It contains information on all subjects or limited in a special field or subject arranged in a systematic order usually alphabetical. The articles in the encyclopaedias are usually compiled and written by experts of the subjects. Sometimes encyclopaedias are called backbone of reference service. Examples:

a. Encyclopaedia Britannica.
b. McGraw Hill Encyclopaedia of Science and Technology.

Bibliographies : Bibliographies can be defined as well organized list of written, printed or otherwise produced records, e.g. books, articles etc. Bibliographies are available in several forms, viz., trade, national or universal bibliographies. The other most useful form is the subject bibliography, which is to be consulted by research workers. Examples:

a. Cumulative Book Index
b. Indian National Bibliography

Biographical Sources : Biographical Sources are those sources which contain information about people.

Geographical Sources : Geographical sources give information concerned with places and provide information like description and location related to places, mountains, rivers, lakes etc. throughout the world. Examples of geographical sources are gazetteers, guide books, handbooks, maps, atlases and globes.

Ready Reference Sources : There are various types of ready reference sources. They are grouped into six major classes. They are yearbooks, almanacs, directories, statistical sources, handbooks, manuals, source books, guide books and advances in etc.

TERTIARY SOURCES OF INFORMATION

Tertiary sources consist of information which is a distillation and collection of primary and secondary sources. Tertiary sources contain both primary and secondary sources. These sources generally provide an overview or summary of a topic. The information is displayed as entirely factual, and does not include analysis or critique. Tertiary sources can also be collections of primary and secondary sources, such as databases, bibliographies and directories.

- Almanacs
- Bibliographies (also considered secondary)
- Chronologies
- Dictionaries and Encyclopedias (also considered secondary)
- Directories
- Fact books
- Guidebooks
- Indexes, abstracts, bibliographies used to locate primary and secondary sources
- Manuals
- Textbooks (also be secondary)

Tertiary sources of information contain information thrice removed from the primary sources. Hence they act as a guide to the secondary and primary sources. Tertiary sources help us in getting original information in an organised way.

Characteristics

- Tertiary sources do not contain the subject knowledge.
- These sources refer to other sources.
- The main function of these sources is to help in searching information in primary and secondary sources.
- These sources are published later to other sources.
- These sources are most important in comparison to other sources.

Tertiary sources are usually compilation drawn from primary or secondly sources, organized and arranged according to a definite plan. Essentially these sources are to aid searchers in using primary and secondary sources. The tertiary sources have been categorized as following on their characteristic features.

1. Bibliography of Bibliographies : Bibliography of bibliographies is essentially a tertiary source of information which acts as a guide to the number of bibliographies published in the form of indexing and abstracting periodicals in locating the documents which list out documents on a particular subject. They assist the searcher in searching documents either in the secondary sources or in the primary sources of information, as it would list out the documents containing similar type of information. Example: A

World guide to Abstracting and Indexing Services, USA, 1963.

2. Literature Guides : These guides are a specific type of reference tool designed to identifying important types of information sources in specific subject. By the use of the subject literature guides, a researcher can either locate a specific Source of information or can identify a specific piece of information or can undertake current or retrospective literature search. They provide information about information and the purpose of such a literature guide is to present the bibliographical structure of subject.

3. Directories : Directories are guides to the sources of information generation, as lists of organizations and institutions and give accounts of their functions. The term directory is also used for a list of events, newspapers, periodicals and so on. They vary in kind, scope, purpose and size. Directories are of learned societies, research institutions etc. Directories of academic and institutions list their publications, research activities, budget, personnel, organizational structures etc. Their features are as following:

i. Directories are also one of the ready reference tools which possess rich information for the users.
ii. Directories are tertiary reference sources which aid the searcher in using the primary and secondary sources.
iii. Directories provide information regarding the name, structure, functions, objectives, operational activities, addresses, officers, members etc. of different types of institutions.
iv. The entries in directories are systematically arranged in alphabetical or classified order.

(a) General Directories : These directories are further divided into following two categories.

i. Topographical directories of cities and towns; and
ii. Telephone, telegraphic, telex directories.

Examples: Kelly's Post Office London Directory, Times's of India Directory, Telephone Directory.

(b) Special Directories : Special directories can be international, national or local in coverage. They are divided into three main groups: Institutional, Professional, Trade and Business Directories. Examples: Commonwealth Universities Yearbook, Directory of Indian Public Libraries, American Medical Directory.

4. Textbooks : A textbook provides assistance in the understanding of a specific branch of knowledge. It is one of the standard works used for instruction. However it is not intended as a source of systematic overview of a topic. Textbooks are graded on their characters such as:

a. Introductory
b. Elementary
c. Advance

Advanced textbooks often possess the characteristics of treaties and monographs. Textbooks are assimilated information written for a particular level of readers with the treatment, concise or comprehensive.

5. Research in Progress : It is a list of research in progress that covers the research activities of a single institution or a particular laboratory, or group of institutions. It consists of a short description of projects, names of investigators, period of investigation, name of sponsoring body, and in some cases, reference to sources of publication of results or results likely to be published. It helps in planning of research, avoidance of duplication and above all, in the anticipation of information. The research in progress helps an individual worker to get additional information about the work or can anticipate where-about regarding the results of an investigation. Example: Directory of scientific research in Indian Universities, New Delhi, INSDOC, 1974.

17

Reference Sources

INTRODUCTION

Reference sources are research tools. Reference sources provide answers to specific questions, such as brief facts, statistics, and technical instructions; provide background information; or direct a user to additional information sources. To find quick, factual information on a topic, we need to consult the reference sources. There are many types of reference sources. For example:

Dictionaries : These contain meanings and definitions of terms.

Encyclopedias : These sources contain concise, factual information on topics or concepts.

Handbooks : The handbooks contain practical information (e.g., how to do something) on a topic.

Almanacs : These sources contain calendars, basic facts, and statistical information relating to people, places, and events.

Biographical sources : These sources contain biographical information on individuals such as birth and death dates and major achievements.

Reference sources, such as encyclopedias, handbooks, and dictionaries, provide conceptual and general information on a topic. Reference sources can be either general or topic-specific. For example, the encyclopedias and handbooks provide systematic general information on a topic. These sources introduce about a concept related to a certain field. The popular reference sources are printed reference books, dictionaries and statistical books. The reference sources are found in electronic format also.

Characteristics of Reference Sources

Non-Circulating : Reference books cannot be issued or taken out of the library.

Quick Facts : Reference books are not read straight through. Users simply "refer" to them when they need quick, basic information.

Overview: Reference books provide a quick introduction to the topic, a brief overview.

Specific Arrangement : Reference sources are organized in very specific ways, depending on the type of source. For example, dictionaries are arranged in alphabetical order by word and encyclopedias are arranged in alphabetical order by subject.

Reference sources are often the best place to start a research because they:

- provide brief, factual information.
- summarize and clarify issues.
- define unfamiliar terms.
- identify additional relevant sources such as books and periodical articles.

Design of Reference Sources

Design of reference sources depend upon:

i. Meant for consultation rather than read through.
ii. The type of information and treatment provided.

Types of Reference Tools

Two major categories of reference sources are:

i. General reference sources: General sources include all subjects and present overviews of topics.
ii. Subject reference sources: Specific subjects based sources provide more in-depth coverage

There are reference sources that provide information on specific subjects as well as general sources that provide information on many subjects. Reference sources are used to obtain a specific answer to a question or to indicate other sources to use during the research process. Although there are several types of reference sources, they all are categorized as either general or specific in scope. Reference works are classified on the basis of their format and the type of information they offer. Various reference sources are described as follows:

Dictionaries

The standard dictionaries give an alphabetical list of words and their definitions. Lots of words are arranged in alphabetical order with their meanings explained or written in another language. Dictionaries also contain information about the form and proper pronunciation of the word. Dialect and slang dictionaries present words and definitions not necessarily found in standard dictionaries. There are also dictionaries of abbreviations and acronyms and dictionaries of quotations. Subject specific dictionaries define terminology and concepts specific to the subject in question. The dictionaries are available in CD-ROM and on the Web too.

Examples:

- Cambridge Dictionaries Online
- Merriam-Webster-Collegiate Dictionary
- How to Find Reference Sources.

Various types of dictionaries are as:

General dictionaries : The general dictionaries are the most familiar to us. The examples include *Webster's International Dictionary*, the *Random House Dictionary of the English Language*, and the *Merriam-Webster Collegiate Dictionary*. The general dictionaries provide definitions, pronunciations, syllabication, and usage.

Historical dictionaries : The historical dictionaries provide the history of a word from its introduction into the language to the present. Example: *The Oxford English Dictionary*.

Etymological dictionaries : These types of dictionaries emphasize the analysis of components of words and their cognates in other languages. These dictionaries emphasize the linguistic and grammatical history of the word usage.

Period or scholarly specialized dictionaries : Such dictionaries focus on a particular place or time period.

Foreign language dictionaries : These dictionaries are fairly self-explanatory.

Subject dictionaries : The subject dictionaries focus on word definitions in a subject area. Subject Dictionaries offer definitions and often short explanations of terms and concepts in specific fields or disciplines, such as finance, law, botany, electronics, physics, etc.

Other dictionaries : Other types of dictionaries include dictionaries of slang, abbreviations, synonyms, antonyms, abbreviations, acronyms, reversals, rhyming, idioms, phrases, and guides to correct usage. Examples are *Dictionary of Acronyms and Abbreviations, The Macmillan Dictionary of Historical Slang, Roget's II: The New Thesaurus, The American Language*.

Other distinguishing types

i. Dictionaries, like other reference sources, may belong to more than one category. For example, an English-Russian engineering dictionary is both a foreign language and a subject dictionary.

ii. Dictionaries may be *abridged or unabridged*. Abridged dictionaries are smaller and contained the most commonly used words. Unabridged dictionaries try to include all words in current usage.

ENCYCLOPEDIAS

Encyclopedias provide general background information. Large subject areas or disciplines are covered in broad articles that explain basic concepts. Encyclopedias are good for fact-finding, getting general background information about a topic or subject. **General encyclopedias** usually arrange articles alphabetically by topic. Encyclopedias may be general or subject specific. Thus we can say that an encyclopedia gives introductory information about a topic, such as history, statistics, description, etc. (*The Encyclopedia Americana*). Encyclopedias traditionally provide comprehensive coverage of an entire area of knowledge. There are general encyclopedias and subject encyclopedias, and they differ as to the level of detail provided and the complexity of the writing.

i. **Encyclopedia Americana** : International ed. 30 vols. Danbury, Conn.: Grolier, 2002.

ii. **New Encyclopaedia Britannica** : 15th ed. 32 vols. Chicago: Encyclopaedia Britannica, 2002.

Subject encyclopedias : Subject Encyclopedias include definitions, description, history, and more about a specific subject, but also offer extensive background information and bibliographies. The subject encyclopedia provides more in-depth and technical information than general encyclopedias. Subject encyclopedias generally assume some prior knowledge of the subject. A few examples of subject encyclopedias include the *McGraw-Hill Encyclopedia of Science and Technology, International Encyclopedia of the Social Sciences, Encyclopedia of World Art, Encyclopedia of Philosophy*, and the *Encyclopedia of Archaeology*. Subject encyclopedias will have subject specific call numbers. Example: *The IEBM Handbook of Human Resource Management* and *Business: The Ultimate Resource.*

Directories

Directories provide names, addresses, affiliations, etc. of people, organizations, or institutions. Directories may be general or focused on a particular subject. Directories are helpful resource to locate and/or contact organizations, companies, people, experts, etc. by listing contact and other information (addresses, phone numbers, names, publications, descriptions, etc.). Example: *Business Organizations, Agencies, and Publications Directory.*

General directories : *Zip Code & Post Office Directory, Encyclopedia of Associations*

Subject directories : *Scholarly Societies Project, Directory of Multinationals, Federal Government Agencies Directory (Hierarchical), Thomas Register of American Manufacturers.*

Biographical Dictionaries

Biographical dictionaries contain short articles about people's lives. Reference sources with biographical information provide information about a person, or references (citations) to other short or full-length biographies written about the person. Biographical sources help patrons locate information about noteworthy persons occur in various formats and types, and differ in depth of information included. The biographical sources are of following types:

General biographical dictionaries : These sources include *Current Biography, Dictionary of American Biography, Who's Who, Encyclopedia of*

World Biography, etc.

Subject biographical dictionaries : The subject specific biographies may focus on a subject area or group. These sources include *Dictionary of Scientific Biography, Contemporary Authors, Biographical Dictionary of Psychology, New Grove Dictionary of Music and Musicians, Women of Science*, etc.

Examples are as following:

i. **McGraw-Hill Encyclopedia of World Biography :** 12 vols. New York: McGraw-Hill, 1973.
ii. **Webster's New Biographical Dictionary :** Springfield, Mass.: Merriam-Webster, 1988. 1130 p.
iii. **Who's Who :** London: Adam and Charles Black, 1894-. Annual.

Geographic Information Sources

Geographical sources are those kinds of reference sources which help in providing information related to place. These sources provide information like description and location related to countries, state regions, districts, cities, mountains, lakes and all places throughout the world. The geographical sources are generally graphic representation of cities, towns, mountains, lakes, river, forests etc. In recent times the geographical sources have become an important part of reference collection of the libraries. Geographic information is located in gazetteers, atlases and maps.

Gazetteers : Gazetteers have two meanings. By the first meaning it is an index to an atlas, and by the second, it is a separately published reference tool which provides information about places of the world or of a particular country. Thus gazetteers are geographical dictionaries, usually of place names. They provide information about the location of a city, mountain, river or other physical features of the earth, population longitude and latitude etc. They also give information about historical, culture political, industrial, administrative details. These sources show where specific physical features are located (e.g. a city, mountain, river, etc.) and may offer information about population and economic characteristics. Gazetteers are sometimes referred to as geographical dictionaries and provide descriptions of places, but no maps. Example: *Texas Gazetteer*. The types of gazetteers are as following:

- **General gazetteers :** are those which provide geographical information in a generalized way. The examples include *Webster's New Geographical Dictionary, The Columbia Lippincott Gazetteer of the World, Gazetteer of Undersea Features, The World Gazetteer, etc.*
- **Regional gazetteers:** focus on a specific geographical region; example includes *Dictionary of Alaska Place Names.*
- **Imperial Gazetteer of India.**

Atlases and Maps : These sources give geographic and spatial information. These sources focus on specific topics of geographic interest like historical, economic, and political matters. Atlases contain collections of maps. They provide information on geographical/political changes. Atlases are to describe a collection of maps bound up in a volume. The globe is a spherical representation of the earth's surface. It is a hollow ball of metal bearing a world map on its surface. The sources may be current or historical. The types of atlases are as following:

- **World atlases:** include *National Geographic Atlas of the World.*
- **National atlases:** *National Atlas of the United States, Atlas of the American Revolution.*
- **Thematic atlases:** focus on a specific subject area. Examples include, *The Oxford Economic Atlas of the World* and the *Environmental Atlas of Alaska.*
- The Times Atlas of the World
- Maps of Mughal India

Maps, atlases and globes are the main sources of geographical information. The map is a graphic document in which location, extent and direction can be more precisely defined and its construction is a mathematical process strictly controlled by measurement and calculation. Map and atlases are needed by common men as well as specialists for satisfying their geography queries. Maps and atlases have a wide variety of their types which have useful geographical information to all kinds of people. Atlases and maps are the main sources of geographical information in libraries; some atlases contain statistics such as population, economic factors, weather, and other facts. There are historical or thematic atlases which show the world at certain dates or during certain events, such as wars.

Travel Guides : Travel guides give information about specific places. Travel guide covers the informations of social, historical, economic aspects. These are used frequently for detailed information about the specific places, historical sites etc, for the travelling point of view. These are meant basically for the people who want to visit various places of the country or the world. These include informations about routes and travel facilities also such as informations about climate of the places, rail roads, highways, hotels to stay and train and airways etc. Examples:

1. Fodder's Guide, India,
2. Hill Resorts of India.

Almanacs

Almanacs contain statistics and facts about countries, events, personalities, or subjects. Almanacs are broader in scope. The types of almanacs are:

- **General almanacs** include the *Statistical Abstract of the United States, The New York Public Library Desk Reference, World Almanac* (an American focus), *Information Please Almanac* (print ed. called *Time Almanac*), *Whitaker's Almanak* (United Kingdom focus).

- Subject almanacs include *The Weather Almanac, The Almanac of Renewable Energy, Political Reference Almanac, Alaska Almanac*, and more.

Yearbooks

Yearbooks provide yearly collections of data and statistics and offer a record of a specific year's activities by country, subject, or other specialized area. Yearbooks are often single volumes. Year books present current and historical events, and popular culture items like sports, entertainment, zip codes. Yearbooks provide a quick update to events occurring during that year. Yearbooks are issued by encyclopedia companies.

i. Britannica Book of the Year : Chicago: Encyclopaedia Britannica, 1938- . Annual.
ii. Facts on File: World News Digest with Index : New York: Facts on File, 1940- . Weekly.
iii. Information Please Almanac: Atlas and Yearbook: New York: Houghton Mifflin, 1947- . Annual.
iv. McGraw-Hill Yearbook of Science and Technology: New York: McGraw-Hill, 1962- . Annual.

Handbooks/Manuals

Handbooks and manuals are subject area tools. Handbooks usually are focused on a particular subject. Manuals provide detailed instructions on a particular subject, such as how-to-do something or how something works. Handbooks offer factual and statistical information, instructions, and quick access to field-specific information.

- Handbooks : Handbook of North American Indians, Guide to Alaska Trees, Words and Ideas: A Handbook for College Writing, Handbook of Mathematical Formulas, MLA Handbook For Writers of Research Papers.
- Manuals : Manual of Photography, Manual for Environmental Impact Evaluation, Alaska Craftsman Home Building Manual, United States Government Manual.

Historical Tables, Chronologies, Historical Yearbooks

Historical tables and chronologies present historical facts in different formats. Chronologies use narrative form to present facts. Historical yearbooks provide facts and statistics for a single year and may be published annually.

- Historical Tables : The Timetables of History.
- Chronologies : Chronology of World History, The New York Public Library Book of Chronologies, Annals of European Civilization, 1501-1900.
- Historical Yearbooks : The Statesman's Year-Book.

Indexes & Abstracts

Indexes and abstracts lead to additional sources of periodical articles. While indexes only provide author, title, and subject information, the abstracts tend to be more descriptive.

Indexes and abstracts supplement the library catalog as described by Bopp and Smith (1995):

Users may come into a library, consult the main catalog, and falsely assume they have searched the entire contents of the library. The catalog may confirm the holdings of a periodical [magazine or journal] but not its contents; a poetry collection but not individual poems; the title of an author's collected works but not the individual work; newspapers but not individual news stories. Indexes and abstracts are created and become extremely useful tools to more fully reveal detailed resources not covered in the more general catalog.

Indexes are arranged usually alphabetically or subject related, of information sources (e.g. books, periodicals, etc.). Examples are as following:

- Ulrich's International Periodical Index
- Canadian Book Trade and Library Index
- Advanced Book Exchange

Searching indexes don't use the same subject classifications as the library catalog. Some indexes provide books of "descriptors" to help searching for key words and key concepts by which the items have been indexed. Types of indexes and abstracts are as following:

- General : Reader's Guide to Periodic Index (FirstSearch), Book Review Index, Periodicals Abstracts (FirstSearch).
- Subject : Art Abstracts (FirstSearch), New York Times Index (ABI Inform), Biography Index (FirstSearch), Chemical Abstracts.

Bibliographies

Bibliographies are lists of books. Bibliography helps identifying sources where information can be found. A bibliography informs to find additional works by a certain author or works on a certain subject. Bibliographies, are lists of books and other materials that provide author, title, and publication information, they lead to other information sources. Another kind of bibliography, the Annotated bibliographies include a brief description or summary of the item. Many bibliographies are selective and do not attempt to include all publications. Bibliographies are sometimes referred to as "Guides to the Literature ..."

Examples: *American Fiction, 1774-1850, A Bibliography of Sir Walter Scott.*

INFORMATION SOURCES

The information sources are the various kinds of sources meant to inform users. These are categorized as following:

i. Primary sources : A primary source is an *original* document containing firsthand information about a topic. The primary sources allow researchers to get as close as possible to original ideas, events, and empirical research as possible. In general, these sources include creative works, first hand or contemporary accounts of events, and the publication of the results of empirical observations or research. Examples are as following:

- Diaries
- Interviews
- Letters
- Original works of art
- Photographs
- Speeches
- Works of literature

ii. Secondary sources : The secondary sources provide the principle sources of analysis about primary sources. The secondary sources offer an *interpretation* of information gathered from primary sources. The secondary sources are the outcome of the process that analyze, review, or summarize information in primary resources or other secondary resources. Sometimes few sources which are presenting facts or descriptions about events are secondary. Examples are as given:

- Biographies
- Dissertations
- Indexes, abstracts, bibliographies (used to locate a secondary source)
- Journal articles
- Monographs

iii. Tertiary sources : A tertiary source presents summaries or condensed versions of materials, usually with references back to the primary and/or secondary sources. These sources provide overviews of topics by synthesizing information gathered from other resources. They can be a good place to look up facts or get a general overview of a subject, but they rarely contain original material. Tertiary resources often provide data in a convenient form or provide information with context by which to interpret it. Examples are as following:

- Dictionaries
- Encyclopedias
- Handbooks

The distinctions between primary, secondary, and tertiary sources can be ambiguous. An individual document may be a primary source in one context and a secondary source in another.

Reference Services and Sources

Reference services fulfill the dissemination purpose of a library. Reference services are provided via the telephone also. Many libraries respond to emailed reference question. There are types of reference assistance as:

- Assistance or instruction in the use of the library, including location of materials, use of the catalog, use of computers to access information, and the use of basic reference sources.
- Assistance in identifying library materials needed to answer a question.
- Providing brief, factual answers to questions, such as addresses, statistics, phone numbers, etc. that can be quickly located.

WEB RESOURCES FOR REFERENCE TOOLS

A good number of Internet reference tools are available as Internet subject directories or virtual libraries. Virtual Libraries, web sites are created by librarians that index quality web links. These can help finding quality Internet reference tools. Many of these sites have specific "general reference" sections. Examples of virtual libraries are:

Reference Desk : Librarian's Index to the Internet. Includes links to other information sources including almanacs, calendars, dictionaries, encyclopedias, holidays, names, phone books, and statistics. Available at http://www.ipl.org/IPLBrowse/GetSubject

General Reference : WWW Virtual Library. One of the first virtual library sites, started by Tim Berners-Lee, the creator of html and the web itself. Available at http://home.istar.ca/~obyrne/

Reference and Periodicals : This virtual library provides separate indexes for teachers, kids, teens, parents, librarians and "community." Available at http://www.awesomelibrary.org/Library/Reference_and_Periodicals/Reference_and_Periodicals.html

Electronic Resources : For The Reference Desk - A selective list of reference sites from the Library of Congress. Available at http://www.loc.gov/rr/elecdesk.html

Academic Info Digital Library site : For a list of subject specific virtual libraries. Available at http://www.academicinfo.net/digital.html

Finding reference sources in library

There are several different ways to find reference sources on the desired topic:

- Asking at the Information & Research Help Desk.
- Browsing the reference area stacks near the Information & Research Help Desk
- Search the Library Catalogue and limit the search to the location: reference.

Reference Services and Goals

- The goal of reference service is to provide an end-product: the information sought by the user. Reference service shall not only meet but also anticipate user needs. The Library staff shall encourage user awareness of the potential of information resources to fulfill individual information needs.

- The Library shall seek to provide users with complete, accurate answers to their information queries regardless of the complexity of those queries.
- The Library shall make available user aids, in print and other media, to help users identify items in the collection relevant to their interests and needs.
- The Library shall provide instruction in the effective use of its resources. Such instruction can range from the individual explanation of information resources or creation of guides in appropriate media to formal assistance through interpretive tours and group presentations designed to provide guidance and direction in the pursuit of information.
- The Library shall collect or provide access to information resources germane to its mission and reflecting the interests of the full spectrum of the population it serves. These information resources shall satisfy, through content, currency, format, organization, and quantity a diversity of user needs.
- The Library shall provide access to the most current reference sources available in order to assure the accuracy of information.
- The Library shall make service areas for reference services highly visible and readily accessible to all users.
- The Library shall design service points to accommodate the needs of all users, including the disabled.
- Reference services staff shall have knowledge and preparation appropriate to meet the information needs of the clientele the Library serves. Staff responsible for the services shall be thoroughly familiar with and competent in using information sources, retrieval techniques, telecommunication methods, and interpersonal communications skills.
- Continuing education of reference service staff is essential to professional growth.
- The Library shall regularly evaluate its service to assure that the service furthers the institution's goals and that the goals reflect the needs and interests of the community served. Results of evaluation shall be used to determine the optimum allocation of resources to provide quality service.

Guidelines for reference service

- The Library's reference collection shall contain current, accurate, and accessible medical, legal, and business information appropriate to the needs of the community served. The reference transaction shall fully satisfy the user's need for information, either by providing accurate sources in hand, or clear and concise referrals to obtainable sources located elsewhere.

- Librarians shall make clear their role as information providers, not interpreters or advisers. They shall provide instruction in the use of resources, enabling users to pursue information independently and effectively, if so desired.
- Libraries may advise patrons regarding the relative merits of sources and make recommendations regarding Library materials when appropriate. Materials recommended shall be the most comprehensive and the most current available.
- The reference librarian shall direct the user to possible sources, both in and out of the library, where the information the user requires will be provided.
- In subject areas where up-to-date information is essential, libraries shall provide the most current information possible, consistent with the needs of the library's primary clientele and within the limitations of the Library's materials budget and collection development policy.
- Referrals shall be made only if the librarian expects that the agency, service, individual, or other source can and will provide the information needed.

18
Encyclopedias

INTRODUCTION

An encyclopedia is a comprehensive reference work containing articles on a wide range of subjects or on numerous aspects of a particular field, usually arranged alphabetically. In other words, an encyclopaedia is a type of reference work. It records the information from either all branches of knowledge or a particular branch of knowledge. Encyclopedias are divided into articles or entries (generally arranged alphabetically). Encyclopedia articles focus on factual information to cover the thing or concept. The word *encyclopedia* comes from the 'Koine Greek' meaning "general education" from *enkyklios*, meaning "circular, recurrent, required regularly, general" and *paideia*, meaning "education, rearing of a child". The meaning of the term has undergone a considerable change during its long history.

The term encyclopaedia was coined by 16th century humanists. The English physician and philosopher, Sir Thomas Browne used the word 'encyclopaedia' in 1646 in the preface to the reader to define his *Pseudodoxia Epidemica*. Now the term encyclopaedia is applied to any reference work of one or more volumes consisting of articles pertaining to all the branches of human knowledge, usually arranged in alphabetical order, which is most easy to use. The encyclopaedias are usually not written by any single author, but by experts in the fields, and contain bibliographies and illustrations. Being major reference sources, encyclopaedias are generally considered as the backbone of library services as they provide answer to (Very reference question about universe of knowledge. They generally contain a comprehensive index at the end to help in tracing information in the articles easily and quickly. The main purpose of the encyclopaedia is to condense current and essential Information in a short and simpler form to make it accessible to the non-specialist. They are secondary sources of information.

Thus in conclusion we can say that an encyclopaedia is a store house or treasury of valuable knowledge giving significant information. They may be comprehensive such as the Encyclopedia Britannica, or subject specific, such as The Encyclopedia of Education

Characteristics

- The modern encyclopedia was developed from the dictionary in the 18th century. Historically, both encyclopedias and dictionaries have been researched and written by well-educated, well-informed content experts, but they are significantly different in structure.
- An encyclopedia article covers a *subject or discipline* and provides most relevant accumulated knowledge on that subject.
- Works containing informational articles on all subjects in all fields of knowledge, usually arranged in alphabetical order.
- Encyclopedias may be concise, complete in one volume, or extensive, published in large multi-volume sets.
- An encyclopedia article also often includes many maps and illustrations, as well as bibliography and statistics.
- Encyclopedia articles are longer, fuller and have more thorough entries.
- Encyclopedias focus more on the thing for which those words stand.
- Encyclopedias may contain material that is also found in dictionaries, and vice versa.

Few examples of General Encyclopedias

American Society of Indexing : General reference sources pertaining to multidisciplinary topics.

Assorted Encyclopedias on the Web : List of online encyclopedias which covers various topics.

Encyclopedia Britannica : An online version of the current edition of the Encyclopedia Britannica is available through the library's website (http://www.library.fgcu.com). Go to the Journal Articles and Databases page, search for database "Encyclopedia Britannica", then click "Connect Now". This service includes access to the entire text of the Encyclopedia Britannica as well as a number of other resources.

Encyclopedia.com : Encyclopedia.com is the Internet's free encyclopedia. More than 1400 articles from the Concise Columbia Electronic Encyclopedia have been assembled at this site for providing free, useful, and quick information.

Infoplease.com : Online version of the popular almanac which can be browsed by topic or searched. Also includes the Random house Webster's College Dictionary and Columbia Encyclopedia.

ELEMENTS OF AN ENCYCLOPEDIA

The following elements describe and define an encyclopedia:

i. Subject matter
ii. Scope
iii. Method of organization
iv. Method of production

The subject matter : Encyclopedias can be general that are covering topics in every field (e.g. *Encyclopædia Britannica)*. Few general encyclopedias cover a wide variety of topics limited to a particular cultural, ethnic, or national perspective.

The scope : The encyclopedic scope is related with the knowledge for their subject domain. The scope defines the reach and boundaries of the subject matters covered. There can be variation in the breadth of material and the depth of discussion.

Method of organization : The systematic method of organization makes an encyclopedia usable work of reference. The two most popular methods of organizing printed encyclopedias:

(a) ***The alphabetical method*:** This method is consisting of a number of separate articles, organized in alphabetical order. This method is today the most common by far, especially for general works.

(b) ***The hierarchical methods* :** The hierarchical method is possible due to fluidity of electronic media. There are possibilities for multiple methods of organization of the same content. Due to electronic media, searching, indexing and cross reference facilities are possible.

Method of production : Due to multimedia and the information technology, the activities such as collection, verification, summation, and presentation have been changed. The choices and preferences of users also matter. The print as well as electronic (online) encyclopedias are found. Encyclopedias are displayed on computer and distributed via computer networks.

Purpose of an Encyclopedia

- To collect knowledge disseminated around the globe
- To set forth its general system to the men with whom we live, and transmit it to those who will come after us, so that the work of preceding centuries will not become useless to the centuries to come

HISTORY

- One of the earliest encyclopedic works, *Naturalis Historia,* was written in ca. AD 77 by Pliny the Elder.
- The first known encyclopedia of the Middle Ages, the *Etymologiae* or *Origines* (around 630) was written by Saint Isidore of Seville.
- The most popular encyclopedia of the Carolingian Age, the *De universo* or *De rerum naturis* was written about 830 by Rabanus Maurus.
- The enormous encyclopedic work in China of the *Four Great Books*

of Song, compiled by the 11th century AD during the early Song Dynasty (960–1279).

- The *De expetendis et fugiendis rebus* by Giorgio Valla (posthumously printed in 1501 by Aldo Manuzio in Venice).
- The 18th century encyclopedias are Chambers' *Cyclopaedia, or Universal Dictionary of Arts and Sciences* (1728), and the *Encyclopédie* of Denis Diderot and Jean le Rond d'Alembert (1751 onwards), as well as *Encyclopædia Britannica*.
- By the late 20th century, encyclopedias were being published on CD-ROMs for use with personal computers (Microsoft's *Encarta* launched 1993, discontinued in 2009).
- Wikipedia, a collaboratively edited, multilingual, free Internet encyclopedia was launched in early 21st century.

Utility and importance of Encyclopaedias

The encyclopaedias are used by people from different walks and backgrounds.

1. Encyclopaedias are consulted for concise, digested information on a topic.
2. These generally present information in an impartial manner, giving all the view points on a subject as well as essential historical background to the topic of enquiry.
3. Encyclopaedias are the only sources for biographical information on an otherwise minor figure not covered in standard biographical dictionaries.
4. Earlier editions of encyclopaedias have their own value also.
5. The role of illustrations in making a subject more comprehensible can hardly be over emphasized. Colour plates, black and white photographs and line drawings in encyclopaedias not only add to their aesthetics but great help in clarifying descriptions.
6. The scholarly treatments of the subject make the general encyclopaedias serve as a gateway to understand the most profound or intricate knowledge.

TYPES OF ENCYCLOPAEDIAS

There are following two types of encyclopaedias:

1. General Encyclopaedias

The general encyclopaedias contain a collection of articles giving essential information about all branches of knowledge. They are most popular and extensively used reference tools. They are arranged either alphabetically or in classified order by subjects or names. They are intended for the general readers. It is a huge and most expensive task to produce as authoritative general encyclopaedia. General encyclopaedias can be classified into different categories according to format, user's age, coverage and language. Here we give below some popular examples of general encyclopaedias.

a) Comprehensive multi-volumed encyclopaedias.
Example : The New Encyclopaedia - 15th ed. - Chicago, 1974.30 Volumes.

b) Popular multi-volumed adult and junior encyclopaedias. Example Encyclopaedia International.- New York: Grolier, 1970,20 Volumes.

c) Multi-volumed junior and children encyclopaedias. Example - Oxford Junior Encyclopaedia. Rev. ed - London: OUP, 1961,12 volumes.

d) One and two volumed adult and junior encyclopedias. Example - The Random House Encyclopaedia.- New York: Random House, 1977.

e) National/Regional encyclopaedias in different languages. Example Encylopaedia Britannica, Encyclopaedia Americana.

2. Subject Encyclopaedias

Subject encyclopaedias are the collection of articles limited to a specific field of area. These encyclopedias aim to serve in a particular subject; hence they are called subject encyclopaedias. Subject encyclopaedias are published for each discipline separately. Subject encyclopaedias are excellent ready reference aids for the specialists who want to trace information about a particular subject. They are very reliable sources to get accurate information on any subject. To get accurate and reliable information on any subject, subject encyclopaedias are the better for use. There are countless subject encyclopaedias available in various subjects. A few important examples are as follows:

- Multi-volumed Subject Encyclopaedias.
  - McGraw-Hill Encyclopaedia of Science and Technology.
  - New York, McGraw-Hill, 1982,15 volumes.
- One or two volumed Subject Encyclopaedias.
  - Van Nostrand's Scientific Encyclopaedia. - 6th ed. -New York: Van Nostrand, 1983.

Uses of Subject Encyclopaedias

When a user frequently wants to know something on or about a particular subject, reference answers can be searched from the subject encyclopaedias. The subject encyclopaedias gives detailed data on a specific subject as well as organised overviews for the purpose of research.

GENERAL DESCRIPTION OF ENCYCLOPÆDIA BRITANNICA

The *Encyclopædia Britannica* is published by Encyclopædia Britannica, Inc. It is a general knowledge English-language encyclopaedia. The *Britannica* is the oldest English-language encyclopaedia still being produced. It was first published between 1768 and 1771 in Edinburgh,

Scotland as three volumes. In 1933, the *Britannica* became the first encyclopaedia to adopt "continuous revision". In March 2012, Encyclopædia Britannica, Inc. announced to discontinue publishing its printed editions and focusing on its online version, *Encyclopædia Britannica Online*. Its final print edition was in 2010, a 32-volume set.

The features of online Encyclopedia Britannica

Encyclopedia Britannica has taken their product much further with their online edition of their classic encyclopedia. This encyclopedia:

i. Accessible 24/7 through the website.
ii. Has all of the information available in the print version.
iii. Enhanced with practical help and extra information, including photos, videos, and sound recordings.
iv. "Expand Your Research" of the online encyclopedia, links to full-text journal articles, online searches that are geared specifically for help in researching the subject, and primary source documents.
v. Ability to double-click any word in the article, which will bring up a box with a definition and an audio pronunciation of the word.

Structure

The 15th and latest edition has a three-part structure:

Micropedia : Set of 12-volumes forms *Micropædia* of short articles.

Macropedia : *Macropædia* is a set of 19-volumes of long articles.

Propedia : *Propædia* is a single volume to give a hierarchical outline of knowledge. The *Micropædia* is meant for quick fact-checking and as a guide to the *Macropædia*; readers are advised to study the *Propædia* outline to understand a subject's context and to find more detailed articles.

Optical disc and online versions : The *Britannica Ultimate Reference Suite 2012 DVD* contains over 100,000 articles inclusive of *Britannica* articles, the *Britannica Student Encyclopædia*, and the *Britannica Elementary Encyclopædia*. It has features such as maps, videos, sound clips, animations and web links and dictionary and thesaurus entries from Merriam-Webster.

EVALUATION OF ENCYCLOPEDIAS

Evaluation Checkpoints for a Reference Source

The different checkpoints for evaluating reference sources are as follows:

1. Authority : The authority is judged by the reputation of the persons responsible for its publication. The editor, consultants, contributors, the publishers and editorial staff such as proof readers, indexers, artists, photographers etc. each one of them has contribution in making a work successful.

2. Scope and Purpose : The scope and purpose is found in the preface and introduction. The work should follow a definite plan such as even in length of articles, completeness of topics in coverage. The facts should be accurate and reliable.

3. Treatment : The three important criteria of topics in any type of reference source are readability, objectivity and style. The explanation and presentation of information should be able to make the unfamiliar subject clear to the user. The standard and the quality of the articles should also be objective without any type of bias.

4. Arrangement : The arrangement of articles can be either in alphabetical or classified order. It depends upon the nature and size of articles as well as the editors' plan for their presentation. The arrangement of the articles should be user friendly. It must be helpful in easy locating the information.

5. Format : The format depends upon the physical make up of the reference source such as:

a) General appearance,
b) Presentation of articles, illustrations, diagrams, tables etc.
c) Quality of paper.
d) Printing, page make-up, binding etc.

6. Revision : The updated and revised information is considered best for the readers' services. So it should be revised and updated at some intervals.

7. Salient Features : The unique features of the publication of the reference source are significant:

a) The bibliography should be current, exhaustive and updated.
b) The appendix and separate lists of abbreviations, pronunciations, errata etc. enhance the value of the reference source.
c) The photographs, sketches, maps, diagrams, charts, tables given at the appropriate places augment the comprehensibility of the reference source.
d) The inclusion of guidelines for using the volumes and contents of each volume in the introductory pages is the important features.

Evaluation of New Encyclopedia Britannica. (Academic edition) Online version

1. Authority : Encyclopedia Britannica, Inc. was originally established in Scotland in the 1700's before reaching Chicago, IL. Printed products of Britannica sets were owned by leading historical figures such as George Washington, Thomas Jefferson, and Alexander Hamilton. Today, its products range in diversity, in order to accommodate for technological needs.

2. Scope : It contains over 75,000 articles, including 23,000 biographies. The full text articles are compiled from over 700 magazines and periodicals. It has links to over 166,000 websites, and more than 27,000 images and maps.

3. Format : Main page can be divided into three sections:

- Left side has "Research tools": the index, A-Z browse, subject browse, world atlas, compare countries, timelines, the year in review browse, world data, video browse, and notable quotations.
- The middle portion gives users the option to review highlights, the biography of the day, or the day in history. Left side column has features news links from the New York Times, the BBC News, and SBS News.
- Across the top of the main screen is a search box, followed by a link to conduct and advanced search. The guided tour section explains the format of the website and provides explanations of each section. The workspace feature allows user to create personal webpages to house articles for research projects.

4. Entries : Entries are in the format of an article and permitting to switch to printable version or email themseives the article. Each entry gives users the option to submit comments or questions.

5. Special Feature : Users are instructed on how to cite each article site they visit in both MLA and APA style format.

Overall Evaluation : The online version features daily updates that would not be possible in a print version. In addition to a "highlights" section, the website also contains a "biography of the day" feature and a "this day in history" section." Similarly, links to the New York Times, BBC News, and SBS World News are provided.

Evaluation of Encyclopaedia Britannica

Encyclopaedia Britannica is one of the most popular encyclopaedia and a general encyclopedia covering all the existing human knowledge. It is most popular and extensively used reference source for the libraries. The first edition of this encyclopaedia was published in 1768-1771 in three volumes. Its 14th edition published with the tide Encyclopaedia Britannica in 1929 and was revised and reorganised till 1973. After it in 1974 its fifteenth edition was published as New Encyclopaedia Britannica consisting of 30 volumes.

1. Authority : The publisher of this encyclopaedia is Encyclopaedia Britannica Inc. The articles contained in this encyclopaedia were written by near more than 400 expert contributors. To make the articles authentic, the writers signatures were also given with article.

2. Aims : The aim of publication of this encyclopaedia is to present suitable material of knowledge and presented the whole knowledge into ten divisions.

3. Arrangement : New Encyclopedia Britannica has been divided into following three parts. In libraries this encyclopaedia is called EB3. The three parts of the encyclopaedia are as follows:

a. **Propaedia :** This is a one volume guide gives outline of knowledge and is a schematic introduction to articles in Macropaedia. It has no index. It is organised according to broad subjects.

b. **Micropaedia :** The first 10 volumes are called micropaedia. This part is a study guide and contains brief information for ready reference. The entries have been arranged in alphabetical order. It provides factual information.

c. **Macropaedia :** This part contains knowledge in depth has lengthy articles. It covers major topics of general interest. The articles are written by well known experts and include selective and annotated bibliographies. It has international approach and universal coverage since 1938 and updated every year by Britannica Book of the year.

4. Special Features : The special features are as following:

i. Its 15th edition represents full revision in general encyclopaedias.

ii. The descriptive bibliography indicates the access of additional information.

iii. Since 1938, it publishes annually its supplement by the title Britannica Book of the Year which updates the whole volume.

iv. Its price is very high so most of the libraries cannot afford it. It is a very useful and best publication in the field of knowledge.

Evaluation of Random House Encyclopedia. Rev. 3d. ed. New York: Random House, 1990.

1. Authority : Based in New York City, Random House was founded in 1927 by Bennett Cerf and Donald Klopfer. The company first began reference publishing in 1947, when it published *American College Dictionary*, followed by its first unabridged dictionary in 1966.

2. Scope : 13,500 illustrations in the special "Colorpedia" section (pictures, paintings, photographs, diagrams, illustrations, drawings, maps and charts).

3. Format : Over 2,000 pages. Color images. 132 page world atlas. "Alphapedia," "Colorpedia," "Time Chart" and atlas/gazetteer sections.

4. Entries : Double pages; connection section for each entry. Limited information.

Evaluation of McGraw Hill Encyclopaedia of Science and Technology

McGraw Hill Encyclopaedia of Science and Technology is a subject encyclopaedia. It has a specific place among subject encyclopaedias in the field of science and technology.

1. Authority : The publication authority of this encyclopaedia is the famous McGraw Hill Book Company, New York (USA). The editing policy is of keeping up-to-date itself with current and right information of science and technology. The international fame subject experts and scientists are in its editorial board and in its advisory committee.

2. Scope : The all topics of 77 subject fields of science and technology are included in it. The coverage is from Acoustics to Zoology. The topics of engineering are also included in it.

3. Arrangement :

a) More than 7000 articles have been included in the present edition.

b) The provision of index is a remarkable task. The two types of indexes are used in it. They are: Analytical index, and Extensive topical index.

4. Style : The presentation of the articles is quite easy and clear. The style and method of writing the entries are very much qualitative. The abstracts of the subject information have been presented in understandable style.

5. Special Features :

i. Entries are presented to relate to each other by the provision of cross-references done in it.

ii. McGraw Hill Yearbook is published every year, which contains reports of activities, incidents and inventions.

iii. The analytical part of its index helps the users in getting the information quickly.

iv. It is reference tool to give identification of current information to the users.

19

Dictionaries

INTRODUCTION

When we look into a dictionary, we find it as a document or source which is a compilation of words ranging from letters A-Z. We use dictionary for deciphering profound word or phrase or understanding the etymology of a word. However, the main purpose is to give meanings to words, it is used for various types of consultation which we will find out later in this chapter. Understanding it, the Oxford English Dictionary defines a dictionary as a "book dealing with the individual words of a language (or certain specified class of them) so as to set forth their orthography, pronunciation, signification and use, their synonyms, derivation and history, or al least some of the facts, for convenience of reference the words are arranged in some stated order, now in most languages, alphabetical, and in larger dictionaries the information given in illustrated by quotations from literature".

Dictionaries are repositories of words. Dictionaries are the first place for looking up spellings and meanings of a broad selection of terms. Depending on purpose and their structure, the dictionaries can be classified into different types. The classification is based on the nature of the lexical entry to the prospective user of the dictionary also. The various criteria for classification of dictionaries are as following:

Purpose : normative or referential.

Arrangement of entries : alphabetical or semantic or causal.

The number of languages involved : monolingual, bilingual, multilingual etc.

The nature of entries : lexical only or also encyclopaedic, the degree of concentration on strictly lexical data.

Density of entries (word list) : general or restricted and special. Coverage of regional and social dialects, jargons and slangs and archaisms.

Axis of time : whether diachronic (dynamic) or synchronic (static).

TYPES OF DICTIONARIES ACCORDING TO NATURE AND SCOPE

Dictionaries have been divided into different categories according to their nature and scope of contents. Here are various popular categories and forms of dictionaries:

General Language or Linguistic Dictionaries : The lexical or linguistic dictionary pertains to linguistic characteristics of the lexical unit viz., pronunciation, definition, etymology, grammatical category, etc. Examples of linguistic dictionaries are the Oxford English Dictionary. Hindi Sabda Sagar, Tamil Lexicon etc. This category of dictionaries deals with the common words of a particular language. They are called general dictionaries and are most popular and readily used. They are grouped according to their purpose, size, volume, and users age.

Special Dictionaries : Special dictionaries are compiled to deal with special purpose or aspect of a language to deal with the special aspects of the words much more comprehensively in comparison to general dictionaries. They are divided into three groups according to their content and scope.

- Dictionaries covering specific linguistic aspects of the words.
- Dictionaries covering a special type or class of words.
- Dictionaries dealing with literary aspects.

Translating Dictionaries : The translating dictionary gives accurate equivalent words in one or more foreign languages. They provide pronunciation, parts of speech and genders so as to enable the learners to follow them easily. Sometimes these dictionaries include slang words, idioms, borrowed and dialect words. These dictionaries are of two types.

- Bilingual Dictionaries
- Multilingual Dictionaries

Subject Dictionaries : Subject dictionaries deal with the words, phrases, expressions and technical words of a particular subject. Some subject dictionaries are meant for two kinds of user i.e. general public, and subject specialists and students. Subject dictionaries are found in various forms according to the size, volume and language as follows:

- Unabridged or abridged
- Single volume or Multi-volume
- Bilingual or Multilingual.

Beginners'/Learners' Dictionaries : The Cambridge University Press has, among its family of online dictionaries, one with simplified definitions; for American English specifically, Merriam-Webster offers Word Central, an online children's dictionary that is helpful for learners of all ages without being juvenile in presentation. For a print version, there is a dictionary for young students (like the *Scholastic Children's Dictionary*) — though the child-oriented design of these books may put off older learners — or one for English-language learners.

Encyclopaedic dictionary : The encyclopaedic dictionary is a combination of an encyclopaedia and a linguistic dictionary. In the amount of the information and the manner of its presentation, again, it combines the features of both.

Historical and Etymological Dictionaries : The historical dictionary records the development of a lexical item in terms of both the form and the meaning of the particular lexical unit. Its focus is also to present the history of a lexical unit. The historical dictionary is concerned with a systematic study of changes affecting a lexical unit during its life i.e. within a period from which there is evidence. The etymological dictionary presents the origin of words by tracing the present day words to their oldest forms. The main function of the etymological dictionary is to present the history of a lexical item. The interest of an etymological dictionary is primarily in the pre-history of the language.

Online Translation Dictionaries : Online translation dictionaries enable visitors to type in a word and they can receive its equivalent in another language abound. For example, Dictionary.com's is Translator site.

Unusual-Words Dictionaries : There are few online repositories of seldom-used and/or offbeat words, for example, the Phrontistery available at http://phrontistery.info/. Such sources are available in print formats also, for example, *The Word Lovers' Dictionary: Unusual, Obscure, and Preposterous Words.*

Visual Dictionaries : Visual dictionaries are provided with illustrations of animate and inanimate things labeled with parts and components, for example, Merriam-Webster's a print visual dictionary.

There are few other types of dictionaries in vogue:

- Anagram dictionary
- Biographical dictionaries
- Concordances
- Crossword Dictionary
- Encyclopedic dictionary
- Etymological dictionary
- Glossary
- Idiom dictionary
- Lexica
- Lexical databases
- Machine-readable dictionary
- Mini-Dictionary
- Monoloingual, bilingual and multilingual dictionaries,
- Phonetic dictionary
- Picture dictionary
- Pocket Dictionary

- Reverse dictionary
- Rhyming Dictionary
- Slang dictionary
- Specialized dictionary
- Terminology dictionaries
- Thesauriý
- Thesaurus
- Translation dictionaries
- Visual dictionary

Properties of the dictionaries

The properties refer to the structure of dictionaries such as:

Microstructure : It is the structure of individual lexical entries. It includes types of lexical information and the way in which types of lexical information are organized,

Mesostructure : It shows the relations between lexical entries and some other source of information. This relation is concerned with:

- a general descriptive section including descriptions of parts of speech, other grammatical information, morphology, pronunciation,
- other lexical entries, in the form of textual or hyperlink cross-references, typically synonyms, antonyms and other lexical semantic relations,
- external materials such as text corpora, datelines describing where and when the word has been used.

Macrostructure : This kind of structure reflects the overall organization of the dictionary, including lexical entries and their microstructure, and the mesostructure.

USES OF DICTIONARIES

The uses of a dictionary depend to a large extent on the type of dictionary. Usually dictionaries are used to verify pronunciation, spellings, meanings or usage of words But these are not the only uses. They can be referred for various purposes. Here we present the uses of dictionaries are presented as follows:

Quick Reference Tool : Dictionaries are used to verity spellings, syllabication, hyphenation, pronunciation and meaning, origin, part of speech and usage of the words. They act as quick reference tools to consult anything about the words.

Tools for Language Standardization : Dictionaries and lexicons have been accepted as the Standardization tools. The standardization is the outcome of carefully scrutinizing words from the recorded sources of the language and the usage of the speakers. Standardization is required to eliminate the variation in spellings and usage of the words.

Vocabulary Builder : The systematic and regular use of dictionaries clears the doubts about the spellings, meanings and usages of words. It enriches the power of the words by helping in building proper vocabulary and ensuring accurate use of words in context.

Language recording tools : Unabridged dictionaries are descriptive type of dictionary. These dictionaries act as a language recorder by tracing the developmental trends of the language by recording etymological details of the words, their history, origin and derivation. The example is Oxford English Dictionary. The historical records of the changes undergone in the meanings and usages of the words from time to time are presented.

EVALUATION OF VARIOUS KINDS OF DICTIONARIES

Roget's International Thesaurus. 5th ed. New York: Harper Collins, 1992

Authority : It has been best selling thesaurus for over fifty years. According to the inside cover, entries are based on "extensive word association research into how words are actually used."

Scope : This edition has 1073 categories. Publication includes 325,000 words and phrases.

Format : Two columns per page. Entries are written in bold, capital letters. Beginning of the work contains a biography of the original author, Peter Roget. Biography is then followed by a "how to use" section, which instructs users to look up a word in the index, find the appropriate sub-entry, follow its number into the text to find the paragraphs on comparable adjectives. Synopsis of categories section preludes actual entries. The entries are not in alphabetical order; they are organized by related categories.

Entries : Each entry word is written in bold, capital letters. A brief definition is given, as denoted italic text surrounded by < >. Parts of speech are listed in the following order: nouns, verbs, adjectives, adverbs, prepositions, conjunctions, and interjections. The most common synonyms are in bold text. Entries are methodically arranged (not alphabetically).

Overall evaluation : It is easy to use, and comprehensive in nature.

Webster's Dictionary of English Usage. Springfield, MA: Merriam-Webster, 1989

Authority : The authority of this dictionary is the American publisher of language related sources. Other publications include *Merriam-Webster's Collegiate Dictionary* (America's best-selling desk dictionary). Company was found in the 1830's by brothers Charles and George Mirriam.

Scope : Entries are examined from historical and present day usage perspectives. Topics were selected from existing books on usage as well as idiomatic English usage. Publication contains more than 500 entries.

Format : Preface is followed by explanatory notes, history of English usage section, pronunciation symbols, entries, bibliography. There are two columns per page. Entry words are written in bold text, and there are spaces between entries. Entire book is just under 1,000 pages.

Entries : Entries are very detailed and contain a lot written text. There are examples, quotations and historical information on the usage.

Overall Evaluation : This dictionary has much more than a book of definitions; it explains *how* to use properly use words. This source has unique qualities that make it a valuable source to understand/learn how to use the language.

Webster's Third New International Dictionary of the English Language. Springfield, MA: Mirriam-Webster, 1993

Authority : The authority is well known among the publishers. This publication cost over $3.5 million to publish. The editorial staff consisted of people from a variety of fields. Over 200 scholars and consultants joined the editorial staff on this project. Extra care was taken in order to produce accurate definitions.

Scope : it is the largest American dictionary. It contains over 476,000 entries. 2,662 pages.

Format : The inside cover has a list of pronunciation symbols. The book itself is quite large in size and has nearly 3,000 pages. The contents section informs readers that there are multiple sections, including tables, illustrations, editorial staff, outside consultants, explanatory notes, etc. Tabs make it easy to find a specific section. The preface attempts to sell the book by stating its credibility, scope, and the effort that went into its publication. Three columns are on each page. Entries are listed alphabetically. Pages have few black and white images. Special color chart section.

Entries : Entry titles are in bold text. In addition to the actual definition(s), entries contain the word's pronunciation, part of speech, and origin. The definitions are succinct, not too wordy, and easy to understand.

Overall Evaluation : It contains the most accurate definitions. The preface is a good indication of the resource's credibility. However, the size and weight of make it cumbersome to use.

20

Introducing Computer in Library

INTRODUCTION

Computer is one of the most revolutionary and powerful tools ever developed because of the tremendous changes it has and still continues to make in our lives. A computer is an electronic device that executes the instructions in a program. Therefore, computers perform complex and repetitive procedures quickly, precisely and reliably. Modern computers are electronic and digital. The actual machinery (wires, transistors, and circuits) is called hardware; the instructions and data are called software. All general-purpose computers require the following hardware components:

Central processing unit (CPU) : This functions as brain of the computer. The CPU executes instructions organized in programs ("software") which tells the computer what to do.

Memory and Storage Devices : The memory supports a computer to store, at least temporarily, data, programs, and intermediate results. The storage devices allow a computer to permanently retain large amounts of data and programs between jobs. Common mass storage devices include external disk drives.

Input device : The input device enters the data and create changes in the work in a computer.

Output device : The output devices support to bring out the result of a process with the help of a display screen, printer, or other device.

Software

The word software refers to instruction or programming sequences that run on the hardware of a computer. Computer software performs the function of the program it implements. It provides instructions to the computer hardware and serves as an input to another piece of software.

Computer software is described as the information processed by the systems. *Software* allow user to perform various tasks. The examples of software are word processors, databases, spreadsheets, antivirus programmes, web browsers. The computer software can be classified into two types:

1. Systems software : It includes basic input-output systems, device drivers etc. System software are those programs that handle the functioning of the computer's hardware. The main categories are:

a. operating systems
b. utility programs
c. network operating systems etc.

2. Applications software : The application software are those programs that processe data for the user. The examples of application software are word processors, database programs, etc. There are many packaged software for various applications.

Operating Systems

The purpose of an operating system is to organize and control hardware and software. The operating system in desktop computer controls operating i.e. working of computer. The operating system (OS) is stored on hard drive. It provides the basic operating platform for other software and peripherals. The operating system (OS) is the first thing loaded onto the computer -- without the operating system, a computer is useless. Operating systems are found on many of the devices we use every day, from cell phones to wireless access points. The examples of OS are DOS, Windows 95 and Windows 98. The basic functions of the Operating System are as following:

1. It manages the hardware and software resources of the system. In a desktop computer, these resources include such things as the processor, memory, disk space, etc.
2. It provides a stable, consistent way for applications to deal with the hardware without having to know all the details of the hardware.

THE GENERATIONS OF COMPUTERS

The history of computer development reflects the generations of computer. These are as following:

First Generation - 1940-1956 : This generation is characterized by Vacuum Tubes. The computers were very big and sizing up to the entire rooms. They were very expensive to operate, generated a lot of heat and depending on machine language. Input was based on punched cards and paper tape, and output was displayed on printouts. Examples are: the UNIVAC and ENIAC.

Second Generation - 1956-1963 : This generation is characterized by transistors. The transistor was far superior to the vacuum tube. The use of transistor allowed the reduction in size of computers. The computers of second generation were faster, cheaper, more energy-efficient and more reliable than their first-generation predecessors. There was no change in input and printouts for output. Second-generation computers moved to symbolic, or assembly languages. The memory moved from magnetic drum to magnetic core technology.

Third Generation - 1964-1971 : The computers of this generation are characterized with the use of Integrated Circuits. Transistors were miniaturized and placed on silicon chips, called semiconductors. This development increased the speed and efficiency of computers. The third generation computers interacted through keyboards and monitors. These computers had an operating system.

Fourth Generation-1971-Present : The Micro-processors are the features of this generation computers. The microprocessor is the thousands of integrated circuits, built onto a single silicon chip. The size reduced at a desirable level and the speed reached to ultimate.

Fifth Generation - Present and Beyond : The Artificial Intelligence has been the feature of this generation computers. The computing devices of this generation are still in development. The goal of fifth-generation computing is to develop devices that respond to natural language input and are capable of learning and self-organization.

TYPES OF COMPUTERS

A. According to Computer sizes and power

Computers can be generally classified by size and power as follows, though there is considerable overlap:

Personal computer : A small, single-user computer based on a microprocessor.

Workstation : A powerful, single-user computer. A workstation is like a personal computer, but it has a more powerful microprocessor and, in general, a higher-quality monitor.

Minicomputer : A multi-user computer capable of supporting up to hundreds of users simultaneously.

Mainframe : A powerful multi-user computer capable of supporting many hundreds or thousands of users simultaneously.

Supercomputer : An extremely fast computer that can perform hundreds of millions of instructions per second.

B. By way of working

i. Analog Computers : The analog systems carry out arithmetic and logical operations by manipulating and processing data which we input such as the weight, temperature, voltage, power density, etc. The Analog System utilizes continuous variables for the purpose of mathematical computation such as mechanical, hydraulic, or electrical energy or operation. The analog computer does not change input data to any such sign language. The analog computer has become obsolete type of computer these days. It is different from a digital computer as it can perform numerous mathematical operations simultaneously.

ii. Digital Computers : The digital systems work on the principle of binary mathematics. In binary mathematics all calculations are represented through "0" and "1". Digital computers function with the help of logic circuits. A digital computer with the help of binary system cannot only perform mathematical problems but also combine the bytes to produce desired graphics, sounds, images and other such commands.

iii. Hybrid computers : These types of computers are, as the name suggests, a combination of both Analog and Digital computers. In the hybrid types of computers the Digital counterparts convert the analog signals to perform Robotics and Process control.

COMPUTER PROGRAM

Computer program is a file or collection of files that instruct a computer what to do. A computer program at the most basic level is a list of events. A computer program is one type of software, other types of software include configuration files that store user preferences, linked or shared libraries, and user files which contain data. In computing, a program is a specific set of ordered operations for a computer to perform. In the modern computer the program contains a one-at-a-time sequence of instructions that the computer follows. Programs can be characterized as interactive or batch in terms of what drives them and how continuously they run. A Web browser is an example of an interactive program. Print jobs are batch programs. When one creates a program, he writes it using some kind of computer language. The language statements are the *source program*. Someone then "compile" the source program (with a special program called a language compiler) and the result is called an *object program* (not to be confused with object-oriented programming). The object program contains the string of 0s and 1s called *machine language* that the logic processor works with. The machine language of the computer is constructed by the language compiler with an understanding of the computer's logic architecture, including the set of possible computer instructions and the length (number of bits) in an instruction.

Computer programs are either written in machine language, which is directly readable by the computer's CPU yet difficult for humans to understand, or in a high-level programming language which is similar to human languages, but must be converted to machine language in order to run. The task of converting the high-level languages to machine language is usually done by a compiler (another program), which is written in an intermediate-level language that was considered a high-level language at the time it was written. Thus as new, more powerful programming languages are developed they can be used to develop newer, yet more powerful languages.

Programming Language

A programming language is an artificial language. The programming languages are used to control the computer. Programming languages are governed by syntactic and semantic rules, to determine structure and meaning respectively. The programming languages are determined by objectives:

- Function
- Target
- Constructs
- Expressive power

First-generation programming language

i. Machine-level programming language is a first-generation programming language is a. It consists of 1s and 0s.
ii. 1GL or first-generation language was (and still is) *machine language.*
iii. Early 1950 brought us machine language without interpreters and compilers to translate languages.

Second-generation programming language

2GL or second-generation language is assembler (sometimes called "assembly") language. A typical 2GL instruction looks like this:

ADD 12, 8

Then an assembler converts the assembler language statements into machine language. Few features are as following:

i. A second-generation programming language is a term usually used to refer to some form of assembly language.
ii. The language is specific and dependent on a particular processor family and environment.
iii. It requires more programming effort and is difficult to use effectively for large applications.
iv. Assembly or machine code could not run on different machines.

Third-Generation Programming Language

Throughout the early 1960's till 1980 saw the emergence of the third generation programming languages. Languages like ALGOL 58, 60 and 68, COBOL, FORTRAN IV, ADA and C are examples of this generation and considered as high level languages. 3GL or third-generation language is a "high-level" programming language, such as PL/I, C, or Java. These languages have following features:

i. A compiler converts the statements of a specific high-level programming language into machine language.
ii. A 3GL language requires a considerable amount of programming knowledge.
iii. Most of the languages had compilers.
iv. Speed and independence were other advantages.

v. The improved portability and simplified debugging, modifications and maintenance were also found.

Fourth-Generation Programming Language

4GL or fourth-generation language is designed to be closer to natural language than a 3GL language. Languages for accessing databases are often described as 4GLs. Features are as following:

i. These language were user friendly, portable and independent of operating systems.
ii. These languages were meant to be usable by non-programmers, having intelligent default options about what the user wants and allowing the user to obtain results fasts using minimum requirement code generated with bug-free code from high-level expressions

Fifth-Generation Programming Language

The 1990's saw the developments of fifth generation languages like PROLOG, referring to systems used in the field of artificial intelligence, fuzzy logic and neural networks. 5GL or fifth-generation language uses a visual or graphical development interface to create source language that is usually compiled with a 3GL or 4GL language compiler. Few features are as following:

i. Microsoft, Borland, IBM, and other companies make 5GL visual programming products for developing applications in Java.
ii. Visual programming allows someone to easily envision object-oriented programming class hierarchies and drag icons to assemble program components.
iii. Without much learning any programming knowledge, and computer aided design with graphics provide an easy to use product that can generate new applications.

ROLE OF COMPUTERS IN LIBRARY

The computers and related technologies make library's life easier, not harder. The role of computers can be explained as:

- Computers and software gives the tools to actually boost library staff's services towards student achievement in a tangible way.
- It saves the time of library staff thus enabling them for other functions and services. It relieves the support load of the staff.
- Improving the services and functions provided by the library.
- Using the computers and technologies for management of library.
- Collecting and organizing basic statistical data in addition to ease of use and stability, library computer and software's technical support team is available any time whenever needed them.
- Library automation software allows to efficiently managing varied library education and management responsibilities.

Library Automation

Library automation is the use and application of computer and networking technologies in the library. The aim of library automation is to provide the right information, to right person, in right manner, in right time with the help of computer and library automation software along with trained staff. While justifying need of library automation more than cost-effectiveness the benefits derived by the library users become the major consideration. There are various areas of library automation such as:

1. House-keeping operations : The housekeeping operations covers acquisition, circulation and serial control, cataloguing. The library automation software has modules for different sections of library.

2. Automated cataloguing system : The automated library cataloguing system is the outcome of creation of bibliographical information in standard format. The automated cataloguing system is helpful in library activities and services such as acquisition, reference, bibliographic service, inter-library loan, cooperating cataloguing etc.

3. To explore human resource : Library automation means eliminating the repetitive work and cumbersome jobs. The library automation supports the housekeeping operation and making the routine and repetitive processes simple. Library automation increases the efficiency and productivity of library staff.

4. Maintaining Library Records : Due to various features present in library automation software, it is easy and very fruitful in maintaining library records, creating reports and sharing of data. It makes the consistency of the record in a standard manner. The areas are such as copy cataloguing, sharing of bibliographical records, making union catalogue, use of other external databases.

5. To Provide Uplift to Library Services : The library keeps itself going with the technologies and providing efficient services to users. The recent changes in library environment and user attitudes have augmented the library automation scenario in the country.

An automated library system usually consists of a number of functional modules, such as acquisitions, circulation, cataloguing, series and an OPAC (Online Public Access Catalogue). An "integrated" library system is an automated system. The most important aspect of library automation software is that the functional modules share a common bibliographic database. Due to technological provisions, the changes to bibliographic records are automatically propagated.

Implementation of Library Automation System: There are several different ways of implementation of an automated library system such as:

- Purchase a complete library automation software, including a number of functional modules, from a single vendor; purchase a variety of modules from a variety of vendors and interconnect them; or

- Open source library automation software are also becoming popular due to very less cost/finances involved. But some expertise is required to implement the system.

Selection of Library Automation Software

There are various library automation software such as KOHA or SOUL. The library can decide the library software that is best suited. The consideration may be as of both the hardware and software. The following criteria may be helpful to select the right software for library housekeeping operations:

- The developers of the software
- Revision of the software
- Number of modules and parameters
- The flexibility and customization of software.
- Ability to improve bibliographic data available in ISO2709 format
- Import and export of data in standard formats
- Training and guidance after installation.
- Availability on major operating systems
- Web interface and OPAC

Barriers in Library Automation

There are many barriers of implementation of Library automation as following

1. Budget constraints
2. The expensive nature of technology
3. Always pressure with competing and changing technology
4. The training and keeping up to date of staff
5. Lack of support from the institutional management
6. Large amount of retrospective conversion of data

LIRBARY NETWORKS

A library network is broadly described as a group of libraries coming together with some agreement of understanding to help each other with a view to satisfying the information needs of their clientele. UNISIST II working document defines Information Network as:

A set of inter-related information systems associated with communication facilities, which are cooperating through more or less formal agreements in order to implement information handling operations to offer better services to the users.

The National Commission on Libraries & Information Science in its National Programme Document (1975) defines a network as:

Two or more libraries engaged in a common pattern of information exchange, through communications for some functional purpose.

Objectives

- To promote and support adoption of standards in library operations.
- To create databases for projects, specialists and institutions to provide online information services
- To improve the efficiency of housekeeping operations
- To coordinate with other regional, national & international network for exchange of information and documents
- To generate new services and to improve the efficiency of existing ones

The objectives of library networks are in the context of following functions:

- Digitization and Preservation
- Professional Training
- Library Tools

21
Concept of Computer Hardware

INTRODUCTION

What we see and touch in a computer system physically, is known as computer hardware. So we can say that Computer hardware is the collection of physical elements that constitutes a computer system. In other words, computer hardware refers to the physical parts or components of a computer. The various physical components we can touch or see in a computer are monitor, mouse, and keyboard. The various kinds of cards and chips such as graphic cards, sound cards, memory, motherboard and chips are also hardware part of computer system. These parts are also known as system unit. What we find that the hardware component is comprised of those parts of computer which are physical objects that can be touched. Hardware provides a base for the computer system on which the software component runs and make computer workable. Various parts and objects which form computer hardware, are described in this chapter.

SERVER

A server is a computer that provides data to other computers. Basically, a server is a device with a particular set of programs or protocols that provide various services, which other machines or clients request, to perform certain tasks. It serves data to systems on a local area network (LAN) or a wide area network (WAN) over the Internet. A server is a system (software and suitable computer hardware) that responds to requests across a computer network to provide, or help to provide, a network service. Together, a server and its clients form a client/server network, which provides routing systems and centralized access to information, resources, stored data, etc. Servers operate within client-server architecture. Servers are computer programs running to serve the requests of other programs, the clients. Thus, the server performs some tasks on behalf of clients. The clients typically connect to the server through the network but may run on the same computer. Server helps in sharing files and resources like fax machines and printers.

The advanced server versions, like Windows Small Business Server 2003 R2 enable the user to handle the accounts and passwords, allow or limit the access to shared resources, automatically support the data and access the business information remotely. For example:

File server : file server is a machine that maintains files and allows clients or users to upload and download files from it. A file server might use Samba or the operating system's built-in file sharing services to share files over a network. A file server needs fast hard drives or SSDs that read and write data quickly.

Web server : Web server hosts websites and allows users to access these websites. Clients mainly include computers, printers, faxes or other devices that can be connected to the server.

Types of Servers

Each type of server runs on software specific to the purpose of the server. The multiple types of servers or types of network servers are as follows:

Server Platform : Server platform is the fundamental hardware or software for a system which acts as an engine that drives the server. It is often used synonymously with an operating system.

Application Server : Also known as a type of middleware, it occupies a substantial amount of computing region between database servers and the end user, and is commonly used to connect the two.

Audio/Video Server : It provides multimedia capabilities to websites by helping the user to broadcast streaming multimedia content.

Chat Server : It serves the users to exchange data in an environment similar to Internet newsgroup which provides real-time discussion capabilities.

Fax Server : It is one of the best options for organizations that seek minimum incoming and outgoing telephone resources, but require faxing actual documents.

FTP Server : It works on one of the oldest of the Internet services, the file transfer protocol. It provides a secure file transfer between computers while ensuring file security and transfer control.

Groupware Server : It is software designed that enables the users to work together, irrespective of the location, through the Internet or a corporate intranet and to function together in a virtual atmosphere.

IRC Server : It is an ideal option for those looking for real-time discussion capabilities. Internet Relay Chat comprises different network servers that enable the users to connect to each other through an IRC network.

List Server : It provides a better way of managing mailing lists. The server can be either open interactive discussion for the people or a one-way list that provides announcements, newsletters or advertising.

Mail Server : It transfers and stores mails over corporate networks through LANs, WANs and across the Internet. A mail server may run a program like Exim or iMail, which provides SMTP services for sending and receiving email.

News Server : It serves as a distribution and delivery source for many public news groups, approachable over the USENET news network.

Proxy Server : It acts as a mediator between a client program and an external server to filter requests, improve performance and share connections.

Telnet Server : It enables the users to log on to a host computer and execute tasks as if they are working on a remote computer.

Virtual Servers : A virtual server is just like a physical computer because it is committed to an individual customer's demands, can be individually booted and maintains privacy of a separate computer. Basically, the distance among shared and dedicated (hosting) servers is reduced providing freedom to other customers, at a less cost. Now, it has become omnipresent in the data center.

Web Server : A Web server may run Apache HTTP Server or Microsoft IIS, which both provide access to websites over the Internet. It provides static content to a web browser by loading a file from a disk and transferring it across the network to the user's web browser. This exchange is intermediated by the browser and the server, communicating using HTTP.

Servers often provide essential services across a network, either to private users inside a large organization or to public users via the Internet. There are few other types of servers, include Open source servers, Gopher server (like a plain document, similar to WWW and the hypertext being absent) and Name server (applies name-service protocol).

Server Dependency

It is significant to note that server software is specific to the type of server, it is important that the hardware should be sufficient to support the demands of the server. Practically, a regular desktop computer can be turned into a server by adding the appropriate software. Servers can be run on a dedicated computer, which is also often referred to as "the server", but many networked computers are capable of hosting servers. Web server runs lots of web scripts in real-time needs to have a fast processor and enough RAM to handle the "load" without slowing down.

Most large businesses use rack-mountable hardware designed specifically for server functionality. Multiple rack-mountable servers can be placed in a single rack and often share the same monitor and input devices. Most servers are accessed remotely using remote access software, so input devices are often not even necessary.

Web server

The web server supports the running and availability of web sites being always connected to the internet. Every Web server that is connected to the Internet is given a unique address made up of a series of four numbers between 0 and 255 separated by periods, for example, 68.178.157.132 or 68.122.35.127.

There are various web servers but among them the popular servers are Apache, IIS, lighttpd and Jagsaw, Netscape's iPlanet, Bea's Web Logic and IBM's Websphere.

Few examples are:

- Internet Information Services
- Sun Java System Web Server

DESKTOP COMPUTER

In the early age of computers, desktop computers were the only personal computers available. A desktop computer is a computer that is designed to stay in a single location. It is found in structure such as tower (also known as a system unit) or an all-in-one machine (such as an iMac). Desktop computers are not powered from an internal battery and therefore must remain connected to a wall outlet.

Advantages of Desktop PC

- A desktop computer has bigger and lot of memory space depending on specifications.
- It is easy to upgrade from current to advanced version.
- A desktop computer is cheaper than a laptop computer of similar specification.
- A desktop computer is easier to upgrade. There's more space for new PCI cards and IDE disks to fit into.
- Faulty accessories and components on a desktop are easy to replace, sometimes without even opening the case!

Disadvantages of Desktop PC

- It has large footprint and needs keyboard, mouse and monitor separately.
- It is bigger and heavier when compared to laptop.
- It is not portable.

PRINTERS

Printer is a device that prints the output or results of a process or task in the form of text or illustrations on paper. Depending on the technologies, usage and requirements, there are many different types of printers. In terms of the technology utilized, printers fall into the following categories:

i. Dot- matrix : The Dot- matrix is an impact printer. It functions by striking pins against an ink ribbon to print closely spaced dots in the appropriate shape. The Dot- matrix printer can print to multi-page forms (that is, carbon copies). There are following aspects which make a dot-matrix printer different from one another:

- **Speed :** Most Dot-matrix printers offer different speeds. The speed depends on the quality of print desired. Given in characters per second (cps), the speed can vary from about 50 to over 500 cps.
- **Print quality :** The best dot-matrix printers (24 pins) can produce near letter-quality type. Determined by the number of pins (the mechanisms that print the dots), it can vary from 9, 18 or 24pins.
- **Ink :** For ink, the Dot Matrix Printer use ribbon.

Compared to laser and ink-jet printers, dot-matrix printers are notorious for making a lot of noise.

ii. Ink-jet : The ink-jet printer works by spraying ionized ink at a sheet of paper. An ink-jet printer provides a resolution of 600 dots per inch, although some newer models offer higher resolutions. Magnetized plates in the ink's path direct the ink onto the paper in the desired shapes. Ink-jet printers are capable of producing high quality print approaching that produced by laser printers.

The features of Ink-jet printers are as:

- **Speed :** Most ink-jet printers offer different speeds depending on the quality of print desired. The speed depends on Pages per Minute (PPM):
- **Print quality :** The print quality is determined by the DPI (Dot Per Inch). The higher the DPI, the better in terms of print quality.
- **Ink :** The Ink-Jet Printers use Ink Cartridges. The ink-jet printers require a special type of ink that is apt to smudge on inexpensive copier paper.

iii. Laser : Laser printer works with the laser beam technology. One of the chief characteristics of laser printers is their resolution that dots per inch (dpi) they lay down. Some laser printers achieve higher resolutions with special techniques known generally as resolution enhancement. There are the standard monochrome laser printer as well as color laser printers. The laser printers come with a certain amount of RAM memory that can be increased by adding memory boards in the printer's expansion slots. The laser printers are also relatively fast, although not as fast as some dot-matrix printers. Laser printers are controlled through page description languages (PDL's).

Other Types of Printers

- **Photo Printer :** It is a type of printer use for printing photographs.
- **Dye-Sublimation Printer :** This printer employs a printing process that uses heat to transfer dye to a medium such as a plastic card, printer paper or poster paper.

- **Thermal Printer :** This kind of printer produces a printed image by selectively heating coated thermo chromic paper, or thermal paper.
- **All-in-One Printer :** This is a popular type of printer available in different brands. This printer does scanning, fax and make copies.
- **Plotter :** This device is used to print large posters and documents.

SCANNERS

Scanning services are available in many libraries. The libraries have optical scanning equipment for the creation of machine-readable text, machine-readable primary source texts, software programs for textual analysis and critical editing, database research tools.

Type of Material Scanned in Libraries

- Text (Books)
- Documents (Handwritten, Ledgers, Receipts)
- Photographs (Prints)
- Photographs (Negatives and Slides)
- Large Format (Posters and Maps) Above 17 x 24 inches (A2)

i. Flatbed Scanners : The most popular type of desktop scanner is the ubiquitous flatbed scanner. It is called because of its flat, glass platen (or bed) which serves as both the scanning area and surface for laying objects down to be scanned. The Entry-level flatbed scanners have the following specifications: 8-1/2" x 11" scanning area, 300 to 400 spi scanning ability (often interpolated to 800, 1200, or 1600 "spi"), 8-bits per color channel, and low cost. They are often come bundled with powerful "value-added" software. The Adobe Photoshop software is most common.

ii. Transparency Scanners : The transparency scanners are the multi-format transparency scanners. These scanners allow scanning everything from 35mm slides all the way up to 4x5-in. transparencies. These scanners are not general and targeted to professionals.

MODEM

Modem is a device that modulates an analog signal to encode into the digital signals and also demodulates it to transmit the information. The types of modem are:

i. Internal Modem : Internal Modem is installed in the desktop or laptop computer to communicate over a network with other connected computers. These modems do not require a power supply or a chassis. Internal modems are more directly integrated into the computer system. The internal modems are not easy to be replaced. There are two types of internal modems:

a. **Dial-up modem :** Dial up works on the telephone cables and requires a network access phone number and log on credentials to make a connection

b. **WiFi® (wireless) modem :** WiFi modem comments to the network without filling any credentials such as phone number.

ii. External Modem : External modems are the simplest type of modem to install and have their own power supply and connected with a cable to a computer's serial port. An external modem's separate power supply does not drain any power from the computer. The examples of these modems are the DSL modems which are used in the broadband connections.

iii. PC Card Modem : These modems are the size of a credit card and fit into the PC Card slot on notebook and handheld computers. These modems are removed when the modem is not needed. The PC card modems have the features of external and internal modems. These devices do not require any wire or cable and plugged directly into an external slot in the portable computer.

Thus we can say that a modem is a device that converts one network protocol to another. Modems only allow one device to connect to the ISPs network.

How modem works?

Modem is abbreviation for Modulator – Demodulator : Modems are used for data transfer from one computer network to another computer network through telephone lines. The computer network works in digital mode, while analog technology is used for carrying massages across phone lines. Modulator converts information from digital mode to analog mode at the transmitting end and demodulator converts the same from analog to digital at receiving end. The process of converting analog signals of one computer network into digital signals of another computer network so they can be processed by a receiving computer is referred to as digitizing.

Types of Modems

1. Directional capacity: half duplex modem and full duplex modem.
2. Connection to the line: 2-wire modem and 4-wire modem.
3. Transmission mode: asynchronous modem and synchronous modem.

Half duplex : A half duplex modem permits transmission in one direction at a time. If a carrier is detected on the line by the modem, it gives an indication of the incoming carrier to the DTE through a control signal of its digital interface.

Full duplex : A full duplex modem allows simultaneous transmission in both directions. Therefore, there are two carriers on the line, one outgoing and the other incoming.

2-Wire and 4-wire Modems : The line interface of the modem can have a 2-wire or a 4-wire connection to transmission medium. In a 4-wire connection, one pair of wires is used for the outgoing carrier and the other pair is used for incoming carrier. Full duplex and half duplex modes of data transmission are possible on a 4- wire connection. As the physical transmission path for each direction is separate, the same carrier frequency can be used for both the directions. 2-wire modems use the same pair of wires for outgoing and incoming carriers. A leased 2-wire connection is usually cheaper than a 4-wire connection as only one pair of wires is extended to the subscriber's premises. The data connection established through telephone exchange is also a 2-wire connection. In 2-wire modems, half duplex mode of transmission that uses the same frequency for the incoming and outgoing carriers can be easily implemented. For full duplex mode of operation, it is necessary to have two transmission channels, one for transmit direction and the other for receive direction. This is achieved by frequency division multiplexing of two different carrier frequencies. These carriers are placed within the bandwidth of the speech channel.

Asynchronous Modem : Asynchronous modems can handle data bytes with start and stop bits. There is no separate timing signal or clock between the modem and the DTE. The internal timing pulses are synchronized repeatedly to the leading edge of the start pulse.

Synchronous Modem : Synchronous modems can handle a continuous stream of data bits but requires a clock signal. The data bits are always synchronized to the clock signal. There are separate clocks for the data bits being transmitted and received. For synchronous transmission of data bits, the DTE can use its internal clock and supply the same to the modem.

Thus every kind of modem acts as the electronic bridge between two worlds - the world of purely digital signals and the established analog world.

Wireless Modem

A wireless modem is a modem that bypasses the telephone system and connects directly to a wireless network, through which it can directly access the Internet connectivity provided by an Internet service provider (ISP). Wireless modems are prebuilt into:

- Smartphones, mobile phones
- personal data assistants (PDAs)

The wireless modem may be distributed in the form of USB, serial or wireless firewall modems. Other types of wireless modems range from the size of a cable modem to the size of a credit card or smaller.

The Difference between Wi-fi Modem and Wi-fi Router

"*Wi—fi*" meaning "wireless fidelity" basically means that the piece of equipment is compatible with the technology. Wide Area Networks (WAN), and the Internet without the physical connection of wires like UTP cables for instance. A wireless modem is a device that is able to connect to a wireless network as provided by an ISP. There are now wireless ready LAN cards and USB devices that receive and transmit radio waves and perhaps the most commonly known wireless devices are wi-fi modems and wi-fi routers. Wireless modem modulates an analog carrier signal to encode digital information, and also demodulates such a carrier signal to decode the transmitted information. Wi-fi routers are devices that perform the same functions of a normal router only wirelessly. They forward data packets along networks and they connect different networks and act as a gateway. According to their nature and function, Wi-fi routers can connect two LANS or WANs, LAN and WAN, or LAN and the internet. Routers are smart devices that determine the best path for forwarding the data packets. Some wi-fi modems are equipped with routing capabilities which can be wireless or wired or both.

Thus we can say that wi-fi modems essentially play the role of modulating and demodulating wireless signals but wi-fi routers connect the user to a wireless network, usually LAN, without any signal modulating and demodulating features. Wifi routers have the capability to determine the best path to take and direct data packets to the correct nodes but wi-fi modems can make signals readable only.

NETWORK SWITCH

A Network switch is a device that filters, forwards, or floods the frames based on the destination address of each frame. A switch is a Layer 2 device and it:

- Replaces a hub as the central point of connection for multiple hosts.
- Moves traffic base on MAC addresses. Each switch maintains a MAC address table in high-speed memory, called content addressable memory (CAM).
- Processes all types of traffic in the same way, regardless of how it is used.
- Creates a different collision domain per switch port, unlike a hub, which allows the sharing of bandwidth by all port, run in half-duplex and is prone to collisions of frames and retransmissions.
- Enables networked devices to talk to each other efficiently.

More technically, a switch is a device in network that filters and forwards packets between LAN segments. Switches operate at the data link layer (layer 2) and sometimes the network layer (layer 3) of the OSI Reference Model and therefore support any packet protocol. LANs that use switches to join segments are called switched LANs or, in the case of Ethernet networks, switched Ethernet LANs. Switches perform their routing functions at the layer 2 model of the OSI. Some switches process data at the Network Layer (layer 3), these types of switches are referred to as layer 3 switches or multilayer switches.

How switch facilitates the communication over a network?

Switches may be connected between WAN routers as places for analytic modules. Some switches provide in built firewall, network intrusion detection and performance analysis modules that can plug into switch ports. A switch serves as a controller. Through information sharing and resource allocation, switches save businesses the money and increase employee productivity.

Types of Switches

There are four main types of network switches. Each different kind of network switche is having its own strengths and weaknesses which also need to be considered given as following:

Unmanaged Switches : Unmanaged Switches manage data flow between a shared printer and multiple computers. These kinds of network switches are the cheapest one and commonly used in various small scale small offices and business houses in order to manage networks. The unmanaged switches need not to be configured. Unmanaged switches have less network capacity than managed switches.

Managed Switches : A managed network switch offers greater flexibility and capacity than an unmanaged switch. The managed switch is configurable; this network switch type have a user interface or software offering which offer its users to the ability to make changes in the settings of the switch.

Smart Types of Network Switches : The smart kinds of network switches are the middle product between unmanaged and managed switch. The user interface in these switches is web-based. Though these switches are set with the most popular default settings, yet these switches provide the facility of an automatic adjustment to the related setting.

Enterprise-Managed Types of Network Switches : The enterprise managed types of network switches have adjustable settings. These types of switches are used in big organizations. These switches are constantly monitored, due to the size and complexity of the network. These network switch types are generally managed by network specialists.

Other types of switches

Modular switches : The modular switches offer more flexibility in their configuration. These switches are classified modular due to inclusion of different sized chassis. These different sized chassis allow the installation of different numbers of modular line cards. The line cards, containing the ports, are fitted into the switch chassis. The number of modules supported depends on the size of chassis. The larger the chassis, the more modules it can support.

Stackable Switches : Cisco introduced StackWise technology in one of its switch product lines. Stack Wise allows interconnecting up to nine switches. Stackable switches are interconnected using a special back cable that provides high-bandwidth between the switches. Switches are connected in daisy chain fashion, thus operating as a single larger switch. Stackable switches use a special port for interconnections and do not use line ports for inter-switch connections. Stackable switches are significant in an environment of fault tolerance and critical bandwidth availability. Using cross-connected connections, the network can recover quickly if a single switch fails.

ROUTER

A router is a device that forwards data packets along networks. A router is connected to at least two networks, commonly two LANs or WANs or a LAN and its ISP's network., Routers are located at gateways. Routers use headers and forwarding tables to determine the best path for forwarding the packets, and they use protocols such as ICMP to communicate with each other and configure the best route between any two hosts. Routers enable computers to communicate and they can pass information between two networks—such as between the home network and the Internet. This capability to direct network traffic is what gives the router its name. Routers can be wired (using Ethernet cables) or wireless. If user just wants to connect the computers, hubs and switches work well; however, if user wants to give all of the computers access to the Internet using one modem, use a router or a modem with a built-in router. Routers also typically provide built-in security, such as a firewall. Routers are more expensive than hubs and switches. Routers are devices meant for routing packets to other networks until that packet ultimately reaches its destination. The packet contains data as well as the destination address. Routers are generally known as intermediate systems, which operates at the network layer of the OSI reference model, routers are devices used to connect two or more networks (IP networks) or a LAN to the Internet. The router is responsible for the delivery of packets across different networks. The destination of the IP packet might be a web server in another country or an e-mail server on the local area network. It is the responsibility of the router to deliver those packets in a timely manner.

Features

Routers are designed to join together multiple local area networks (LANs) with a wide area network (WAN). Routers receive incoming network packets, look inside each packet to identify the source and target network addresses, then forwarding these packets to the final destination. The features of a router are as following:

- A router acts as a dispatcher, choosing the best path for information to travel so it is received quickly.
- A router includes a 4 - 8 port Ethernet switch (or hub) and a Network Address Translator (NAT).
- They include a Dynamic Host Configuration Protocol (DHCP) server, Domain Name Service (DNS) proxy server.
- They include a hardware firewall to protect the LAN from malicious intrusion from the Internet.
- All routers have a WAN Port that connects to a DSL or cable modem for broadband Internet service.
- Some routers even have USB ports, and more commonly, wireless access points built into them.

- Ethernet switches and hubs can be connected to a router with multiple PC ports to expand a LAN.
- The connection between the router and switches/hubs may require either straight-thru or crossover (null-modem) cables.
- Few routers permit configuring TCP/UDP ports for games, chat services, and the like, on the LAN behind the firewall.

It is significant to note that Wi-Fi wireless networks also utilize routers. These networks do not have the concept of a wireless switch or hub. Technically, a wireless access point is provided and functioning as a wired switch. Due to technological advances, the routers, being added to satellites in space, will route IP traffic between satellites in space in much the same way that packets are moved on Earth. This technique will offer greater networking flexibility.

Advantages of a Router

Though, initially, the routers were designed to forward the packets, the router began to provide other services as well such as:

- Ensuring steady, reliance availability of network connectivity.
- Providing integrated services of data, video, and voice over wired and wireless networks.
- Helping in mitigating the impact of worms, viruses, and other attacks.
- The routers have the control on the network and they permit or deny the forwarding of packets.

Difference between Network Switch and Router

- Switches create a network. Routers connect networks.
- A network router is a more sophisticated network device compared to either a network switch or a network hub.
- Like hubs and switches, routers are typically small, box-like pieces of equipment that multiple computers can connect to.
- While routers, hubs and switches all share similar physical appearance, routers differ substantially in their inner workings.
- Switches (and hubs) are not capable of joining multiple networks or sharing an Internet connection. Routers are designed specifically to join the LAN to the WAN for the purpose of Internet connection sharing.

22

Automatic Identification Techniques and Applications in Libraries

AUTOMATIC IDENTIFICATION

During the last 4-5 decades, the automatic identification procedures (Auto ID) have become very popular. Many service industries, purchasing and distribution logistics, industry, manufacturing companies and material flow systems are using the automatic identification support. Automatic identification procedures exist to provide information about people, animals, goods and products. The omnipresent barcode labels triggered a revolution in identification systems some considerable time ago. Because of the procedures used for the transfer of power and data, the Bar Code system and RFID systems (Radio Frequency Identification) became popular. RFID systems can be used just about anywhere a unique identification system is needed. The RFID tag can carry information. RFID is similar to barcode technology in that it employs coded labels to communicate information about a specific item (e.g. a library book) to a central server. The present chapter discusses Barcode system and RFID system in libraries.

BARCODE TECHNOLOGY

Computers nourished and revolutionized the work culture of libraries. Due to computer technology, performance of library jobs is being done with efficiency. The ultimate satisfaction of their users is also achieved. In the inclusion of various technologies, Barcode technology has been implemented in the libraries.

Barcodes : The barcode is an identification tool and it provides an accurate and timely support of data transferring for sophisticated management systems. Basically, the barcodes are self contained machine-readable identification labels. These labels contain information encoded in a series of black bars and white spaces of varying widths. These back bars and white spaces represent digits and other punctuation symbols. These bars and spaces are readable only through a reader or a scanner.

Barcode Scanner : The function of a scanner is to scan a barcode symbol and provide an electrical output that corresponds to the bars and spaces of a barcode. A basic barcode scanner consists of a decoder and a scanner. Barcode scanner functions like a keyboard, it sends a signal to the computer. It reads the barcode and signal are sent to the processor in the similar manner.

Types of scanners : There are three basic types of barcode scanners:

i. **Fixed :** Fixed scanners are attached to their host computer or terminal and transmit one data item at a time as the data is scanned.

ii. **Portable batch :** Portable batch scanners are battery operated. These types of scanners store data into memory for later batch transfer to a host computer.

iii. **Portable RF :** Portable RF scanners are also battery operated. These scanners transmit data online in real time. The real-time two-way communication provides the instructions.

ROLE AND ADVANTAGES OF BAR CODE TECHNOLOGY IN LIBRARY OPERATIONS

Barcode technology plays a vital role in systematizing the tasks of the library such as:

i. Circulation System : The use of barcode technology has been found resulting in rapid and accurate circulation processes. The work of circulation in automated library involves series of operations and a large amount of data. Due to large amount of data entry, sometimes error occurs, the library staffs have to rectify the same. Thus use of barcode system avoids queues at circulation desk.

ii. Inventory Control and Easy Access : The information related to each and every item in the collection is stored. Libraries adopted this technology to retrieve and collect the data quickly and efficiently. For example, the retails stores and big industries use the barcode technology to take inventory control.

iii. Stock Verification : Use of barcode technology in the library helps in stock verification and data entry. The easy and accurate information access supports such functions in library.

The goals of barcode system in a library are the efficient and accurate functioning. Various other advantages are as following:

- Accuracy in circulation
- Time saver

- Easy process for stock verification
- Reduces operational cost
- Improve operational efficiency
- Establish quality standard
- It is mature and proven Technology
- Easy to use

BASIC REQUIREMENTS FOR BARCODE APPLICATION

To implement a barcode system in library, following hardware and software are required:

- Personal computers
- Barcode Scanner
- Printer/ Printing Software
- Database of Library Holdings/members
- Library Management Software

The implementation of Barcode system is a conglomeration of various equipment, computer hardware and software described as following:

Library Management Software : The library management software acts as an interface between the computer and printer/scanner, it covers all the operations of libraries of different sizes including web-enabled search facility. It must be able to comply with the conditions of international standards such as options for MARC implementation, client-server architecture, facility to run on various operating systems, multimedia support such as images, videos, music, etc. The user interface should be interactive, screen-oriented, and menu driven along with the facility to set user-defined security at function level. The indexing features might help in bibliographic searches even for large databases. The circulation module of the library management software supports front desk operations like check-outs and check-ins, renewals, students/membership records keeping, etc. It provides an option to generate and print barcoded ID cards (with an optional 'add-on' facility to attach members' photograph thereon). The system monitors overdue items and generates reminders for the same. Whole organization provides greater flexibility in operations. It also keeps a complete log of all circulation transactions for future reference.

Printer : For printing barcodes, high quality of printing is required. Defects in printing will lead to wrong reading or nil reading of data. In that context, laser printer is essential to achieve the required precision in the barcodes.

Barcode Labels : Labels are printed on a customized A4 sheet of self adhesive labels. These sheets have usually 65 labels per page format. For security purpose, lamination of bar-coded label is done with the help of cello tapes.

Barcodes : Usually one dimensional numeric barcodes are prepared.

Smart/Spine Labels : It is placed on the spine of the book about 1½ inch above from the bottom. These labels are also called smart labels as these have both the call number and accession numbers.

Hand-held Barcode Scanner : Hand-held barcode scanners are popular. They scan the barcodes of the ID cards and the books, e.g. Charged Coupled Device (CCD).

- **CCD :** The scanning through CCD is automatic, although the scanning range is seldom more than an inch or two. CCD scanners have no moving parts. CCD scanners use LEDs for illumination, which is quite safe for direct viewing. Further, CCD scanners have scan rates of 45 scans per second or faster. Usually a keyboard wedge is used as an interface between the CCD scanner and the computer.
- **Portable Barcode Scanner for Stock Verification :** Use of portable scanner for the stock verification, serves the dual purpose of scanning the barcodes and storing that data in its memory.

BARCODE FORMAT & SYMBILOGICS

The language used to represent or arrange the bars and spaces is called symbology. It defines the technical details of a particular type of barcode:

- The width of the bars
- Character set
- Method of encoding
- Checksum specifications

Some of the popular symbologies areas are as follows:

Universal Product Code : It is the common code extensively used in retail trade. Its standardization in a form that allows many organizations throughout the world to interpret the same data is its prominent advantages. It also uses the space efficiently to record the data. Its limitation is that it can only record certain length of numbers.

Interleaved 2 of 5 (I 2 of 5) : It is very compact. But it can only record numbers. The code represents the number of even length. It is possible to scan only a part of the barcode and obtain something that looks like a valid result.

Code 39 (Code 3 of 9) : It is alpha and numeric and can represent even some special characters such as ' $ ',' / ', ' . ', ' : ', ' + ', ' – ', ' % ' and can enclose ' space '. The code can be of any length. It can enclose all the capital letters of the alphabets but lower case letters can't be enclosed. The code 3 of 9 is always started / ended with an asterisk (*), known as start / stop character. Bars and spaces are used to encode an individual character. 5 bars and 4 spaces, three of which are wide, represent each character and six are narrow.

European Article Number (EAN) : The EAN is only numeric but Code

Bar is having facilities to enclose ' $ ', ' / ', '. ', ': ', '+ ', '– ', '% ' in addition to numerals. Code Bar is used by Geac in library circulation system. Code 48, which include alphabetic characters, are used by many American Libraries. There are two-dimensional barcodes also which can store large quantity of data in a small area. The European Article Number is a superset of the UPC and encodes digits. It is available in two variations: EAN 8 to encode 8 digits and EAN 13 to encode 13 digits.

CODE 128 : It is a continuous alphanumeric symbology of variable length encoding full 128 ASCII character set. Every symbol starts and stops with a unique start/stop character.

Coda bar : It is a discrete, self-checking numeric symbology including six other characters and four unique start/stop characters. Each character has three bars and four spaces. It encodes only numeric and few special characters and is most widely used coding symbology. Generally libraries use this symbology to encode books and borrowers card.

Code 49 : Code 49 is a first two-dimensional barcode symbology. It is a multi-row, continuous and variable length symbology encoding the full ASCII 128 character set. Each row is composed of 18 bars and 17 spaces. Each row contains a row number and the last row contains information regarding the row number in the symbol.

While observing the various languages as above, Code 3 of 9 is alpha numeric and it encodes characters bi – directionally. This means that whether an operator scans a barcode from left to right or right to left, the reader can interpret the symbol and transmit the data in proper sequence. These features of code 3 of 9 have been the dominant consideration in its adoption by libraries and information centers.

RADIO FREQUENCY IDENTIFICATION

Radio Frequency Identification (RFID) is part of a broad category of automatic identification (Auto-ID) technologies. Auto-ID technologies include RFID, barcodes, optical character readers and some biometric technologies, such as retinal scans. Auto-ID technologies enable machines to scan, capture and "recognize" identification for an object. R*adio Frequency Identification*, RFID is a *dedicated short range communication* (DSRC) technology. The term RFID is used to describe various technologies that use radio waves to automatically identify people or objects. With RFID, the electromagnetic or electrostatic coupling in the RF (radio frequency) portion of the electromagnetic spectrum is used to transmit signals. Radio-frequency identification (RFID) is the use of an object (typically referred to as an RFID tag) applied to or incorporated into a product, animal, or person for the purpose of identification and tracking using radio waves. An RFID system consists of an antenna and a transceiver, which read the radio frequency and transfers the information to a processing device (reader) and a transponder, or RF tag, which contains the RF circuitry and information to be transmitted. The antenna provides the means for the integrated circuit to transmit its information to the reader that converts the radio waves reflected back from the RFID tag into digital information that can then be passed on to computers that can analyze the data.

Usage of Radio Frequency Identification

Radio Frequency Identification (RFID, for short) is a technology used for tracking and identification of objects in many areas of commerce, shipping, manufacturing, and, beginning in the late 1990's, in the circulation, inventory and security processes of libraries. RFID technology is being implemented in a number of industries. Supply chain implementation is perhaps one of the most frequently mentioned applications of RFID tags and equipment.

Significance of RFID in various areas

There are a few groups defining standards and regulating the use of RFID, including: International Organization for Standardization (ISO), International Electrotechnical Commission (IEC), ASTM International, DASH7 Alliance, and EPCglobal. RFID has many applications; for example, it is used in enterprise supply chain management to improve the efficiency of inventory tracking and management. RFID technology continues to spread in various industries, consumers around the world stand to gain. There will be a better availability of products; stolen items will be easier to recover; and it will be much simpler to recall defective products.

1. High-speed inventory management : A unique advantage of RFID systems is the ability to scan items on the shelves without tipping them outward from the shelves or removing them. Using wireless technology, it is possible not only to update the inventory, but also to identify items which are out of proper order. This helps to identify items that have been misplaced in the stacks or shelves.

2. Automated materials handling : RFID technology enables automated materials handling. This includes conveyor and sorting systems that can move library materials and sort them by category into separate bins or onto separate carts. This significantly reduces the amount of staff time required to ready materials for re-shelving.

Disadvantages of RFID Systems

1. High cost : The major disadvantage of RFID technology is its cost. RFID tags cost more than barcodes tags.

2. Exit sensor problems : The performance of the exit sensors is more problematic. They must read tags at up to twice the distance of the other readers.

3. Perceived Invasion of Patron Privacy : The invasion of privacy often revolves around the idea that the RFID tags contain patron information or that the RFID tags might be read by a device other than devices authorized by the library. It is important to educate library staff and patrons about the RFID technology.

THE TYPICAL WORKING OF RFID SYSTEM

RFID tags consist of a microchip attached to a radio antenna mounted on a substrate. The antenna is typically attached to a microchip, although not all RFID tags use silicon chips. The chip can store data. Some chips store only a unique numeric identifier. Or chips may store data about an object (an asset, a product or a shipment) - for example, the date of manufacture, destination and product information, all of which may be written to a tag. Retrieving the data stored on an RFID tag requires a reading device called a reader or an interrogator. A typical reader is an electronic device that has one or more antennas that emit radio waves and receive signals back from the tag. The reader then passes the information in digital form to a computer system. RFID system is made up of two components:

- the *transponder*, which is located on the object to be identified,
- the detector or *reader* , which, depending upon design and the technology used, may be a read or write/read device.

A reader contains a high frequency module (transmitter and receiver), a control unit and a coupling element to the transponder.

The transponder, which represents the actual data carrying device of an RFID system, normally consists of a coupling element and an electronic microchip.

RFID FREQUENCIES

RFID tags and readers need to be tuned into the same frequency to enable communications, as in Radio communications. RFID systems can use a variety of frequencies to communicate, but because radio waves work and act differently at different frequencies, a frequency for a specific RFID system is often dependant on its application. High frequency RFID systems (850 MHz to 950 MHz and 2.4 GHz to 2.5 GHz) offer transmission ranges of more than 90 feet, although wavelengths in the 2.4 GHz range are absorbed by water, which includes the human body, and therefore has limitations. Types of RFID in the context of Frequency are:

i. HF, Long range applications : The high frequency, long-range RFID applications operate within one meter from the reader and typically involve a large number of tag transponders (100+), requiring reliable anti-collision mechanisms and full interoperability. The products comply with ISO 15693 standard.

ii. LF, Short-range Applications : The low frequency, short-range applications use transponders embedded in plastic cards or paper tickets developed through partners. Transaction security is ensured by an optional state-of-the-art anti-clone algorithm. The products comply with the ISO 14443-B standard, 13.56 MHz carrier frequency.

How RFID Functions?

RFID is defined as a method of identifying unique items using radio waves (http://www.rfidjournal.com). RFID technology allows the automatic collection of product, place, time and transaction data quickly and easily. An RFID system includes a reader, a transponder, and their associated antennas. A typical RFID system is made up of several system elements:

1. Tags
2. Provisioning Devices (Printing/Encoding Devices)
3. Interrogating Devices (Readers, Reader/Writers)
4. Antennas
5. RF Signal (Using specific frequencies and air interface protocols)
6. Backend Processing Systems

RFID Tags : Most RFID tags contain at least two parts. One is an integrated circuit for storing and processing information, modulating and demodulating a radio-frequency (RF) signal, and other specialized functions. The second is an antenna for receiving and transmitting the signal. Until recently, the high cost of RFID has limited its use. In general the RFID tags or RFID transponders are small low cost items. These are attached to items that need tracking or other forms of data collection to be performed. The RFID tags are the small plastic elements. Most RFID tags are used for RFID location and RFID tracking systems.

RFID Provisioning Devices : RFID provisioning devices set up the RFID tag with a unique serial number so that the tag can be used as a unique identifier. The provisioning device may be a RFID writing device or a printer that can write to a tag (known as a transponder). Tag provisioning (tag commissioning) device encodes information on the chip within the transponder to verify that the tag received the correct information.

RFID Interrogating Devices : RFID interrogating devices are called readers or may be reader/writers. A reader is an electronic device used to communicate with RFID tags. A reader has one or more antennas, which transmit radio waves and receive signals back from the tag. RFID readers may be either fixed (stationary) or mobile. An antenna "transmits" when it radiates an electromagnetic field in response to an applied alternating current. An antenna "receives" when it induces an alternating current in response to an ambient electromagnetic field. Antennas may be embedded as part of a RFID reader/interrogator or they may be physically separated from a reader.

RF Signal : RF signals are driven by two factors:

- Frequency
- Air Interface Protocol

RFID systems can use a variety of frequencies to communicate. High frequency RFID systems (850 MHz to 950 MHz and 2.4 GHz to 2.5 GHz) offer transmission ranges of more than 90 feet. The wavelengths in the 2.4 GHz range are absorbed by water, which includes the human body, and therefore has limitations. RFID operates in several frequency bands and the exact frequency is controlled by the Radio Regulatory body in each country. The generic frequencies for RFID are:

- 125 - 134 kHz
- 13.56 MHz
- UHF (400 – 960 MHz)
- 2.45 GHz
- 5.8 GHz

RFID Backend Processing Systems : RFID systems have interfaces and a layer of software (often called middleware) will sit between the RFID system and the organizational systems. Middleware is used to place RFID data in context of the organizational setting. It is used to identify the relevant event and require passing on to organizational applications.

APPLICATION IN LIBRARIES

The libraries are using RFID to speed up the self check in/out processes, to control the theft and to ease the inventory control in library. The RFID tag can be read even when it is embedded in an item, such as in the cardboard cover of a book or in the packaging of a product. It stores data such as stack number, accession number, book number, author information etc., but barcode is limited to just an identification number.

There is, however, a key difference to the library's inventory as compared to that of a warehouse or a retail outlet. In the warehouse and retail supply chain, goods occasionally are returned. The retail sector is looking at RFID as a "throwaway" technology that hands an item to a customer which gets discarded. In libraries, items are taken out and returned many times. Thus the same RFID tag is re-used many times. The application is described as following:

Various areas of applications of RFID in Libraries

Checkout : RFID technology's helps in reading ID tags regardless of position or orientation. It detects signals through physical materials. This feature is advantageous for library circulation processes. Several items are read at once so the checkout procedures is implementation of RFID in libraries generally leads:

- to greatly-reduced queues at the checkout counter,
- enhanced customer service, and
- less repetitive strain injuries for library staff.

Check-in : RFID is beneficial for check-in processes. This system is able to check in multiple items simultaneously. The RFID readers are affixed sometimes to the book return slots and this fixation allows effectively checking in items when they pass through the slot. An automated materials handling (AMH) system supports the sorting. A conveyor carries items past an RFID reader, which checks them in and then sorts them by category into bins or onto carts. RFID system saves time in this process.

Inventory : RFID helps in inventory processes in libraries. By passing the reader alongside the books on the shelves, inventory is taken with a portable, hand-held wand (reader). Without removing or even tipping the books outward from the shelves, the reader picks up the individual signals from each item's tag. For example, RFID has enabled the library at California State University, Long Beach to inventory 5,000 books per hour, and the Vatican Library in Rome estimates the ability to inventory 120,000 tagged items in its collection in half a day. The inventory with RFID has been helpful in locating lost or wrongly shelved items.

Security : The RFID based LMS facilitates the fast issuing, reissuing and returning of books with the help of RFID enabled modules. The monitoring module monitors the movement of books across the gates. The books taken out without prior issuing are traced out easily and alarm the librarians. Item security is the area in which RFID technology benefits a library. RFID tags can be enabled with a theft-detection bit that is deactivated upon proper checkout. As the items pass an RFID reader upon being checked back in, the security bits are reactivated.

DIFFERENCE BETWEEN BARCODE AND RFID SYSTEM

- Information can be read from RFID tags much faster than from barcodes.
- Several items in a stack/counter can be read at the same time using RFID.
- IRFID can stand more than 10,000 read/write.
- RFID can have theft bit which can be in two states "ON/OFF".
- More information can be written in the RFID tag on incremental basis.

The various differences are displayed in the following table:

	RFID	Barcode
Line of Site	Not required (in most cases)	Required
Read Range	Passive RFID: - Up to 40 feet (fixed readers) - Up to 20 feet (handheld readers) Active RFID: - Up to 100's of feet or more	Several inches up to several feet
Read Rate	10's, 100's or 1000's simultaneously	Only one at a time
Identification	Can uniquely identify each item/asset tagged	Can typically only identify the type of item (UPC Code) but not uniquely
Read/Write	Many RFID tags are Read/Write	Read only
Technology	RF (Radio Frequency)	Optical (Laser)
Interference	Like the TSA (Transportation	Obstructed barcodes cannot

	Security Administration), some RFID frequencies don't like Metal and Liquids. They can cause interfere with certain RF Frequencies.	be read (dirt covering barcode, torn barcode, etc.)
Automation	Most "fixed" readers don't require human involvement to collect data (automated)	Most barcode scanners require a human to operate (labor intensive)

Source: http://www.inlogic.com/rfid/rfid_overview.aspx

23

Library Automation Software

To automate the library, specialized software are required. The library automation software may be chosen on the basis of the type and needs of library. Library automation can be defined simply as the use of computer and networking technologies in the library. The various areas of library automation are:

- Automation of library functions
- Office automation (e.g. word-processing, spreadsheets, databases, etc.)
- Patron services (e.g. computer laboratory, multimedia center)

This chapter describes two major library automation software in India.

SOFTWARE FOR UNIVERSITY LIBRARIES - SOUL

Software for University Libraries (SOUL) is state-of-the-art integrated library management software. The software has been designed and developed by the INFLIBNET Centre. It is based on requirements of college and university libraries. This user-friendly software is developed to work under client-server environment. The software is suitable for all types and sizes of libraries. The first version of software (SOUL 1.0) was released during CALIBER 2000. The next version of the software (SOUL 2.0) was released in January 2009. The database for new version of SOUL is designed for latest versions of MS-SQL and MySQL (or any other popular RDBMS). SOUL 2.0 is compliant to international standards for bibliographic format, records and NCIP 2.0 and SIP 2 based protocols for electronic surveillance and control.

Major Functionalities and related technologies

- It has UNICODE based multilingual support for Indian and foreign languages.

- It has Client-server based architecture and user-friendly interface that does not require extensive training.
- It supports multi-platform for bibliographic database such as My SQL, MS-SQL or any other RDBMS.
- It supports cataloguing of electronic resources such as e-journals, e-books, virtually any type of material.
- It is compliant to International Standards such as MARC21, AACR-2, MARC XML.
- It is compliant to NCIP 2.0 protocol for RFID and other related applications especially for electronic surveillance and self check-out & check-in.
- It provides freedom to users for generating reports of their choice and format along with template and query parameters.
- It supports ground-level practical requirements of the libraries such as stock verification, book bank, vigorous maintenance functions, transaction level enhanced security, etc.
- It provides facility to send reports through e-mail, allows users to save the reports in various formats such as Word, PDF, Excel, MARCXML, etc.
- It has highly versatile and user-friendly OPAC with simple and advanced search. OPAC users can export their search results in to PDF, MS Excel, and MARCXML format.
- It supports authority files of personal name, corporate body, subject headings and series name.
- It supports data exchange through ISO-2709 standard.

FEATURES OF SOUL

User friendly software : It has windows based user friendly software. It has well-designed screens, logically arranged functions with extensive help messages make the software user friendly.

Client server architecture : It is based on client server architecture allowing scalability to the users.

RDBMS : It uses RDBMS to organize and query the data.

Large Academic Libraries : It is specially designed to work in the large academic libraries, capable of handling large number of records.

Multi-user and access : It is multi-user software and there is no limit on simultaneous accesses.

International standards : It supports internationally known standards such as CCF and AACR II. Etc. It provides export and import facility and adheres to ISO 2709 format.

Powerful OPAC : OPAC is versatile and very user-friendly with all options in-built, accessible over the web using any GUI based browsers.

Language Support : It provides facility to create, view and print records in regional languages.

MODULES

The functions in this software have been grouped into six categories, looking into the functional divisions of Indian University libraries. At present SOUL uses RDBMS on Windows N.T. operating system as back end to store and retrieve the data. However, keeping in view the trends in IT towards Linux operating system, efforts are under way also to provide SOUL to work on Linux platform. The SOUL has been divided into following six broad modules:

1. Acquisition Module

The acquisition module provides facilities to handle work relating to acquisition of reading materials of all types except serials. Acquisition module comprises following six broad sub-modules.

Suggestion : This sub-module enables creation / updation of databases of new items suggested by a faculty member along with bibliographical details.

Order Processing : This sub-module helps in selecting the items for ordering, vendor/publisher selection, assigning order and reference number, setting deadlines for supply.

Receiving / Accessioning : This function supports cross checking with order, receiving partial/ full supply of items listed in order, duplicate checking with an existing title, assigning accession numbers along with further necessary details required and merging the records with existing database, if items are already in the collections.

Payments : Payments sub-module allows processing of the regular invoices, advance payments, and recording of information pertaining to each invoice including conversion rates, handling charges discounts etc.

Master Databases : In this sub-module, publisher, vendor, Currency and budget codes (both source wise and department wise) are few major master databases that are frequently handled/created.

Reports : This sub-module supports in report generation.

2. Cataloguing Module

Catalogue module functions for some aspects as per AACR-II rules. The major aspects covered are user services such as recent addition services, CAS, creation and updation of authority files etc. It has the facility to create database in the regional languages, using respective scripts. It has following sub-modules:

- Catalogue Process
- Catalogue Search
- User Services
- Authority File Maintenance

- Retrospective Conversion
- Reports

3. Circulation Module

Circulation module has been designed to achieve transactions within minimum possible time. This module has provision for membership, issues, returns, ILL, reminders, over dues, reservations, recall etc. It has following sub-modules:

Membership : This sub-module provides the facility to create all types of member records, assigning unique membership code, borrowing privileges, renewal, issue of no-due certificates, master databases for codes etc.

Transactions : This handles all major functions such as issue, return, renewal, reservation, recall or reminder of an item etc. This module also handles cancellation of reserved books, lost/missing books, searching the member status and searching catalogue module etc. Transaction is based on Accession number and Member code.

Inter Library Loan : This sub-module allows lending of items to specified member library and also borrowing items from other libraries, issues, reminders etc.

Over due collection : This generates daily, weekly, monthly reports to find out as to how much overdue charges have been collected.

Reminder : This sub-module handles individual and group reminder generation for all overdue materials. Comprehensive listing of materials that are overdue can also be generated within a specific period giving from and to dates.

Search : The status enables the library circulation desk staff to check the status of a member or items borrowed by a user and overdue items.

Maintenance : This sub-module covers binding, lost and cost recovery of books, damaged books, withdrawn books etc.

Reports : This sub-module allows the generation all possible reports that a large library expects are provided for.

4. Serials Module

This module allows the smooth functioning of serial control. This facilitates creation of an exclusive database for different serials. This module has been designed to handle serials. It helps in keeping track of every title received in the library. It has following sub-modules:

- Suggestion
- Subscriptions
- Payment
- Master Databases
- Check-in
- Sending reminders

- Binding
- Status search
- Title history
- Export/Import
- Reports

5. Online Public Access Catalogue Module (OPAC)

SOUL has the facility of library's OPAC terminals by allowing the users to access the internal as well as external resources. This enables the users to access various databases developed at INFLIBNET. Some of the major features of OPAC are:

Boolean Search : SOUL includes Boolean operation when more than one search option is to be used. Search key fields, such as, author, title, keywords, class number, accession number, etc. are available.

Sorting and displaying : Search results can be sorted according to the preference of search item. User has option to select variety of display formats. Display of records is according to AACR-II format.

Status of book : Status of each book from acquisition module is reflected. User can see the status of currently borrowed items by entering his/her borrower number.

Access through web browsers : Accessible through the GUI based web browsers like Netscape Communicator, Internet Explorer etc. Search results can be saved and printed.

6. Administration Module

Administration module authorizes users i.e., the library staff to use various modules. Assigning login and password to use each module of the system is done by the system administrator. The security function, backups, recovery of data and other utility functions are some of the features added under this module.

STANDARDS SUPPORTED BY SOUL SOFTWARE

SOUL follows the internationally acceptable standards like AACR-2, CCF, MARC 21 and ISO 2709. Adoption of Standards in SOUL makes user's database globally acceptable and interchangeable.

Anglo American Cataloguing Rules-2 (AACR - 2) : The Anglo-American Cataloguing Rules 2 are designed for use in the construction of catalogues and other lists in general libraries of all sizes. It is popular due to the rules provided for the description of, and the provision of access points for, all library materials commonly collected at the present time. It has two parts; part I deals with the provision of information describing the item being catalogued, and part II deals with the determination and establishment of headings (access points).

Common Communication Format (CCF) : The Common Communication Format (CCF) was developed under the auspices of United

Nations Educational, Scientific and Cultural Organization (UNESCO). It has the goal to facilitate the exchange of bibliographic data between organizations. The first edition of the CCF in 1984, the second edition in 1988 and third edition was published in 1992. Later, it was developed as an ISO-2709 exchange format. It has adapted the AACR 2 as a standard for data entering.

ISO 2709 : The ISO 2709 computer format is the universal standard which is used in the library world for bibliographic records. ISO 2709 is a content-independent specification of fielded text for data exchange. It is widely used by libraries, archives and visual resource collections worldwide.

MARC 21(MAchine Readable Catalogue) : MARC 21 formats are standards for the representation and communication of bibliographic and related information in machine-readable form. The Library of Congress and the Library and Archives Canada serve as the maintenance agency for the MARC 21 formats for bibliographic, authority, holdings, classification, and community information data for the MARC 21 user community. The MARC Forum, an electronic discussion list, provides a platform for open discussion of proposed changes.

NISO Circulation Interchange Protocol : NCIP is NISO Circulation Interchange Protocol. It is also known as Z39.83. It is a North American standard with implementations in the US, Canada, and many other countries around the world. NCIP services facilitate activities such as: the automation of tasks, the exchange of data, the ability to provide information to library staff, and the empowerment of patrons. The original vision for NCIP identified three main application areas: Direct Consortial Borrowing (DCB), Circulation / Interlibrary Loan Interaction (C-ILL), and Self-Service Circulation.

E-GRANTHALAYA

e-Granthalaya is a library automation software designed by National Informatics Centre, Department of Electronics & Information Technology, Ministry of Communications and Information Technology, Government of India. The software can be implemented either in stand-alone or in client-server mode where database and WebOPAC are installed on the server PC while the data entry program is installed on client PCs. The software provides LOCAL/LAN/WAN based data entry solutions for a cluster of libraries where a centralized database can be created with Union Catalog output. The software provides Web OPAC interface to publish the library catalog over Internet/Intranet. The software runs on Windows paltform Only, UNICODE Compliant thus, supports data entry in local language.

e-Granthalaya was started as an in-house project at 'Karnataka State Centre of NIC,Bangalore'. The first version of the software was designed for the Public Libraries in the State. Later, NIC HQs 'Library and Informatics Services Division' took over the designing of the software. The software emerged with improved user interface. It had simplified the work-flow of library functions. The composition and functioning is suitable for all kinds of libraries.

Versions : Following table shows the release of various versions of the software:

Technology/Platform used	Version	Year	DBMS
Visual Basic 6/ASP/HTML	1.0	2003	MS SQL Server 7
Visual Basic 6/ASP/HTML	2.0	2005	MS SQL Server 2000
VB.NET/ASP.NET 2.0	3.0	2007	MS SQL Server 2005
ASP.NET 4.0/AJAX/Silver Light (Hosted in NIC Server in Cloud Computing Environment) (*Under Development)	4.0	2014	MS SQL Server 2008R2/ PostGresql

Features of e-Granthalaya

e-Granthalaya has a number of features and facilities for library automation such as:

- It runs on Windows Platform Only (Win XP/vista/7/8/Server 2003/ 2008).
- It provides Local/LAN/WAN based Data Entry Solution.
- It is UNICODE Compliant, supports data entry in local language.
- It arranges Module - Wise Permission to the software Users.
- It facilitates Retro-Conversion as well as Full Cataloging Modes of Data Entry.
- It permits Authority Files/ Master tables for Authors, Publishers, Subjects, etc.
- It has Z39.50 Client Search Built-in.
- It allows merger databases of eG3 into Single Database.
- It facilitates Common/Centralized Database for N Number of libraries, minimize data entry.
- It is useful for Main/Branch Libraries Acquisition/Cataloging.
- It allows printing of Accession Register.
- The Search Module is built-in with basic/advance/boolean parameters.
- It is useful for Library Statistics Reports.
- It supports CAS/SDI Services and Documentation Bulletin.
- It classifies and generates Compact/Summary/Detailed Reports Option.
- It generates Bibliography in AACR2.
- It facilitates Digital Library integration with uploading / downloading of pdf/html, etc documents.

- It permits Micro-Documents Manger (Articles/Chapter Indexing).
- It has SERIALS Control System for Subscription with Auto-Generate Schedule.
- It permits Budget Modules with Bill Register Generation, manages Multi-Budget Head.
- It facilitates importing of Data from any structured Source (MARC21/EXCEL).
- Well exhaustive Web Based OPAC Interface with separate Membership module.
- It facilitates Multi-copies of Accession No. can be accessioned in bulk with single click with Auto-Accession Number.

System Requirements

For Stand-Alone Mode (All the Components to be installed on a Single PC):

Hardware: P IV or above with backup device, Min 1 GB RAM, 40GB HDD

OS: Windows XP (SP2)/Vista/win 7/8

DBMS: MS SQL Server 2005/2008/R2/2012 (Express Ed) - FREE

Connectivity: LAN/Internet Connectivity

For Client-Server Mode, system requirements are as following :

- Server PC
- *Hardware* : A Server Pc with Min 4GB RAM, 80GB HDD
- *OS* : Windows Client OS (Win 7/8) or Windows Server 2008/R2/2012 (Standard/Enterprise Edition)
- *RDBMS* : MS SQL Server 2005/2008/R2/2012 (Express Edition/Standard Edition)
- *Connectivity* : LAN/Internet Connectivity
- BarCode Printer (Any Model/Make) with Barcode Reader

Distribution and Availability

The software is provided at zero cost to the Ministries/Departments of Central Government and State Government and Centre of Excellence under Direct Control of Government. The support, training, Data Entry, Maintenance, Migration, etc. are provided on Payment basis by the *NICSI* Emapnelment Agency. Government Libraries Hosting may also be done in NIC Server as per NIC hosting policy. The e-Granthalaya software can be get from any District/State Centres of NIC or from NIC Hqs, New Delhi.

e-Granthalaya (ver. 3.0)

The e-Granthalaya is popular library software among academic libraries. This software has been developed by NIC, India. The third version of e-Granthalaya (ver. 3.0) has been released recently. This version is popularly called as eG3. This version is based on the recent technologies from Microsoft. Due to the requirements in the libraries and received feed back form the users and experts, more features have been added. Following are the main features of the latest version of the software:

Multi-lingual Version : The "eG3" is a multi-lingual version. It supports data entry in all the 10 Indian Scripts/languages. Technically it is supported by the Windows XP / Windows 2000/2003 Server and Vista platform from Microsoft. The back end database is supported by MS SQL Server 2005. It supports the data in UNICODE while the labels can be displayed in the user's own language/script. The following table displays the list of the script/languages supported by the software.

Script	Font	Remarks	Languages
Devanagari	Mangal	UNICODE/Open Type Font	Sanskrit, Hindi, Marathi, Knkani, Nepali
Tamil	Latha	UNICODE/Open Type Font	Tamil
Telugu	Gautami	UNICODE/Open Type Font	Telugu
Gujarati	Shruti	UNICODE/Open Type Font	Gujarati
Gurumukhi (Punjabi)	Raavi	UNICODE/Open Type Font	Punjabi
Malayalam	Kartika	UNICODE/Open Type Font	Malayalam
Bengali	Vrinda	UNICODE/Open Type Font	Bengali, Assamese, Manipuri
Oriya		UNICODE/Open Type Font	Oriya
Kannada	Tunga	UNICODE/Open Type Font	Kannada

State-of-the-art platform : The design of "eG3" is supported by the Microsoft technologies. The VB.NET and ASP.NET (Ver.2.0) are the key design environment. These platforms have been chosen as they support the UNICODE data storage, retrieval and display. Visual Studio 2005 of the Microsoft Office Productivity Tools provides the base to design a multi-lingual design.

DBMS and Server Platform : The "eG3" has been using the DBMS from the Microsoft. It uses "Microsoft SQL Server 2005". This RDBMS supports UNICODE data. This is very user-friendly and provides a strong support for library applications. When the e-Granthalaya is implemented in Stand-ALone mode, MS SQL Server (Express Edition) is needed. The client/server mode implementation with Intranet publishing of the library catalog, the 'Standard Edition' of the MS SQL Server 2005 is sufficient.

Installation and Updation : The eG3 deployment is based on Microsoft technology called as 'ClickOnce'. The e-Granthalaya software is kept in NIC server and it can be deployed/ installed automatically on the target/client PC. It is not cumbersome to update the software. Updation is also downloaded automatically when the application runs on the Client PC every time.

Architecture : The software has the 3-tier layers structure:

i. the BLL and

ii. the DLL layer

iii. the Presentation layer

The BLL and the DLL layers are hosted on the NIC server. These layers are responsible for the database. The third layer "Presentation layer" is installed on the client PCs. This architecture and design suite the requirements of the NIC Network/infrastructure, there databases for group of libraries are hosted in NIC server. There are the server components as well such as web services; Reports Services and Web OPAC interface are present. The client's components such as data entry software are installed automatically on the target/client PCs. The web services based aspect supports LAN/WAN based connectivity. Architecture of eG3 supports the creation of a common database for a cluster of libraries. It facilitates the Union Catalogue services for a specific group of libraries.

Appendices

1. UNDERSTANDING DEWEY DECIMAL CLASSIFICATION PRACTICAL

Various Indian universities are using the 19th edition of Dewey Decimal Classification (DDC). The present chapter explains the rules of classifying titles/documents according to 19th edition. These rules contribute to uniformity in the Interpretation of entries and consequently achieve much desired consistency in application of the DDC in libraries in various countries. The 19th edition of DDC is divided into following 3 volumes:

Volume 1: Introduction, Tables

Volume 2: Schedules

Volume 3: Relative Index

Main classes and mapping of Universe : In Dewey Decimal classification, whole universe of knowledge is divided into 10 main classes which are numbered 0,1,2,3,4,5,6,7,8,9. Here 9 are main classes and 0 is used to represent General works not belonging to a single particular subject. Each of the main classes 1-9 consists of a major discipline or group of related discipline. Each main class is again divided into 10 divisions to occupy the second place in the notation. this division process moves further again and again. These divisions are further divided into subdivisions.

Some Rules

1. The first significant rule is that DDC uses decimal fractions.
2. The class number does not consist of less than 3 digits. For example 6 will be written as 600 and 74 as 740.
3. When a class number extends beyond the 3 digits, a dot is put after 3 digits. For example 325.3; 362.14; 386.242. The dot used in these class numbers after 3 digits is not a decimal point as it is usually considered. It is used only to ease the transcription and remembering.
4. If a class number extends beyond 6 digits, then after 3 digits a space is left. In other words after 6 digits, the remaining digits are transcribed in groups of three, leaving a space between each group.

5. The ascertaining of the specific subject of a document is followed by finding out appropriate class number for that specific subject from the Schedules and Tables of DDC. The Relative Index helps us in this respect.
6. DDC is primarily an enumerative scheme of classification, so most of the subjects in DDC have readymade class numbers.
7. Various number building Devices and Add Instructions have been supporting to build class numbers for compound and complex subjects. Therefore we should be familiar with these number building devices.
8. Any class number in the schedules may be further extended by any number taken from Table-1 of the Standard Subdivisions. For this there is no need for instructions. Whenever a subject warrants, this can be done by the classifiers on their own.
9. The other kinds of number-building is done as per instructions given under the entry in the Schedules When a number is to be farther extended by any other number either from the schedules or any of the auxiliary Tables 2-7, then there are specific instructions.

VARIOUS NOTES

In tables as will as in schedule of DDC (Ed. 19), a large number of various types of Notes have been used. These notes help us to understand and interpret the definitions scope and limitations of a subject covered by an entry. The notes given in schedules of DDC at different place s help to correctly classify a document. The notes help also to understand the position, boundaries and scope of these subjects.

1. Add to... of a Full Number : It is a simple device in which we add a full number anywhere from the schedules to any other full class number designated as a base number. Usually this note is given in the following form: Add 001 -999 to base number..........

2. Addition of a Segment : In this kind of number-building, only a segment of another number is added to a designated base number, but not the Main number. Sometimes a segment is added to a base number not from a distant place in the schedules but from the same division or section or from the same subsection in which the base number exists.

3. Addition from the Same Division/Section with a Facet Indicator : Sometimes a segment number from the same division/section is added to a designated base with the help of a facet indicator digit which is usually 0 or 04. These additional digits are added to avoid cross classification i.e. a class number may not mean two different subjects.

4. Class Here Notes : Some topics apparently do not seem a part of a given subject. These are broader or narrower than a topic to which they are attached with the note Class here. They are not very logical, yet it provides a class number to an otherwise un-accommodated topic.

5. Class Elsewhere Notes : Sometimes a subject, seemingly a part of another subject or related to that, is accorded an independent number, then there appears a note in various forms. Such a note sometimes refers to a more appropriate class number to the scattered topics of a subject. Such a not is analogous to a See cross reference in an alphabetical list of subject headings.

6. Class ...in Notes : The following types of notes are also written on some places in the schedule.

7. For...See... Notes : This is another kind of note which cross-references to a related number. In such a case it takes the form of **For...See....**

8. Class Comprehensive Works in... Notes : This types of note is appended to a centered entry, which is covered by a continuous span of numbers. To assign a single class number to a work covering all the topics, a not gives one number for such a work.

9. Note appearing under Discontinued (Bracketed) Entries : When a number is discontinued in the present edition then there appears a note indicating its new class, numbers this types of notes are of following types:

a. **Class Number not be used:** The notation of required headings are indicated in square brackets [ ] and instructions are **Not to use class in...**, then it means that do not use this class number and class in............

b. **Number discontinued:** When the class number was given in square brackets and it is also directed that this class number discontinued. It simply means that the new number for this topic is other.

c. **Unassigned Class Number:** At some places, some class numbers are indicated in square brackets and by indicating the term written in front of the class number is square bracket has been directed to unused class number.

10. Formerly Notes : In some places, in front of the headings or under them. Formerly notes are given in square brackets.

11. Collective Add Notes : Sometimes Add to device is given at one place in the schedules, when a continuous span of number is susceptible to addition of facets from another continuous span of numbers. It emphasized that such numbers are continuous and occur on a single page of the schedule. All such numbers are marked with an asterisk, and asterisk is explained on the same page in the foot note.

12. Scope Notes : Sometimes instead of formally defining a subject, its scope is explained with illustration.

13. Inclusion Notes : There are such topics, on which no amount of literature is still not present and also there is no provision of their class number in schedules separately. Actually such topics are not fully developed, and their literary warrant does not demand a full and separate number for them. Hence these topics are given a standing room on ad hoc basis in a class with which it may have affinity.

14. Add from Auxiliary Tables Notes : Out of 7 Auxiliary Tables, such notations have been given in Tables 2-7, which can be used easily with some certain class number of the schedules and they are provided some specialty.

AUXILIARY TABLES

There are various types of auxiliaries (tables) in volume-1 of DDC (19th edition). There are 7 auxiliaries in DDC which are contained in different tables. The special concepts are represented constantly by the same notation in all the disciplines. They are called Auxiliaries in DDC. They are never used alone in number building, but have to be added to a subject irrespective of its scope or depth. The auxiliary tables have numbers which are used in classifying, after ascertaining the specific subject of a document we have to assign the class number with the help of schedules and tables. These tables provide numbers for special concepts repeatedly with a variety of subjects and disciplines.

Table-1: Standard Subdivisions

There are internal and external characteristics of a document. The examples of internal characteristics are the subject i.e. philosophy, theory, history, methodology etc. and the examples of external characteristics are the format and content i.e. journal, pamphlet, micro card, microfilm, video-tape etc. A subject can be embodied in any one of these internal forms and a document may be in any one of the external forms.

The standard subdivisions (abbreviated as SS) have been presented in Table-1 as follows:

-01 Philosophy and theory
-02 Miscellany
-03 Dictionaries, encyclopaedias, concordances
-04 Special topics of general applicability
-05 Serial publications
-06 Organisations and management
-07 Study and teaching
-08 History and description of the subject among group of persons
-09 Historical and geographical treatment

Identification of the Standard Subdivision is followed by the assignment of the class number.

Adding of SS to Main Class/Division : Whenever we have to use a SS add a zero to the main class. This is the general principle with few exceptions of this principle.

Adding a SS to Division Number : In the case when a SS have to add to a division number, only one zero is filling the vacant place, hence only one zero is dropped while adding a SS)

Use of Two Zeros : Generally one zero is added for a SS to a main class, But there are many cases where a SS is added with two or even three zeros. For adding more then one zero, there are instructions directly or indirectly in the schedules, under many class numbers.

Use of Three Zeros : In some cases 3 zeros are used to add a SS, when the subject divisions begin with two zeros.

Add-to-instruction about SS : Some of the Standard Subdivisions can be further extended with an add-to-instruction by a number or its segment either taken from the schedules or any of the Tables 2-7. In such cases, clear instructions are available to do so in that particular entry.

Two or More Standard Subdivisions : Sometimes a title may include 2 or more Standard Subdivisions.

When SS are not used : There are certain cases when SS are not used. When a SS is 'a part of the subject of the document, for example history, encyclopaedias, dictionaries etc. the SS is not used.

Table -2: Areas

Table-2 lists geographical areas, population clusters and natural, geographical and geophysical divisions of the world. These area numbers are added to the basic core subjects. These area numbers are obtained from Table-2. The summary of the Areas table is given below :

1. Areas, regions, places in general
2. Persons, regardless of area, region, place
3. Ancient world
4. Europe (Western Europe)
5. Asia Orient (Far East)
6. Africa
7. North America
8. South America
9. Other parts of World

Each digit has been hierarchically divided into countries and further to provinces. For example:

50. Asia / Orient Far East
51. China and adjacent area
52. Japan and adjacent islands
53. Arabian Peninsula and adjacent areas
54. South Asia India
55. Iran (Persia)
56. Middle East
57. Siberia (Asiatic Russia)
58. Central Asia
59. South East Asia

Adding an Area Number

The area numbers can be added to class number in following three ways:

i. When Area Number already a part of the Class Number : Many a time the area is so important to a subject that it is a primary characteristic of division for that subject. In these types of cases the subject itself is divided by the area number.

ii. Through Standard Subdivisions : Area number can be added to any class number through the Standard Subdivision-09. Some topics warrant the addition of an area number but there are no instructions for this in the schedules. In. these cases the area number car be added through the SS-09.

09.	In Standard Subdivision tab-Le - 09 have
091	Treatment by area, regions, places in .general
093-099	Treatment by specific^ continents. countries, localities extraterrestrial world.

These entries have the instructions, which are as fallows;

"Add Area notation... From Table-2 to base number-Off-

It means that the area numbers covered by the span 1 or 3-9, may be added. So any area number may be added to any class number without any difficult.

On Add-to Instructions

In the schedules of DDC, under several entries on "Add to" instruction is given.

iii. Adding of Two Area Numbers : Sometimes two areas may be present in a subject. In such cases, the numbers for both the areas are added, which are usually joined by a 0 (zero).

iv. Area Number interposed between two Subject Facets : There are some classes like Law, Public administration, Political Science etc. in which the base number, after the area number, can be further extended by some subject subdivisions. It means that here the area number forms the intermediate facets, whereas it usually forms the last facet.

v. Extension of Area Number by another Number : In the subjects like Desert of Asia or Forests of Africa there two areas are present. These are the cases of compound area numbers. In these cases, for both the area numbers, one from notation 1, and the other from notation 3-9, can be synthesized to form a compound area number for areas. For this situation the instructions are, under -1 Areas, regions, places in general or to any of its subdivision, add 0 and then add Area notation 3-9 from Table-2.

vi. Addition of Area Number to a Standard Subdivision except – 09 : In Table-1 of Standard Subdivisions, under some of the SS, there appears an Add- to-note which permits the addition of a number from Table-2. As per rules and the required number of zeros, the compound number can be added to any number in the schedules.

vii. Use of Standard Subdivisions after an Area Number : A standard subdivision can be added to any number extended by Area Number from Table-2 on add-to instructions then it is a part of the subject. It may be further extended by any SS from Table-1, just like any enumerated number in the schedules.

Table-3: Subdivisions of Individual Literatures

Table-3 is used only with the main class 800 Literature. The notations of this table cannot be used alone, they are used with some base numbers of the main class literature. The specific instructions are given for the subjects tabled in the schedule under class number 808.

A class number in 800 literature is usually completed with the help of Table-3. The main class 800 literature has been treated as the most faceted schedule in the DDC. This table is a table of literary forms further bifurcated into two tables viz. 3 and 3A. Table- 3 lists the various themes of literature to be added on instructions to the numbers in the schedule 800.

Table-3 has been summarized as follows:

-01-07	Standard Subdivisions	-08	Collections
-09	History, description, critical appraisal	-1	Poetry
-2	Drama	-3	Fiction
-4	Essays	-5	Speeches
-6	Letters	-7	Satire and human
-8	Miscellaneous writings		

Each of the above literary forms (-1 to -8) has been further divided as follows by three processes:

(a) By Standard Subdivisions attached with two zeros, such as -100 1 - 100 7, Standard subdivisions of poetry.

(b) By varieties of that Literary form, such as

-1	Poetry	-3	Fiction
-102	Dramatic	-301	Short stories
-103	Epic	-306	Cartoon fiction
-106	Descriptive	-308	Specific types of fiction
-108	Light and ephemeral		

(c) By period divisions as taken from the schedules, such as

-11-19	Poetry of specific period
-31-39	Fiction of specific period

1. Works of Individual Authors : To provide class number to works of an individual literary author is very easy and simple. It is obtained through a formula, which is as follows:

Base number + Form + Period

2. Works of some English Writers : The class numbers for some of the well known English writers, can be obtained.

Works of Indian Language Writers

For Indian literatures, the Period Table has been given on Page 1422 under base number 891.4 of the schedules, which is as follows:

1. Upto 1345
2. 1345-1645

3. 1645-1845
4. 1845-1895
5. 1895-1920
6. 1920-1940
7. 1940-

3. Literature in specific Languages and Forms displaying specific themes : In the examples of such cases, both language and forms are present.

4. Anthologies, History, Critical Appraisal of Literatures of a Specific Language, Form and Period.

Obviously in such cases the language, form and period facets are present along with a theme or a viewpoint facet. The use of Table-3A is done.

Base number + Form (Table-3) + Period (as taken from the schedule of concerned language literature + 080/09 + Theme/Viewpoint (Table 3A).

5. Use of Table-3A with other classes : The Table-3A, the supplement of Table-3, is used for specific number 792.0909 special aspects of theatre. Under this base number, instructions are to add notation 1-3 from Table-3A.

Table-4 : Subdivisions of Individuals Languages

Table-4 has the elements of the languages. This table has been formally defined as a table of notations designating regularly recurring topics applicable to any language. It may be added as directed to individual languages in 420-490.

Table-4 is as follows:

1. Written and spoken codes of the standard form of the language.
2. Etymology of the standard form of the language.
3. Dictionaries of the standard form of the language
4. Structural system (Grammar) of the standard form of the language.
5. Non-standard forms of the language
6. Standard usage of the language.

All these numbers and their subdivisions can be add to the umbers in the schedules as per instructions under 420-490.

Using Table-4

In asterisked number in the main class 400 of the schedule via a footnote, leads us to the instructions under 420-490 specific languages. The instructions can be read under each language identified by, add subdivisions of individual languages' notation 01 - 86 from Table-4 to designated Base Number.

Dictionary of English language idioms 42* + 31 = 423.1

Bilingual Dictionaries : In building class numbers for bilingual dictionaries, the Table-6 is also used with Table-4 to which it supplements for many linguistic subjects. In bilingual dictionaries, the words are given in one language and their meaning in another. The formula for number building of bilingual dictionaries is as follows:

Base number + 3 (Table4)+Table-6

The dictionaries are classified under the language which is more useful in the library concerned.

Table-5 : Racial, Ethnic, National Groups

The Table-5 is concerned with the persons according to their ethnic, racial and national origins have systematically been arranged. This table has been defined as a table of notations designating specific, racial, ethnic or national groups. On add to instructions, the notations of this table is usually applied, and can also be added to any class number. SS - 989 functions as a facet indicator. The summary ofTable-5 is as follows:

1. North Americans
2. Anglo - Saxons, British, English
3. Nordics
4. Modern Latins
5. Italians, Romanians, related groups
6. Spanish and Portuguese
7. Other Italic peoples
8. Greeks and related groups
9. Other racial, ethnic, national groups.

Each of the above division has been subdivided hierarchically. For making use of these divisions, Relative Index can be freely used. Each notation from Table- 5 is preceded by an abbreviated symbol r.e.n. for example.

Negroids r.e.n. - 36	Where r.e.n. stand for
Russian, people r.e.n. - 917.	Racial, Ethnic and National

1. Use on Instructions : Table-5 can be used on instructions. The notations of Table-5 are used on instructions under the base number.

2. Extension of Table-5 by Area Notation from Table-2 : As-per instructions preceding Table-5, each number in this notation may further be extended by a notation from Table-2. This addition can be by following two ways: through 0 (zero) as a facet indicator and on instructions.

3. Directly extending Table-5 by Table-2 : There are some such divisions in Table-5, which are further directly, divisible by Table- 2.

4. Using Table-5 through Standard Subdivisions : The numbers of Table-5 can be freely added to any class number in the schedules through a Standard Subdivision namely, -089 Treatment among specific, racial, ethnic.

5. Using Table-5 through Table-3A : In Table-3A under the subdivision 8 literature for and by various specific, racial, ethnic, national group, we are expectedly invited to add notation from Table-5 for further specification.

Table 6

Table-6 has notations designating specific languages. The summary of Table-6 is as following:

1. Indo European (Indo-Germanic) Languages.
2. English and Anglo-Saxon Languages.
3. Germanic (Teutonic) Languages.
4. Romanic Languages.
5. Italian, Romanian, Rhaeto Romanic Languages.
6. Spanish and Portuguese Language.
7. Italic Languages.
8. Hellenic Languages.
9. Other Languages.

This table can be applied in many places in the schedules and auxiliary tables, with sufficient and clear add-to-notes under the entries requiring addition of notation form Table-6.

Table-7: Persons

The table 7 has the persons, categorized into different groups according to their various characteristics. This table has been defined as a table of notations designating persons by specific occupational and other classes as follows:

1. Persons occupied with philosophy and related disciplines.
2. Persons occupied with or adherent to religion. It also pertains to persons as religious scholars religious officials/leaders and followers of a religion.
3. Persons occupied with social sciences, etc.
4. Persons occupied with linguistics, lexicography.
5. Persons occupied with pure sciences.
6. Persons occupied with applied sciences.
7. Persons occupied with the art.
8. Persons occupied with creative writing and speaking.
9. Persons occupied with geography, history, and related disciplines.

i. Use on Instructions : Table-7 can be used on Add-to instructions also. For Example, 390.4 Customs of people of various specific occupations.

ii. Use in Conjunction with other Tables : When there is no instruction under the required base number and the use of the notation ofTable-7 is essential, that they can be used with following ways.

iii. Through the Notation - 088 of SS of Table-1 : If a situation demand the use of Table-7 (Persons) but there is no official invitation to use it, then a notation from Table-7 may be added to the class number in the schedules through the Standard Subdivision.

Examples of Dewey Decimal Class numbers

Add to... of a Full Number

Add 001 -999 to base number..........

Libraries on Science 026 + 500 = 026.5AO=026.5

Libraries on Algebra 026 + 512 = 026.512

Libraries on pedagogical algebra 026 + 512.9 = 026.512 9

Museums on medical science 069 + 610 = 069.61(1= 069.61

Curriculums in mathematics 375 + 510 = 375.51)0= 375.51

Addition of a Segment

Add to.... A Segment from a Distant Part.

Wages in textile industries.

331	Labour economics
331.2	Wages, hours, other conditions of employment
331.28	Wages in specific industries and occupations
331.282-289	Extractive, manufacturing, construction

331.28 + 77 = 331.287 7

Wages in agricultural occupation will be 331.28 + 630 = 331.2830 = 331.283

Trade in rice well be 381.41 +3.18 = 318.41318

'Add to..." From the same Division /Section

Reference service in school libraries

020	Library science
027.8	School libraries
025.527	Reference and information service

Add to the base number 025.527 the number following 02 in 026 - 027

It means that the base number is 025.527. To this base we are directed by Add to .i4 above, to add the number coming after 02 in 025-027. Hence the desired number is 025.527+ 027.8 = 025.527 78

Reference service in public libraries 025.527 + 027.4 = 025,527 74

Embryology of Microbes 576.13 + 0.3 = 576.133

Addition from the Same Division/Section with a Facet Indicator

Teaching methods for the mentally retarded students.

370	Education
371.928	Mentally deficient students

Mentally retarded. Add 0 [zero] to base number 371.928 and to the result add the number following 371.904 in 371.904 2 - 371.9046.

This base number is 371.928

Adding the zero as instructed 371.928 + 0

The teaching methods as in 371.904 2 - 371.9046 is 371.904 3

The number following 371.904 in 371.904 3 is 3.

Hence the required class number is 371.928 + 0 + 3 = 371.928 03

Facilities towards the education of mentally retarted students. 371.928 + 0 + 5 = 371.928 05 Genetics of insets 595.70 + 0.15 = 595.7015

Ecology of insects 595.70 + 0.5 = 595.705

Genetics of fishes 597.0 + J56Ll5 = 597.015

Class Elsewhere Notes

361.61 Social policy

If welfare reform, class under 361.68

Class ...in Notes

523.302.22 Moon pictures and designs

Class charts and photographs in 523.39

It clearly means that 523.30222 Moon Pictures and Designs does not include charts and photographs of moon, for the latter there is a distinct class number 523.39 Similarly under

1817.4 Indian Philosophy

Class philosophy of Pakistan and Bangladesh in 181.15. Relation between these two subjects is obvious, so is the need of this note.

Adding a SS to Division Number

Encyclopaedia of mathematics 510+ 03 = 510.3

Symbols and abbreviations in mathematics 510+ 0148 = 510.148

History of mathematics 510+09 = 510.9

Use of Two Zeros

When Area Number already a part of the Class Number

914 Geography of Europe

Through Standard Subdivisions

09. In Standard Subdivision tab-Le - 09 have

091 Treatment by area, regions, places in .general

093-099 Treatment by specific continents. countries, localities extraterrestrial world.

Addition of Area Number to a Standard Subdivision except - 09

Colleges and universities teaching in India.

-0711 +54 = 0711 54 = 711.54

Works of famous writers

Charles Dickens (1812-1870): David Copper field.

= 82 + 3 (Form - Fiction] + 8 (Period: Victorian period) = 823.8

Poems of R.W. Emerson

81+1 (From, Poetry) + 4 (Periods: Latter 19 the century) = 811.4

Works of Indian Language Writers

Geetanjali by Ravindra Nath Tagore.

891.44 (Bengali) + 1 + 5 (Period 1895 -1920 = B91.441 5

A journal of English dramatic poetry.

82 +102 + 05 (SS for Journal as under -1 - 8) = 821.020 5

An anthology of 20th century English poetry.

82 + 1 + 91 (Period) + 08 (From 1008 Table-3) = 821.910 8

Treatment of social themes in theatre.

792.0909 + 355 (Table-3A) = 792.090 935 5

Bengali alphabets. 491.44* +11 = 491.4411

German grammar. 43* + 5 (Table-4) = 435

Sanskrit grammar. 4912* + 5 (Table-4) = 491.25

Sanskrit dictionary. 491.2' + 3 (Table-4) = 491

Dictionary of English language idioms. 42* + 31 = 423.1

Dictionary of German abbreviations. 43* + 31 = 433.1

Hindi - English Dictionary. See the difference in two numbers as:

In India (English is more useful)

42* + 3 + 91431 = 423.914 31

In (USA Hindi is more useful)

491.43* + 3 + 21 = 491.433 21

English German dictionary 42* + 3 + 31 = 423.31

French - German dictionary 44' + 3131 = 443.31

Where r.e.n. stand for Racial, Ethnic and National

Russian, people r.e.n. - 917.

Social stratification of German people.

305.8 + 31 (Table-5) = 305.831

Social welfare services to Indians. 362.797 + 914 11

A social Study of German nationals in USA.

305.8 + 31 (Table-5) + 0 + 73 (Table-2) = 305.831 073

Chilean nationals

-68 (Table-5) + 83 (Table-2) = - 688 3

Development of Puppetry among Bengalis.

791.530 + 089 (Table -1) + 9144 (Table-5) = 791.530 899 144

Biography of Russians.

920.009 2 + 9171 = 920.009 291 71

Bible in Sinhalese language.

220.5 + 9148 (Table-6) = 220.591 48

Kadambari a Hindi magazine.

059 + 91431 = 059.91431

Persons

Customs of poets 390.4 + 81 (Table-7) = 390.481

Contributions to music by blind persons

780 + 088 (Table-1) + 08161 (Table-7) = 780.880 816 1

2. UNDERSTANDING COLON CLASSIFICATION PRACTICAL

Colon Classification devised by Dr. S.R. Ranganathan was first published in 1933. The 6th edition is very popular for classifying documents. The 6th edition was first published in 1960 and then it was reprinted in 1963,1964,1969,1976 and 1989. The division of 6th edition is as following in 3 parts follows.

Part-1 : This part provides rules, definitions, explanations and examples.

Part-2 : This part provides the schedules of classification with an alphabetical index, and index to the schedules of Space Isolates, and of the Personality isolates in Botany and Zoology.

Part-3 : This part provides worked out class numbers of classics in Indology. It also provides schedule of Sacred books with special names, followed by an index.

NUMBER BUILDING IN CC

CC is different from other schemes of enumerative pattern of classification; it is an analytico-synthetic scheme. The number building in CC involves two major steps.

1. Analysis of the subjects into facets and transforming them into five fundamental categories.
2. Synthesis of the facets.

Use of Index : In the end of Part 2, an index has been provided at Page No. 2.124, which is to the fundamental constituent terms in the schedules of classification. This index helps in recognising the main class and facet of a given isolate term. At the beginning of the index, instructions to use the index and key to the contractions are given. Here we give below an entry from the index by which we can understand the meaning and implications of a given entry of the index.

Methodology for making Class Numbers

As we have already known that CC is an analytico- synthetic scheme of classification, thus the class number for a given subject is prepared in it by analyzing the subject into its facets and synthesize them. According to Ranganathan, we have to analyze the concepts of the subject first for classifying the book, and then the concepts are separated according to their characteristics. Then we have to try to know the main class of the subject that would be the Basic class of the book (title) which is to be classified. In finding out the basic class of the subject we can take help of the index given in the end of Part II of CC. The index is most helpful in determining the Basic Class of the subject.

1. Facet Analysis of the Subject : First analysis of the subject is done by dividing it into its facets. We see that facets are present in this subject as follows:

Time facet (It is known easily)

Space facet (It is a place and known easily)

Matter facet (It is seen a thing/matter)

Energy facet (It is regarded as an action)

Personality facet (The remainder is the Personality)

2. Determination of the Basic Class : On analyzing the subjects into its facets (concepts) we have come to know that the subject is of the main class. After analyzing the subject we have to know the basic class of the subject.

3. Notations : reaching to main class, the notations according to facet formula are found and determined.

4. Synthesis by Facet Formula : In the end we have to synthesize all the facets by facet formula given to each main class. The facet formula of each main class is given at the top and running of the main class sometimes.

Systems and Specials

(a) Systems : Systems occur in so many main classes such as Physics, Agriculture, Medicine, Psychology, Education, History and Economics. Using the CD the system facet for other main classes can be constructed. Systems are treated as the Basic classes. The facet formula for the main class to which the system belongs is also applicable to the System Basic class. But, in case of System Basic class, the Personality isolate should always be preceded by a comma, even if the facet formula does not provide comma after the main class. System refers to exposition of basic subject according to some special school of thought. Thus system denotes a division of a main class expounded after a school of thought. A school of thought is a group, or succession of persons devoted to some cause or philosophy. The class number for a system is derived by the Chronological Device, i.e., by using the date of origin of the system as the epoch. An example of system facets is:

SN14 Individualistic Psychology. It means a school of psychology that came into beinginN14i.e.in 1914.

(b) Specials : The specials refer to specific areas of a subject. It also means specialization in a particular aspect which deals with the entire subject. Special facet have been enumerated at the end of some the main classes such as Physics, Chemistry, Biology, Agriculture, Medicine and Economics.

Example : L9C Child medicine

(c) Systems and Specials : If both systems and specials are to be used for classifying documents, system should precede specials and should be separated by a comma.

COMMON ISOLATES

Common Isolates are defined as an isolate idea which is denoted by the same isolate term and represented by the same isolate number. In other words common isolate is an isolate which is common to all the main classes. In CC, there are two types of Common Isolates.

(A) Anteriorising Common Isolates (ACI) : The isolates those should precede the general treatment of subject and are the approach materials such as historical material, periodicals, dictionaries, encyclopaedias, conference proceedings etc. ACI are those isolates which can be attached to the host class number directly without any connecting symbol. There are 3 types of ACI.

i. **Applicable before Space facet :** These ACIs are applicable before the Space. Those which have their facet formula, they are attached to the class number according to their facet formula, and those, which do not have their facet formula can be attached directly to the class numbers of the books.

   Examples—

   Annual Conference Proceedings of ILA 2p44,N3

ii. **Applicable only after Space Facet:** ACI which are applicable only after Space ^- facet consists of two divisions.

iii. **Applicable only after Time facet:** There are some ACIs which are used only after Time facet. These are 10 in numbers. There is no facet formula to them. They can directly be joined after Time facet. They are as follows:

s	Statistics (if stray)	v	source material
t	Commission Report	v5	Literature
t4	Survey	v6	Tradition
t5	Plan	v7	Archive (as in V History)
t6	Ideal	v8	Archaeology (as in V History)

(B) Posteriorising Common Isolates (PCIs) : To join PCIs, a connecting symbol is needed. By adding the PCI to any class, the extension of the class decreases. The resulting class is arranged posterior to the original class i.e. it comes after the original class. First the host class is to be worked out on the basis of the facet formula and then the PCI number is added. PCIs are of two types as follows:

i. **Energy PCIs :** There is no facet formula for these types of PCIs, they are joined directly after their connecting symbols colon (:).

b1	Calculating	f3	Experiments
b2	Designing	f4	Discussion
b6	Measuring	g	Criticism
cl	Weighing	p	Drafting
f	Investigation/Research	r	Reporting
f2	Observation	u	Surveying

ii. **Personality PCIs :** The personality PCIs are added after Space Isolate and a comma should precede it. There is a facet formula given for these PCIs, which is (Cl), |P|, (P2):(E1).

   The isolate in [P] is obtained by AD in case of localised body and in case of non ¬localised body the isolate in |P| is got by CD and it should be preceded by 9. These PCIs are as follows:

b	Profession	f3	Experimenting
d	Institution	f4	Discussional
e	Educational (in which the subject represented by the host class is taught)	f7	Yogic (Asrama)
		g	Learned society
		h	Industrial body
		k	Commercial body
e2	Lower	w	Administrative department of the government
e4	Higher		
f	Investigating		
f2	Observational		

VARIOUS DEVICES

Due to new subjects always have been emerging and a scheme of classification should be able to accommodate these new emerging subjects within its frame work. For this purpose a number of devices can be used. The purpose of such a device is to form a new isolate or to sharpen an existing isolate in an array. There are many devices in CC as follows:

Chronological Device (CD) : CD is a device in which a chronological number can be joined from the schedule of the Time isolate for sharpening a facet number. It can sharpen an isolate or can form a new isolate. In the main class 0 Literature, all numbers for authors are derived by CD.

Geographical Device (GD) : GD is a device in which a geographical number can be employ from the schedule of the Space isolate for sharpening a facet number. Like DDC, it can also sharpen an isolate or can form a new isolate. This device has been used in Library Science, Fine Arts, Religion, Linguistics, History and in several other classes.

Subject Device (SD) : This device is used to form or sharpen a facet by adding to it another class number from elsewhere in the scheme. It is also used in several main classes whenever required. The part of the number derived by the SD is enclosed in circular brackets.

Alphabetical Device (AD) : AD is also used to form or sharpen an isolate number. In this device, the first, or the first two or three letters of the names of persons or objects are used. It can be used wherever warranted.

Superimposition Device (Sup D) : By this method two isolate numbers occurred in a facet of a main class can be represented. Out of these two isolates, one is the principal isolate is taken first and the secondary isolate is taken later, and both the isolates are joined with the connecting symbol hyphen (-).

PHASE RELATIONS

Nowadays we have been seeing several interdisciplinary subjects. The interdisciplinary subjects should be represented by their correct class numbers. For this purpose, CC has provided a method called Phase Relation. A class which comprehends two or more classes brought into mutual relation is called a phased or complex class. The constituent classes are called its phases and their relation is known as Phase relation. A phase relation may be between two or more main classes, within one and the same facet of a main class or within one and the same array in isolates. The phase relations are organized at following three levels:

1. Inter Class or Subject Phase Relation
2. Intra-Facet Phase Relation
3. Intra- Array Phase Relation

Each of the above phase relations, has five kinds of relations as shown in the following table with their connecting symbol.

Nature of Relation	Inter class	Intra- Facet	Intra-Array
1. General relation	0a	0j	0t
2. Bias relation	0b	0k	0u
3. Comparison	0c	0m	0v
4. Difference	0d	0n	0w
5. Tool	0e	0p	0x
6. Influencing	0g	0r	0y

1. Inter Class or Subject Phase Relation : Relation between two or more main classes (subjects) is called Inter Class Phase Relation. As discussed above there can be six types of different relations between the subjects.

2. Intra-Facet Phase relation : Intra-Facet phase relation is the interrelation between e isolates of a facet in a main class. These relations are also of six types.

3. Intra-Array Phase Relation : Intra-Array phase relation is the interrelation between e two isolates of a facet which belong to the same array. This relation is again of six types.

Various examples discussed to explain class number building in Colon Classification

Epidermis G [P], K[P2], L[P], 871

G871 K,871 L871

Example of the Chapter-2 Library Science:

	2[P];[M]:[El[2Pl.[S] '(T)
University libraries	is in [PI category whose notation is 34.
Books	are in [M] category whose notation is 14.
Circulation	is in [El category whose notation is 6.
Uttar Pradesh	is a isolate of [S] category, whose notation can be obtained from the Space Isolate table given on Page 2.10 of CC.
1999	is a isolate of [T] category, whose notation can be obtained from the Time Isolates table given on Page 2.7 of CC.

Now putting all notations in the above facet formula,

We get the class number 234;14:6.4452'N99

Some examples of system facets are:

B6M8 Hyperbolic geometry, where B6 is geometry and M8 means the year 1880s, which means that a system of geometry expounded in the 1880s.

LB Ayurveda, L is the Medicine and B means 9999 to 1000 BC, i.e. a system of medicine that came into being prior to 1000 BC.

Homeopathic treatment of diarrhea

The facet formula for the main class L is L[P]: [E] [2P]

Homeopathy has been enumerated under the System facet at the end of the schedule for main class Medicine. The basic class for homeopathy is LL. Therefore the class number for the above title will be LL, 25:452:6

Examples of Specials are:

G9Up Marine Biology

J9B Dry fanning

L9C Child medicine

S9XX Industrial psychology

Small industry export

The main class is X Economics. The facet formula for Economics main class is X[P],[M|:[E)[2P1. Small industry has been enumerated under the special facet at the end of the schedule for main class Economics. Therefore the class number for the above title will be:

X9B, 9(A): 545

Examples of Anteriorising Common Isolates (ACI)

i. **Applicable before Space facet**

Cyclopaedia (Facet Formula is k [P),(P2), where

[P] = Geographical area of preview which is obtained by GD.

[P2] = Epoch of origin which is obtained by CD.

Examples—Encyclopaedia Britannica

In this encyclopaedia, the information all about the world is contained, thus its area is whole world, the isolate number for which is 1. It was started in 1768 which will be used as epoch of origin of it. Thus the class number is kl, L68.

Encyclopaedia Americana k73, M29 (Each is 1829)

(In this encyclopaedia, the information is about only of America)

International Encyclopaedia of Science published in 1826.Akl,M26

Periodical (Facet Formula is m[P], [P2D, where,

[P] = Geographical area of purview which is obtained by GD.

[P2] = Epoch of origin which is obtained by CD.

Examples—

Indian Journal of Botany (1978). Im44,N78

Herald of Library Science (India, 1962). 2m44,N62

Journal of American Chemical Society (1879). Em73,M79

Serial (Facet formula is n[P|,[P2]), the rules are the same as of m periodical. Examples-

Statesman's Yearbook (UK, 1864) nl,M64

India: A reference annual (Started 1953) n44,N53

Directory of medical doctors (India, 1925) Ln44,N25

Yearbook of secondary education (UK, 1921) T2n56,N21

Conference Proceedings (Facet Formula p[P],[P2], where,

[P] = Geographical area of purview which is obtained by GD.

[P2] = Year of the conference, if an isolated one, to be got by GD (worked to three digits). Epoch of origin, if it is held periodically.

Examples—

Annual Conference Proceedings of ILA 2p44,N3

(Held at Lucknow, 1995). Indian Science Congress. Ap44,N4

(Held at Delhi, 1955)

Both of the above conferences are held annually each year, hence the decade number is given. The origin of ILA is 1933, hence it is given N3; similarly 1947 is the establishment year of Science Congress for which decade number N4 is given.

When the conference does not organise yearly, the year is given in 3 digits. Examples—

Conference proceedings of pharmacists of India (Delhi, 1975). LX3p44,N75

Conference of librarians of UP (Agra, 1990). 2p445,N90

National conference on Hindu Law (Delhi, 1984). Z(Q2)p44,N84

Biography: It is further divided into following divisions:

General (Facet Formula w[S], [T], where [S] = space, [T] = Time).

Biography of Indian farmers (youngest born in 1933). Jw44,N3

Biography of American Scientists (youngest born in 1959). Aw 73,N5

If there is no information is available in title about [P2] facet, only the [PJ facet is used. Examples —

Biography of Indian economics. Xw44

Biography of American cartographer. Ullw73

Individual (Facet Formula w [P]), where,

[P] - Date of year of the person by CD in 3 digits.

Biography of Raman (1895) CwM95

Biography of Ramanujan (1887). BwM87

Life of Charles Darvin (1809). GwM09

Autobiography	**Facet Formula**	w[P], 1
Ana	Facet Formula	w[P],2
Letters	Facet Formula	w[P],4

where [P] = Date of the birth.

Autobiography of Melwil Dewey (Born 1851). 2wM51,l

Autobiography of Ranganathan (Born 1892). 2wM92,l

Ana of Ranganathan (Bom 1872). 2wM92,2

Letters of Melvil Dewey (Bom 1851). 2wM51,4

Letters of C.V Raman (Born 1895). CwM95,4

Works : It is further divided into the following two divisions:

General	(Facet formula	x[S],[P2] were P2 = LED
Individual	(Facet formula	x [PI

Collection of works of Indian scientists.

(youngest born in 1932) Ax44,N3

Works of Ranganathan (Born in 1892). 2xM92

Selected works of Ramanujan (Born in 1887). BxM87

Case Study (it has facet formula same as for w)

Biography of Jawaharlal Nehru, V44y7M89

(PM of India, born in 1889).

Life of Kennedy (President of USA, Bom in 1917).

V73y7N17

Correspondence of Dr. Rajendra Prasad, (India President).

V44y7M80

ACI Applicable only after Space Facet

r Administrative Report : no facet formula for this ACI, hence it can be used without any connecting symbol after space facet.

Administrative report on education is India. T.44r

Adm. Report of Finance Dept, of UP x7.4452r

s Statistics (if periodical) (Facet Formula s[T]): here those statistical data are entered which are published serially after a section interval. [T) is taken from CD.

Periodical on secondary education in India (started in 1948)

T2,44sN48

Quarterly statistics on American trade, 1989. X:5.73sN89

ACI Applicable only after Time facet

Statistics of educated adults in Japan, 1971. T3.42'N71s

Commission reports of Indian labour (1950). X:9.44'N50t

Posteriorising Common Isolates (PCIs)

Energy PCIs:

Calculating solar month.	B9:123:bl
Designing of dresses.	M8:b2
Measuring of rain fall.	U2855:b6
Observations on wheat agriculture.	J382:f2
Experiments in Physics.	C:f3
Discussion on Indian culture.	Y73(P15):l:f4
Criticism of Shakespeare.	0111,2J64:g
Reporting on practice of prostitution.	Y15:44:r

Personality PCIs

Examples— Facet Formula Cl, [PI, [P2|: [E]

Medical profession in India.	L.44,b
Educational institution of UK.	T.56,d
Delhi College of Engineering.	D.4481,e4,D
Tata Iron and Steel Works.	F1823.44,k,T
Observational comments of Indian constitution.	W:2.44,l2:g
Ministry of Industries, Govt, of India, New Delhi.	X:5.44,w,N

Examples of Chronological Device (CD)

Colon Classification	2:51N33	(N33= 1933 Birth of CC)
Decimal Classification	2:51M76	(M76=1876 Birth of DDC) Shakespeare
	0111,2J64	(J64=1564 Birth of Shakespeare)

Examples of Geographical Device (GD):

Indian law	Z44	(44 is for India)
British philosophy	R856	(56 is for Britain)
Russian theatre	NT58	(58 is for Russia)
American society	Y773	(73 is for America)
Sikhism	08441	(441 is for Punjab)
Indian architecture	NA44	(44 is for India)

Examples of Subject Device (SD)

Medical libraries	24 (L)
Religious libraries	24 (Q)
Computer machine	D6,8(B)
Hindu law	Z(Q2)
Mathematical Biology	G:(B)

Educational psychology T:(S)

Examples of Alphabetical Device (AD)

D5125He (He for Hero make of cycles)

J3751D (D for Dasheri mangoes)

J381B (Basmati rice where B is for Basmati)

Examples of Superimposition Device (Sup D)

Nerves of eyes. L185-74'

Working class women. Y15-49

Examples of Inter Class or Subject Phase Relation

Deference between Engg. and Technology. D0dF

Influence of Religion or working class. Q0gy49

Statistical analysis in library management (Tool). 2:80eB28

Botany compared to Zoology (Comparison). I0cK

Relation between Philosophy and Religion (General). Q0aR

Mathematics for Economists (Biased). B0bX

Examples of Intra-Facet Phase relation

Electronics for nuclear engineers (Biased). D650k7

Study of special and university libraries (General). 23:60j8

Different: Adult education and university education (difference). T30n4

Jainism compared to Buddhism (Comparison). Q30m4

Indian music through painting (Tool). NR440eNQ

Influence of Christianity on Buddhism Influencing. Q60r4

Examples of Intra-Array Phase Relation:

Chemical method used for examination of urine (Biased). L:4030u5

Study of insane and criminal psychology. (General). S630t5

Carnatic music through Hindustani Music (Tool). NR4410x5

Rural sociology compared to urban sociology (Comparison). Y310v5

Difference between Saivism and Saktism (Difference). Q230w5

Influence of humidity on temperature (Influencing). U2840y5

3. CATALOGUING PRACTICE: BASIC RULES

ANGLO-AMERICAN CATALOGING RULES 2

AACR 2 or AACR II is a code meant for a dictionary catalogue. In the dictionary catalogue all the entries (author, title, subject, series, etc) and their related references are arranged together in one general alphabet.

There are following kinds of entries in AACR 2:

- Main Entry
- Added Entries

Besides main entry and added entries, there are references or cross reference entries.

Main Entry

According to the provisions in AACR 2, main entry is the complete catalog record of a bibliographical entity. The main entry normally includes the tracing of all other headings under which the record is to be represented in the catalogue. The main entry is the basic entry, with sometimes title occupying heading of a main entry. The last section contains the tracings, which indicate headings under which added entries have been prepared for a given document.

Elements of Main Entry

In AACR 2 practice, main entry of a book would generally consist of the following elements:

- Call number (Class number and book number), accession number;
- Heading3. Title, Subtitle
- Author statement
- Edition statement
- Imprint (place of publication, publishers name and date of publication or copyright)
- Collation (pagination or number of volumes; illustration; size; etc. Illustration is general term which includes maps, diagrams, charts, tables, etc.);
- Series statement;
- Notes (cover special quality about a book);
- Tracing

Added Entries

An added entry is an entry, additional to the main entry, under which a bibliographical entity is represented in a catalog. Added entries are prepared for subordinate authors like joint authors, editors, translators, and illustrators. These are also prepared for title, series, and subject(s). A reference entry is prepared for editor of a series.

For References : The Sears list of subject headings is used for deriving the standard subject terms or key words as subject headings. The see reference and see also reference entries are provided as added entries.

X See reference:

XX See also reference:

See reference: Reference is a direction from one heading or entry to another.

See also reference: A See also reference directs the user from one heading to a related heading.

CLASSIFIED CATALOGUE CODE

According to Classified Catalogue Code, classified catalogue has two parts: the classified part and the alphabetical part. As discussed in the main chapter, the classified part contains main as well as cross reference entries. These entries are prepared by call number and class number respectively. These entries are called as number entries also. The arrangement of the entries is based on the call numbers and class numbers. The alphabetical part is comprised of word entries and they are arranged in alphabetical manner as in dictionary working and helping the information retrieval as alphabetical index to the classified component. Several index entries such as Book index entries, Class Index entries, and Cross Reference index entries are prepared as:

i. Main entry

ii. Added entry

a. Class Index Entries

b. Book Index Entries

i. Author Entry

ii. Joint Author Entry

iii. Collaborator Entry

iv. Title Entry

v. Series Entry

c. Cross Reference Index Entries

i. Alternative name Entry

ii. Variant Form of Word Entry

iii. Pseudo-Real Name Entry

iv. Editor of Series Entry

d. Cross Reference Entries

Bibliography

1. "A Brief Introduction to the Dewey Decimal Classification". OCLC. http://www.oclc.org/dewey/resources/summaries.en.html
2. AACR2. http://www.aacr2.org/
3. "Abridged". OCLC. 2012. http://www.oclc.org/dewey/versions/abridged/default.htm
4. Abrera, J.B. 1974. Traditional Classification: Characteristics, Uses and Problems. Drexel Library Quarterly, Vol. 10, No. 4, pp. 21-36.
5. Adams, W.J., Jansen, B.J., & Smith, T. (1999). Planning, building, and using a distributed digital library. Third International Conference on Concepts in Library and Information Science. Dubrovnik, Croatia. http://ist.psu.edu/faculty_pages/jjansen/academic/pubs/colis99/colis99.html
6. Ahmet ALTAY, Ammar TEKIN, Bahtiyar DURSUN, Mustafa YAYLA. The Role of the Libraries in the Information Society.
7. Al-Ansari, H (1999). 'Improving the organizational structure for an electronic environment: a case analysis of Kuwait University libraries' Library Review 48 (3) pp131-139.
8. Alabaster, Carl (2010). Developing an Outstanding Core Collection: A Guide for Libraries. ALA.
9. ALIA's submission: http://www.aph.gov.au/house/committee/laca/digitalagenda/Sub47.pdf
10. ALCTS Newsletter article on RDA http://www.ala.org/ala/mgrps/divs/alcts/resources/ano/v16/n6/nws/rdaqs.cfm
11. Alsop, J. (2007). Bridget Jones meets Mr. Darcy: Challenges of contemporary fiction. Journal of Academic Librarianship, 33, 581-585.
12. Alvi, Wajih A. (2001). Jammu & Kashmir. In. Library and Information Services in Indian States and Union Territories edited by P.B.Mangla, et.al. New Delhi: Shipra.
13. American Library Association Council. (1970). Library education and personnel utilization (LEPU): A statement of policy adopted by the ALA council, June 30, 1970

14. Amudhavali, A and N. Sumithra (2001). Tamil Nadu. In. Library and Information Services in Indian States and Union Territories edited by P.B.Mangla, et.al. New Delhi: Shipra.
15. Anbarasan and R. Ramasmy (2001). Union Territories. In. Library and Information Services in Indian States and Union Territories edited by P.B.Mangla, et.al. New Delhi: Shipra.
16. Anderson, R. (2011, May 31). What patron-driven acquisition (PDA) does and doesn't mean: An FAQ.
17. A Student's Guide to Evaluating Libraries in Colleges and Universities. http://www.ala.org/acrl/issues/marketing
18. Academic Library by WBDG Staff. http://www.wbdg.org/design/academic_library.php#over
19. Ajibero, M.I. (2004). Donor support and sustainability: the experience of university libraries. In Proceedings of SCAULWA 2003 conference, Erata Hotel, Accra, Ghana, p.11.
20. American Society of Indexing: http://asindexing.org/site/refbooks.shtml#general_collect
21. Anderson, J.Q. & Rainie, L. 2006. The future of Internet II: Pew Internet and American Life project. www.elon.edu/e-web/predictions/2006survey.pdf.
22. Anderson, R. (2011, May 31). What patron-driven acquisition (PDA) does and doesn't mean: An FAQ.
23. Anderson, Dorothy (1974). Universal bibliographic control : a long term policy, a plan for action. Pullach/München : Verlag Dokumentation.
24. Anil Singh (2002).Application of Bar Code Technology in Libraries. Library Herald. V.40, N. 1, p 43-47.
25. Apotiade, J. K. (2002). Ibadan distance learning centre series: LSE 302 cataloguing and classification. Ibadan: Distance learning centre University of Ibadan. Pp. 5
26. Assorted Encyclopedias on the Web http://edis.win.tue.nl/encyclop.html
27. Automation Systems Installed Counting by Library organizations. http://www.librarytechnology.org/lwc-ils-marketshare.pl?SID=20120527624877929
28. AVAL's submission: http://online.anu.edu.au/caul/gov-inqu/dig-agenda99.html
29. Avrin, Leila (1991). Scribes, script, and books: the book arts from antiquity to the Renaissance. New York, New York: American Library Association; The British Library.
30. B. D. Kumbar. GROWTH AND DEVELOPMENT OF PUBLIC LIBRARY SYSTEM IN INDIA WITH SPECIAL REFERENCE TO KARNATAKA. International workshop on "Democratization of Information: Focus on Libraries"

31. B. Ramesh Babu, Ann O'Brien, (2000) "Web OPAC interfaces: an overview", Electronic Library, The, Vol. 18 Iss: 5, pp.316 - 330
32. Baker, D. (1997). 'Document delivery: access versus holdings' Librarian Career Development 5 (3) pp84-93.
33. Barber, E., Pisano, S., D'Alessandro, S., Romagnoli, S., Parsiale, V., De Pedro, G. ve Gregui, C. (2006). Information society and information technology: The situation of the public libraries in Buenos Aires city and surrounding areas, Argentina. The International Information & Library Review, 38; 1-14.
34. Bavakutty, M. (2001). Kerala. In. Library and Information Services in Indian States and Union Territories edited by P.B.Mangla, et.al. New Delhi: Shipra.
35. Bayram, H. (2010). Bilgi toplumu ve bilgi yönetimi, Etap Yayýnevi, Ýstanbul.
36. Barua, B. P. (1994). Raja Ram Mohan Roy Library Foundation and Library Movement in India. Presented at 39th All India Library Conference. Delhi: Indian Library Association.
37. Basil Enemute Iwhiwhu, Patience Obotayire Okorodudu (2012), Library Philosophy and Practice 2012
38. Batt, C. (1999). 'I have seen the future and IT works' Library Review 48 (1) pp 11-17.
39. Beals, Jennifer Benedetto (Winter 2006). Assessing library collections using Brief Test methodology. Electronic Journal of Academic and Special Librarianship, 7(3).
40. Béjoint, Henri (2000). Modern Lexicography. Oxford University Press.
41. Ben White (2012). Guaranteeing Access to Knowledge: The Role of Libraries. WIPO Magazine.
42. Bengtson, B. and J.S. Hill (1990). Classification of Library Materials. New York: Schuman Neal. Berthon, H & Webb, C. (2000). 'The moving frontier: archiving, preservation and tomorrow's digital heritage', Books and bytes: Conference Proceedings: 2000 VALA Biennial Conference and Exhibition, VALA, Melbourne.
43. Bert Roest (1997). "Compilation as Theme and Praxis in Franciscan Universal Chronicles". In
44. Bergenholtz, H., Nielsen, S., Tarp, S., ed. (2009). Lexicography at a Crossroads: Dictionaries and Encyclopedias Today, Lexicographical Tools Tomorrow. Peter Lang.
45. Bettina H. Wolff (1979). Finding the Library's Role in an Information Society, Public Library Quarterly, Volume 1, Issue 2.
46. Beulah Muller. Challenges Facing Special Libraries In South Africa.
47. Bhaskar Raj, A.S. (1995). The barcode Technology and Its application. Electronics For You.
48. Bhatt, R.K. (2001). Delhi. In. Library and Information Services in

Indian States and Union Territories edited by P.B.Mangla, et.al. New Delhi: Shipra.

49. Bhattacharjee, R. (1999). Role of Raja Rammohan Roy Library Foundation in the promotion of public library movement in India.Herald of Library Science 38 (1-2).

50. Bisa berbagi itu indah dan mulia. Advantages and disadvantages of the difference physical forms of the library catalogue. http://widodo.staff.uns.ac.id/

51. Bischoff, Bernhard (1990). Latin palaeography antiquity and the Middle Ages. Dáibhí ó Cróinin. Cambridge: Cambridge University Press.

52. Blair, Gerard M. (2009). "Presentation Skills." Basic Management Skills. University of Edinburgh, School of Engineering. Web. 06 May 2009. <http://www.see.ed.ac.uk/~gerard/Management/art1.html>.

53. Blom, Phillip (2004). Enlightening the World: Encyclopédie, the Book that Changed the Course of History. New York; Basingstoke: Palgrave Macmillan.,99-105

54. Bob, M. L. (1982). The case for quality book selection, Library Journal, 107, 1707-1710.

55. Bobal, Alison M., Mellinger, Margaret, Avery, Bonnie E. (2008). Collection assessment and new academic programs. Collection Management, 33(4), 288-301.

56. Bolner, Myrtle S. and Gayle A. Poirier. The Research Process: Books and Beyond, 2nd ed. Dubuque, IA:Kendall/ Hunt Publishing Company, 2001.

57. "Books of the world, stand up and be counted! All 129,864,880 of you.". Inside Google Books. August 5, 2010. http://booksearch.blogspot.com/2010/08/books-of-world-stand-up-and-be-counted.html

58. "Book". Dictionary.com.

59. Bureau of Public Personnel Administration. (1927). Proposed classification and compensation plans for library positions: Report of the Bureau of Public Personnel Administration to the Committee on the Classification of Library Personnel of the American Library Association. Washington, DC: Author.

60. Bush, V. (1945). As we may think. Atlantic Monthly (July)

61. Carp, Douglas, Donald Leslie and James Lichtenberg. 2004. Tiny trackers: use of RFID by libraries and booksellers. Newsletter on Intellectual Freedom 53(5): 169, 206-215.

62. Cataloging Policy & Support Office, Library of Congress. Descriptive Cataloging Manual : Z1 : Name and series authority records. http://www.loc.gov/catdir/pcc/naco/z1.pdf

63. Cataloger's Desktop. http://desktop.loc.gov/

64. Cathro, W 1999, 'Digital libraries: a National Library perspective' in Strategies for the next millennium: proceedings of the ninth Australasian Information Online & On Disc Conference and Exhibition, ALIA, Sydney. http://www.nla.gov.au/nla/staffpaper/cathro4.html

65. Chakraborty A. R. and Chakraboty B. (1978). Giants in library and information science, Annals of Library Science and Documentation, 29, 52-54.

66. Chambers' Cyclopaedia, 1728, with the 1753 supplement.

67. Chan, Lois Mai (1994). Cataloging and Classification: An Introduction. 2nd ed. New York: McGraw-Hill.

68. Chandok, Seema (1998). Application of Barcode Technology in Libraries. Library Science Slant with Documentation.V.35, N.4, p.247-50.

69. Changing Roles of Academic and Research Libraries (2007). http://www.ala.org/acrl/issues/value

70. Chatterjee, Amitabha (2001). West Bengal. In. Library and Information Services in Indian States and Union Territories edited by P.B.Mangla, et.al. New Delhi: Shipra.

71. Chatoopadhyay, D. P. (1998). Chattopadhyay Committee on NPLIS.CLIS Observer 15(1-2), 12.

72. Chattopadhyay, Anjana (2001). Bihar and Jarkhand. In. Library and Information Services in Indian States and Union Territories edited by P.B.Mangla, et.al. New Delhi: Shipra.

73. Chan, Lois Mai (2007), Cataloging and classification (Third edition ed.), The Scarecrow Press, Inc., p. 321.

74. Chen, Kristine (October 2010). Given them what they want. School Library Journal, 56(10), 29.

75. Chindlund, J., Chochrek, D., Scanlan, J. et al. (2005). The future of librarians in the work-force: Business librarians. Institute of Museum and Library Services (IMLS) White Paper, 15 December.

76. Chinwe M.T. Nwezeh (2011). Students Use of Academic Libraries in Nigeria: A Case of Obafemi Awolowo University Library, Ile-Ife. Library Philosophy and Practice 2011.

77. Christie Hoerneman, Wed, 12/01/2010 - 15:44. Features of the Online Encyclopedia Britannica. http://www.librarypoint.org/

78. Clack, Doris H. Authority control: principles, applications, and instructions. Chicago: American Library Association, 1990.

79. Clack, Doris H., ed. (1980). The Making of a Code: The Issues Underlying AACR2. Chicago: American Library Association.

80. Clark, S. O. (2000). Fundamentals of library science. Warri: COEA puplishers.

81. Clarke, Rachel Ivy (May 7, 2013). "Picturing Classification The Evolution and Use of Alternative Classification in Dutch Public Libraries". Public Libraries Online.

82. Collection Development & Management by Irwin and Albee (2012)

83. Collison, Robert Lewis (1966). Encyclopaedias: Their History Through out the Ages (2nd ed.). New York, London: Hafner. OCLC

84. Collins, Donald, Diane Catlett, and Bobbie Collins (1994). Libraries and Research: A Practical Approach, 3rd ed. Dubuque. IA: Kendall/ Hunt Publishing Company.

85. Colish, Marcia L. (1997). Medieval Foundations of the Western Intellectual Tradition, 400-1400 Yale University Press, New Haven and London.

86. Colon classification - ISKO. www.iskoi.org/doc/colon.htm

87. Colon Classification: A Requiem - DRDO Publications

88. Colon Classification (6th Edition) by Dr. S.R. Ranganathan, Delhi: Ess Ess Publications.

89. Colon classification (CC) from 1928 to 1987. Publications.drdo.gov.in/ ojs/index.php/djlit/article/download/.../2839 by MP Satija - ý2013 –Jul 22, 2013 -

90. "Colon Classification." Encyclopædia Britannica. 2003. Encyclopædia Britannica Online. 27 Jul, 2003 http://search.eb.com/ eb/article?eu=25223.

91. Comaromi, John P. (1976), The eighteen editions of the Dewey Decimal Classification, Albany, N.Y: Forest Press Division, Lake Placid Education Foundation, p. 43, ISBN 0-910608-17-2

92. Committee on Culture, Youth, Education and the Media to the European Parliament titled 'Report on the Role of Libraries in the Modern World' http://www.publiclibraries.fi/publications/ report.htm

93. Concise Encyclopedia (1997). Dorling Kindersly Limited.

94. Corsaro, James. "Control of Cartographic Materials in Archives."

95. Council of Australian State Libraries submission: http:// www.aph.gov.au/house/committee/laca/digitalagenda/ Sub10councilstatelib.pdf

96. Cowie, Anthony Paul (2009). The Oxford History of English Lexicography, Volume I. Oxford University Press. p. 22.

97. Coyle, Karen (2011). "MARC21 as Data: A Start". The Code4Lib Journal (14).

98. Coyle, Karen (2005). Management of RFID in libraries. The Journal of Academic Librarianship 31(5): 486-489.

99. Crawford and Gorman (1995) provide a hypothetical example of digitising the New Yorker and PC Magazine to 'prove' the

impracticality of universal conversion of printed resources into digital resources.

100. Crawford, W. (1998). 'Paper persists: why physical library collections still matter', Online, vol22, no1, pp42-44, 46-48. http://www.onlineinc.com/onlinemag/OL1998/crawford1.html
101. Crawford, W & Gorman, M. (1995). Future libraries: dreams madness & reality, American Library Association, Chicago.
102. Creth, S. D. (1989). Personnel issues for academic librarians: A review and perspectives for the future. College & Research Libraries, 50(2), 144-152.
103. "Countries with libraries that use the DDC". OCLC. 2009.
104. Cunnington, D. (1998). 'Building better gateways: Buddy at the University of Melbourne Library', Robots to knowbots: the wider automation agenda: Conference Proceedings: 1998 VALA Biennial Conference and Exhibition, VALA, Melbourne. http://www.vala.org.au/valaweb/num322.pdf
105. "Cutter Classification". Forbes Library Subject Guides. Forbes Library.
106. What Are Card Catalogs? http://www.ehow.com/info_8082360_card-catalogs.html
107. "Cyclopædia". Collier's New Encyclopedia. 1921.
108. "Cyclopædia". The American Cyclopædia. 1879." encyclopaedia" (online). Oxford English Dictionary http://www.oed.com/search?q=encyclopaedia
109. Darnton, Robert (1979). The business of enlightenment : a publishing history of the Encyclopédie, 1775–1800. Cambridge: Belknap Press.
110. Darzentas, J 1999, 'Sharing metadata: enabling online information provision', OCLC Systems & Services 15 (4) pp172-178.
111. Das, V.K. (2001). Arunachal Pradesh. In. Library and Information Services in Indian States and Union Territories edited by P.B.Mangla, et.al. New Delhi: Shipra.
112. Dasgupta A. (2007). Library staff and Ranganathan's Five laws. IASLIC Bulletin , 52 (4), 195-204.
113. David Baker, Wendy Evans. Libraries and Society: Role, Responsibility and Future in an Age of Change.
114. Datta, B K. (2004). Libraries and Librarianship. Quoted by Jashu Patel and Krishan Kumar In. Libraries and Librarianship in India. Westport: Greenwood.
115. De expetendis et fugiendis rebus – First Renaissance encyclopedia. http://www.dm.unipi.it/~tucci/index.html
116. Dewey, M. (1876). 'The profession', American Library Journal, vol1, September 30, p5-6, quoted in Rice-Livey, M. & Racine, J. 1997. 'The role of academic librarians in the era of information technology' Journal of Academic Librarianship 23 (1) p32.

117. Denis Diderot and Jean le Rond d'Alembert Encyclopédie. University of Michigan Library: Scholarly Publishing Office and DLXS.
118. Dewey, Melvil (1876), Classification and Subject Index for Cataloguing and Arranging the Books and Pamphlets of a Library (Project Gutenberg eBook). http://www.gutenberg.org/files/12513/12513-h/12513-h.htm
119. "Dewey Web Services". OCLC. http://www.oclc.org/en-US/dewey/webservices.html
120. "Dewey Decimal Classification/Linked Data". OCLC. http://dewey.info/
121. "Dewey Services". OCLC. 2009. http://www.oclc.org/dewey/default.htm
122. Dewey, Melvil (1930). Speech given to the Lake Placid Education Foundation (LPEF) Trustees on July 28.
123. Dewey, Melvil (1920). Decimal Classification Beginning. Library Journal, Vol. 45, February 15, pp. 151-152.
124. Dewey Decimal Classification. 20th. ed. 1989. Albany: Forest Press.
125. Dewey, Melvil (1876), A Classification and Subject Index for Cataloguing and Arranging the Books and Pamphlets of a .., [s.n.]. http://www.worldcat.org/oclc/78870163
126. "Dewey decimal classification and relative index (1971)". Internet Archive.
127. Dewey Decimal Classification and Fundamental Laws Governing Knowledge by Moya K. Mason. DESIDOC Bulletin of Information Technology 17 (6) (November 1997) (Special Issue on Digital Libraries).
128. Dictionary.com Unabridged Based on the Random House Dictionary, © Random House, Inc. 2014. http://dictionary.reference.com/cite.html)
129. Digital Library (1995). Communication of the ACM. (April).
130. Digital encyclopedias put the world at your fingertips. http://reviews.cnet.com/1990-3118_7-6378998-1.html
131. Digital Library. (2008). Wikipedia. http://en.wikipedia. org/wiki/Digital_library
132. Dr. Jyotsna Gupta. Types Of Libraries. Course Material.
133. Drabenstott, Karen M. (1994). Analytical review of the library of the future, Washington, DC: Council Library Resources.
134. Dugdale, C. (1999). 'Managing electronic reserves: new opportunities and new roles for academic librarians?' Librarian Career Development 7 (12) pp150-163.
135. Dutta, Bimal Kumar (1970).Libraries and librarianship of Ancient and Medieval India. Delhi: Atma Ram.

136. Ehrenberg, Ralph E. (1982). Archives & Manuscripts: Maps and Architectural Drawings. Chicago: Society of American Archivists..
137. Encyclopædia Americana, 1851, Francis Lieber ed. Boston: Mussey & Co. at the University of Michigan Making of America site
138. Encyclopædia Britannica, articles and illustrations from 9th ed., 1875–89, and 10th ed., 1902–03.
139. Encyclopedia Britannica http://www.britannica.com/
140. Encyclopedia.com. http://encyclopedia.com/
141. Encyclopedia at Encyclopædia Britannica
142. "encyclopaedia", Chambers Reference Online; "encyclopaedia". AskOxford.
143. "encyclopaedia", Bartleby.com; "Encyclopaedia", Merriam Webster.
144. "Encyclopaedia". Encyclopædia Britannica.
145. Encyclopedia – Diderot's article on the Encyclopedia from the original Encyclopédie.
146. Encyclopedias online University of Wisconsin – Stout listing by category. http://web.archive.org/web/20080112134535/http:/www.uwstout.edu/lib/reference/encycl.htm
147. "Encyclopædia". Encyclopedia Americana. 1920.
148. "Encyclopædia". The New Student's Reference Work. 1914.
149. "Encyclopaedia". Encyclopædia Britannica (11th ed.). 1911.
150. "Encyclopædia". The Nuttall Encyclopædia. 1907.
151. "Encyclopædia". New International Encyclopedia. 1905.
152. "Encyclopedia.". Archived from the original on 2007-08-03. Glossary of Library Terms. Riverside City College, Digital Library/Learning Resource Center.
153. http://web.archive.org/web/20070803182506/http:/library.rcc.edu/riverside/glossaryoflibraryterms. htm#e
154. "Encyclopaedia". Encyclopædia Britannica. http://www.britannica.com/EBchecked/topic/186603/encyclopaedia
155. "Encyclopedia". Dictionary of the Middle Ages.
156. Quintilian, Institutio Oratoria, 1.10.1, at Perseus project. http://www.perseus.tufts.edu/hopper/text?
157. Henry George Liddell, Robert Scott, A Greek–English Lexicon, at Perseus project. http://www.perseus.tufts. edu/hopper/text?doc=Perseus%3Atext% 3A1999.04. 0057% 3Aentry%3De%29gku%2Fklios
158. Errors and inconsistencies in several printed reference books and encyclopedias. http://kennedy.byu.edu/staff/peterson/multivol/multibooks.html
159. Erwin, Emmit and Christian Kern (2005). Radio frequency identification in libraries. Australaisian Public Libraries and

Information Services 18(1) (March): 20-28.

160. Espranza, S. M. (1999).Public Libraries and Academic Libraries. Jaipur: Printwell.

161. Evaluation of Information Sources tutorial. http://www.lib.lsu.edu/instruction/evaluation/evaluation00.html

162. Evans, Linda J., and Maureen O'Brien Will (1988). MARC for Archival Visual Materials: A Compendium of Practice. Chicago: Chicago Historical Society.

163. Evans, G.E. and S. Heft, (1994). Introduction to Technical Services. Englewood, Co.: Libraries Unlimited.

164. Evans, G. Edward & Saponaro, Margaret Zarnosky (2012). Collection Management Basics. Libraries Unlimited.

165. Fayen, Emily Gallup(1983). The online catalog : improving public access to library materials. White Plains, NY : Knowledge Industry Publication,.

166. Fandino, Marta (2008). "UDC or DDC: a note about the suitable choice for the National Library of Liechtenstein". Extensions and Corrections to the UDC. http://www.ukrbook.net/UDC_n/st_16.pdf

167. "Features - Law Librarians and their Evolving Role as Information Technology Managers | LLRX.com." LLRX.com | Legal and Technology Articles and Resources for Librarians, Lawyers and Law Firms. Web. 05 May 2009. <http://www.llrx.com/features/evolving.htm>.

168. Fialkoff, F. (2005). Balancing act. Library Journal, 130, 8.

169. Fister, B. (1992). The research process of undergraduate students. Journal of Academic Librarianship 18 (3):163-169.

170. Fister, Barbara (October 1, 2009). "In the search for better browsability, librarians are putting Dewey in a different class". The Library Journal.

171. Foo, S., Chaudhry, A.S., Majid, S.M., & Logan, E. (2002). Academic libraries in transition: Challenges ahead. Proc. World Library Summit, Keynote address: Academic Library Seminar, National Library Board, Singapore, April 22-26.

172. Fox, Michael J. "Descriptive Cataloging for Archival Materials."

173. Fox, E.A. (1999). The Digital Libraries Initiative: Update and discussion. Bulletin of the America Society for Information Science 26 (1): October/November.

174. Frey, T. (2007). The future of libraries: Beginning the great transformation. www.davinci-institute.com/page.php

175. Schachter, D. (2006). The learning organization. Information Outlook, 10(12): 8–9.

176. "10 tips for time management in a multitasking world." Web log post. Penelope Trunk's Brazen Careerist. 10 Dec. 2006. Web. 9 May 2009.

<http://blog.penelopetrunk.com/2006/12/10/10-tips-for-time-management-in-a-multitasking-world/

177. Gardner, Richard K. (1981). Library collections: their origins, selection, and development. McGraw Hill.
178. Gallimore, A. (1999). 'Managing the networked public library' Library Management 20 (7) pp 384-392.
179. Garrod, P & Sidgreaves, I. (1998). Skills for new information professionals: the SKIP Project, LITC, London. http://www.ukoln.ac.uk/services/elib/papers/other/skip/
180. Glassel, Aimee (1998). "Was Ranganathan a Yahoo!?"" Internet Scout. March.
181. Gopal, K. (2000). Digital libraries in electronic information era. New Delhi: Author Press.
182. Gordon Dunsire, Chris Pinder, (1991). "Dynix, automation and development at Napier Polytechnic", Program: electronic library and information systems, Vol. 25 Iss: 2, pp.91 - 103
183. Gordon, Moran (2001). "Ethics, strengths and values: a review article", Journal of Librarianship and Information Science, 33, no. 2: 98-101.
184. Gordon-Till, Jonathan (2002). "Ethics: the professional challenge", Business Information Review, 19,: 46-54.
185. Gorman, M. (1991). 'The academic library in the year 2001: dream or nightmare or something in between?' Journal of Academic Librarianship 17 (1) March, pp 4-6.
186. Gorman, Michael (1989). The Concise AACR2, 1988 Revision. Chicago: American Library Association.
187. Graham, P. (1995). 'Requirements for the digital research library' College & Research Libraries 56, July pp 331-339.
188. Grantham, C. (2007). Virtual library: e-ssential. ACCESS. 21 (3) 5-8.
189. Greenstein, D.I., & Thorin, S.E. (2002). The digital library: A biography. Digital Library Federation.
190. Gregory, Vicki L. (2011). Collection Development and Management for 21st Century Collections. Neal-Schuman Publishers, Inc.
191. Gunn, H. (2002). Virtual Libraries Supporting Student Learning.
192. Haines, Helen Elizabeth (1935). Living with Books: The Art of Book Selection. Columbia University Press.
193. Haley, Daniel Joseph (2010). The Use of Print Materials in the Internet Age: A Comparative Study of Academic Library Circulation Patterns. Dissertation, University of California Los Angeles.
194. Harbour, Denise (March/April 2002). Collection mapping. Book Report, 20(5), 6-10.
195. Hannabuss, Stuart (2008). "Book Review: Librarianship and Human Rights: a Twenty-First Century Guide by Toni Samek 2007, Oxford: Chandos Publishing", Journal of Librarianship and Information

Science, 40, no.1, 59-60.

196. Hanson, James C. M. (1908). Catalog rules; author and title entries (Chicago: American Library Association.
197. Hartmann, R. R. K.; James, Gregory; Gregory James (1998). Dictionary of Lexicography. Routledge. p. 48.
198. Hartmann, R. R. K.; James, Gregory; Gregory James (1998). "Encyclopedic definition". Dictionary of Lexicography (Routledge): 48–49.
199. Hastings, K & Tennant, R. (1996). 'How to build a digital librarian' D-Lib Magazine November. http://www.dlib.org/dlib/november96/ucb/11hastings. html
200. Hawkins, B. L. (1998). 'The unsustainability of traditional libraries' in New thinking on higher education: creating a context for change, ed J Meyerson, Anker Publishing, Bolton, pp 148-177.
201. Haycock, K., & Sheldon, B. E. (Eds.). (2008). The portable MLIS. Westport, CT: Libraries Unlimited.
202. Henry George Liddell, Robert Scott, A Greek–English Lexicon, at Perseus project http://www.accesswave. ca/~hgunn/special/papers/virlib/print.html
203. Hensen, Steven L. (1986). "The Use of Standards in the Application of the MARC Format." American Archivist 49, 31-40.
204. Hensen, Steven L. (1988). "Squaring the Circle: The Reformation of Archival Description in AACR2." Library Trends 36, 539-552.
205. Hensen, Steven L. (1993). "The First Shall Be First: APPM and Its Impact on American Archival Description." Archivaria 35, 64-70.
206. Hensen, Steven L. (1988). "Squaring the Circle: The Reformation of Archival Description in AACR2." Library Trends 36, 539-552.
207. Hensen, Steven L. (1986). "The Use of Standards in the Application of the MARC Format." American Archivist 49: 31-40.
208. Hoffert, Barbara (2007). Who's selecting now? As Phoenix Public Library boldy passes on selection responsibilities to its vendors, some libraries follow - and others dig in. Library Journal, 40.
209. http://searchdatacenter.techtarget.com/sDefinition/0,,sid80_gci211604,00.html
210. http://eduscapes.com/collection/4.htm
211. http://www.mit.gov.in
212. http://eduscapes.com/collection/3.htm
213. http://www.lib.uchicago.edu/e/net/types.html
214. http://library.eb.com.proxy.crrl.org/
215. http://web4lib.org/archive/1997-October/022268.html
216. http://www.thefreedictionary.com/_/search.aspx? charset=utf-8&SearchBy=0&Word=library&tab= 1&Search=Search&TFDBy=0

217. http://www.library.ca.gov/about/cslgen1.html
218. http://web.uri.edu/library/collections/collection management and policies
219. http://www.is.uwa.edu.au/information-resources/collections/management
220. http://uri.libguides.com/cml
221. http://www.aiim.org/Research-and-Publications/Glossary
222. http;//www.nlindia.org/history.html
223. http;//hkmsl.gov.in/glance.htm
224. http;//razalibrary.gov.in/index.asp
225. http;//www.sarasvatimahallibrary.tn.nic.in/library/library.html
226. http://digitalcommons.unl.edu/libphilprac/747/
227. http://www.nationallibrary.gov.in/nat_lib_stat/modernisation.html
228. http://www.nationallibrary.gov.in/nat_lib_stat/services.html
229. http://www.nationallibrary.gov.in/nat_lib_stat/index2.html
230. http://www.nationallibrary.gov.in/nat_lib_stat/history.html
231. http://www.nationallibrary.gov.in/nat_lib_stat/collection.html
232. http://www.ncip.info/index.html
233. http://www.loc.gov/marc/overview.html
234. http://www.iso.org/iso/en/ISOOnline.frontpage
235. http://msdn.microsoft.com/msdnmag/issues/04/05/ClickOnce/
236. http://www.techterms.com/definition/server
237. http://www.techterms.com/definition/computer
238. http://www.nairaland.com/41492/advantages-desktop-computers-versus-laptops#990302
239. http://library.columbia.edu/locauons/dhc.html
240. http://ecomputernotes.com/Computernetworking notes/computer-network/explain-about-modem
241. http://www.differencebetween.net/object/difference-between-wifi-modem-and-wifi-router/
242. http://www.orbit-computer-solutions.com/Switches. php
243. http://switchpipe.org/detailed-review-describing-detail.html
244. http://www.orbit-computer-solutions.com/Routers. php
245. http://compnetworking.about.com/cs/wireless/g/bldef_ap.htm
246. http://www.library.illinois.edu/export/ugl/about/dewey.html
247. http://lcweb.loc.gov/faq/
248. http://www.oclc.org/dewey/versions/webdewey.en. html
249. http://www.oclc.org/dewey/versions/print.en.html
250. http://www.oclc.org/dewey/versions/abridged. en.html
251. http://www.oclc.org/content/dam/oclc/dewey/versions/print/intro.pdf

252. http://www.oclc.org/dewey/resources/summaries. en.html#hist
253. http://www.oclc.org/dewey/news.en.html
254. http://kelschindexing.com/colonclassification.html
255. http://www.isibang.ac.in/~library/portal/Pages/chp1.pdf
256. http://skil.stanford.edu/module1/index.html
257. http://www.clark.edu/Library/iris/find/library_ catalog/ library_catalog_p2.shtml
258. https://www.lib.odu.edu/genedinfolit/1infobasics/ subjective_vs_objective.html
259. http://www.academicinfo.net/digital.html
260. http://home.istar.ca/~obyrne/
261. http://www.loc.gov/rr/elecdesk.html
262. http://www.ipl.org/IPLBrowse/GetSubject?vid=13& tid=6996& parent=0
263. http://www.awesomelibrary.org/Library/Reference_ and_ Periodicals/Reference_and_Periodicals.html
264. http://ipl2server-1.ipl.org/IPLBrowse/GetSubject? vid=13&tid= 6996&parent=0
265. http://www.ipl.org/div/aplus/bibliography.htm# Bopp%201995
266. http://www.aquinas.edu/library/ge103/pdf/Typesof Reference Sources.pdf
267. http://www.thomasnet.com/index.html
268. http://www.lib.lsu.edu/gov/index.html
269. http://www.scholarly-societies.org/
270. http://www.merriam-webster.com/
271. http://www.library.mun.ca/guides/howto/index.php
272. http://www.webology.org/2004/v1n2/a8.html
273. http://www.ipl.org/div/aplus/bibliography.htm# Bopp%201995
274. http://www.library.yorku.ca/eresolver/?id=151
275. http://acsweb2.ucis.dal.ca/HBICDB/english/cbti.html
276. http://www.unige.ch/biblio/ses/IFLA/rol_lib_ 030526. pdf#page=2&zoom=auto,0,426
277. http://www.ala.org/ala/mgrps/divs/rusa/awards/outstanding referencesources/index.cfm
278. http://www.ala.org/alcts/mgrps
279. http://www.actuaries.org.uk/research-and-resources/pages/ library-services
280. http://www.abebooks.com/
281. https://www.lib.odu.edu/genedinfolit/1infobasics/subjective_vs_ objective.html
282. http://www.ipl.org/div/aplus/bibliography.htm# Bopp%201995

283. http://www.oed.com/
284. http://global.oup.com/
285. http://library.dce.edu/pdf/OPAC.pdf
286. http://www.aquinas.edu/library/ge103/pdf/Typesof Reference Sources.pdf
287. http://dictionary.cambridge.org/dictionary/learner-english
288. http://OneLook.com
289. http://www.wordcentral.com/
290. http://www.infovisual.info/
291. http://translate.reference.com/
292. http://phrontistery.info/http://schools.natlib. govt.nz/school-libraries
293. http://www.unesco.org/webworld/libraries/manifestos/school_manifesto.html
294. http://www.library.fgcu.com
295. http://www.historylearningsite.co.uk/research.htm
296. http://www.historylearningsite.co.uk/secondary_ sources.htm
297. http://www.sccollege.edu/Library/Pages/guides tutorials.aspx
298. http://polaris.gseis.ucla.edu/gleazer/462_readings/mitchell.PDF
299. http://www2.curriculum.edu.au/scis/connections/issue_79_2011/articles/dewey_decimal_ classification_-_edition_23.html
300. http://www.sccollege.edu/Library/Pages/guides tutorials.aspx
301. Hunter Eric J. and KGB Bakewell (1983). Cataloguing. 2nd ed. London : Clive Bingley.
302. Iannella, R. (1998). 'Mostly metadata: a bit of smarter technology', Robots to knowbots: the wider information agenda: Conference Proceedings, 1998 http://www.vala.org.au/valaweb/num8011.pdf
303. IFLA UBCIM Working Group on Minimal Level Authority Records and ISADN. Mandatory Data Elements for Internationally Shared Resource Authority Records. http://archive.ifla.org/VI/3/p1996-2/mlar.htm
304. IFLA Working Group on GARE Revision Guidelines for authority records and references 2nd ed. 2001.
305. Important Notice: MSN Encarta to be Discontinued. MSN Encarta. http://encarta.msn.com/guide_page_ FAQ/FAQ.html
306. India. Ministry of Education (1961).Report of Advisory Committee for Libraries. New Delhi: Manager.
307. Infoplease.com. http://www.infoplease.com/
308. International Federation Of Library Associations And Institutions (Ifla) World Summit On The Information Society Information For All: The Key Role of Libraries in the Information Society Report prepared

for: LIBRARIES @ the HEART of the Information Society Prelude to the World Summit www.ifla.org

309. IFLA/UNESCO (2001). The Public Library Service; IFLA/UNESCO Guideline for Development. Munchen: K G Saur.
310. Ijari, S.R. (2001). Karnataka. In. Library and Information Services in Indian States and Union Territories edited by P.B.Mangla, et.al. New Delhi: Shipra.
311. ILA. (2004). Indian Library Association, Sixty-third Annual report. Quoted by Jashu Patel and Krishan Kumar In. Libraries and Librarianship in India. Westport: Greenwood Press. p.182.
312. International Federation of Library Association's (IFLA) Manifesto. http://www.unesco.org/webworld/libraries/manifestos/school_manifesto.html
313. Internet Accuracy Project – Biographical errors in encyclopedias and almanacs. http://www.accuracy project.org/cbe-errors-books.html
314. Introduction to the Dewey Decimal Classification . Hermann Memorial Library / Sullivan County Community College Information Literacy Guides
315. Ithaka S+R Library Survey 2010: Insights from U.S. Academic Library Directors.
316. Jagdish, M. (1979).Histories of Libraries and Librarianship in Modern India since 1850. Delhi: Atma Ram.
317. Jain M K and Jain N K (2007). Five laws of library science, DLIBCOM, 2 (8-9) 20-22.
318. Jayaswal, P.K. (1997). Dr. B P Barua: An assessment of his Role in Institutional- Building. In. Public Libraries in Developing Countries: Status and Trends edited by P K Mahapatra and V K Thomas. New Delhi: Vikas.
319. Jebaraj, D., & Deivasigamani, M. (2003). The electronic library: An Indian scenario. Library Philosophy and Practice 5 (2). http://unllib.unl.edu/LPP/jebaraj.html
320. Jill Powell (2014). Books & Bytes: Librarians as Information Managers.
321. J Mitchell - ý2001 Relationships in the Dewey Decimal Classification.
322. JSC (Joint Steering Committee for Development of RDA) http://www.rda-jsc.org/
323. Joachim, Martin D., Ed. Historical Aspects of Cataloging and Classification, Volume 2 The Haworth Information Press, Binghamton, NY, 2003, p. 460.
324. Joseph T. Tennis. Function, Purpose, Predication, and Context of Information Organization Frameworks.
325. Juceviciene, P, Tautkeviciene, G. (2002). Triangle of Competences" as one of the basic characteristics of the university library learning environment. European Conference on Educational Research,

Lisbon, 11-14 September 2002 / European Educational Research Association. Lisbon, 2002, p. 1-9. Access via Education-line: http://www.leeds.ac.uk/educol/documents/00002343.htm

326. K. Bhattacharyya, (1972) "Some General Characteristics Of Special Libraries In Science And Technology In The UK", Journal Of Documentation, Vol. 28 Iss: 3, pp.214 – 232

327. Kafker, Frank A., ed. (1981). Notable encyclopedias of the seventeenth and eighteenth centuries: nine predecessors of the Encyclopédie. Oxford: Voltaire Foundation.

328. Kafker, Frank A., ed. (1994). Notable encyclopedias of the late eighteenth century: eleven successors of the Encyclopédie. Oxford: Voltaire Foundation.

329. Kakai M., Ikoja-Odongo, R., & Kigongo-Bukenya, I. M. N. (2004). A study of the information seeking behavior of undergraduate students of Makerere University, Uganda. World Libraries 14(1): 1-24.

330. Kaplan, Tali Balas. "Done with Dewey". ALSC.

331. Karen Coyle, "Management of RFID in Libraries" , Preprint version of article published in the Journal of Academic Librarianship, v. 31, n. 5, pp. 486-489

332. Karn, Sanjay Klumar, et.al. (2006). Status of State (Public) Libraries in Jharkhand; An Analytical Study. ILA Bulletin. XLII(2), Apr.-Jun.. p.25.

333. Kawatra, P.S. (2000). Textbook of information science. New Delhi: APH Publishing Corporation.

334. Kelley, Michael (September 15, 2012). A toolkit for taking stock; libraries leverage new metrics driven by data from collectionHQ. Library Journal, 137(15), 18.

335. Khanna, J K (1987). Library and Society. New Delhi: Ess Ess Publications. 89

336. Khanna, J.K. (1986). Colon Classification. New Delhi, India: Ess Ess Publications.

337. Khursid, Anis (1972). Growth of Libraries in India. Quoted by Jashu Patel and Krishan Kumar. In. Libraries and Librarianship in India. Westport: Greenwood, 2004, p.6.

338. Kinds of Card Catalogues By Chris Joseph, eHow Contributor .

339. Klemperer, K & Chapman, S. (1997). 'Digital libraries: a selected resource guide' Information Technology & Libraries 16 (3). http://www.lita.org/ital/1603_klemperer.htm

340. Kneale, R. (2009). You don't look like a librarian! Shattering stereotypes and creating positive new images in the Internet age. Medford, NJ: Information Today, Inc.

341. Koehler, Wallace, Jitka Hurych, Wanda Dole, and Joanna Wall (2000). "Ethical Values of Information and Library Professionals – An

Expanded Analysis." International Information & Library Review 32 (3/4), 485–506.

342. Krajewski, Markus (2011), Paper machines, Cambridge, Mass: MIT Press
343. Kumar, P.S.G. (1987). Introduction to Colon Classification, Edition 7. Nagpur, India: Dattsons.
344. Kumar, P.Y.Rajendra (2007). Network of Rural Libraries in Karnataka. Proceedings of National Seminar on Legislation Based Rural Library service in India. Organized byRanganathan Society for Book Culture, Library and Information Studies, North East Chapter on 8-10 Sept., 2007 at Imphal. pp.117.
345. Kumbar, B. D. (2005). Growth and Development of Public Library System in India with Special Reference to Karnataka. http://www.nigd.org/libraries/mumbai/reports/article-4.pdf.
346. Kurzeme, I 'Technology and dust mites' The Australian Library Journal, May 1997, pp147-153.
347. Lakshmi, R., Suma, P. (1998). A step towards developing a digital library. Library Science with a Slant to Information Studies 35 (1).
348. "Latest versions". OCLC. http://www.oclc.org/dewey/versions.en.html
349. Law, D. (2009). Waiting for the (digital) barbarians. Information Outlook, 13(8), 15–18.
350. Leila Avrin. Scribes, Script and Books.
351. Lerner, Fred (2009). Story of Libraries: From the Invention ofWriting to the Computer Age Continuum International Publishing Group, New York, 2009, p. 48.
352. Library Catalog History and Function. http://consortiumlibrary.org/ls101/unit4/slide02/
353. Library classification. http://www.thefreedictionary. com/library+classification
354. Library Classification: Intro, Need and Purpose. http://www.skuastkashmir.ac.in/index.php
355. Library classification. http://www.britannica.com/EBchecked/topic/339461/library-classification
356. Library of Congress. http://www.loc.gov/index.html
357. Library Support Staff in an Age of Change: Utilization, Role Definition, and Status. http://www.ala.org/offices/hrdr/librarysupportstaff/library_support_staff_in_an_age_of_change
358. Lim, E. (1996). 'The virtual library meets the virtual campus: strategies for the 21st century' in Electronic dream? Virtual nightmare: the reality for libraries.
359. Lim, E. (1998). 'Building a virtual national serials collection using

the MEADS system' Australian Academic and Research Libraries, 29 (4) December, pp165-175.
360. Littlefield, J. (2008). A cataloguing carol. http://www.librarystudentjournal.org/index
361. Loertscher, David & Wimberley, Laura H. (2010). Collection Development Using the Collection Mapping Technique: A Guide for Librarians. Hi Willow Research and Publishing.
362. Luo, Michael (2003). "Where Did Dewey File Those Law Books?". The New York Times.
363. Luzeckyj, A. (1999). The vital link: library staffing in the 21st century.
364. Lynch, C & Garcia-Molina, H. (1995). Interoperability, scaling, and the Digital Libraries Research agenda. http://www-diglib.stanford.edu/diglib/pub/reports/iita-dlw/main.html
365. Lynch, C.A. (1994). The integrity of digital information: Mechanism and definitional issues. Silver Spring, MD: ASIS.
366. M. Buckland. (1992). Redesigning Library Services: A Manifesto. Chicago: American Library Association; Internet edition 1997 at http://sunsite.berkeley.edu/Literature/Library/Redesigning/html.html.
367. Majumder, Apurba Jyoti; Gautam Sarma (2007). Webdewey: The Dewey Decimal Classification in The Web. ISI Bangalore Planner 2007.
368. Malwad, N.M., et al. (Ed.) (1996). Digital libraries: Dynamic storehouse of digitalized information. New Delhi, New Age International.
369. "Managerial skills/competencies." Get Satisfaction - People-Powered Customer Service. Web. 10 May 2009. <http://getsatisfaction.com/smutel/topics/managerial_ skills_competencies>.
370. Mangla, P.B. (2000). The role of libraries in global village with particular reference to India: Reading in library and information science (Dr SP Sood Festschrift). Vyas, S.D., et al. (Eds.). Jaipur: Raj Publishing House.
371. Mangla, P.B. (2000). National Policy on Library and Information Systems and Services; An overview in 50 Years- Library and Information Services in India. Edited by M.K.Jain, et.al. p.3.
372. Manish Kumar. Special Libraries In Electronic Environment: March Towards Users Bliss. ICoASL 2011, Poster.
373. Martin, S. K. (1993). Achieving the vision: Rethinking librarianship. Journal of Library Administration, 19(3-4), 209-227.
374. Mark Nichol. 5 Types of Specialized Dictionaries. http://www.dailywritingtips.com/
375. Mary Edna Anders. Reference Service In Special Libraries
376. Mason, M. (1998). 'The yin and yang of knowing', in Books, bricks &

bytes: libraries in the twenty-first century, ed. S. Graubard & P. LeClerc, Transaction Publishers, London, pp161-171.

377. Matarazzo, James and Toby Pearlstein (2010). "Survival Lessons for Libraries: A Microcosm Points to Broader Implications — Positions Advertised in For-Profit Libraries in New England 2006–2009," Searcher, Vol. 18, No. 10, December 2010, pp. 12–14.

378. Mark Nichol. 5 Types of Specialized Dictionaries. http:// www.dailywritingtips.com/

379. Matters, Marion (1990). "Reconciling Sibling Rivalry in the AACR2 'Family': The Potential for Agreement on Rules for Archival Description of All Types of Materials." American Archivist 53 (Winter 1990): 76-93.

380. Maxwell, Margaret F. (2002). Handbook for AACR2: Explaining and Illustrating the Anglo-American Cataloguing Maxwell, Robert L. Maxwell's guide to authority work. Chicago : American Library Association, 2002.

381. McCarthy, Laena (2009). "New Classification System for Public Libraries?". The Public Library Association Blog.

382. McMillan, G. (1999). '(Digital) libraries support (distributed) education. http://www.ala.org/acrl/mcmill.html

383. McMillan, G. (2000). 'The digital library: without a soul can it be a library?' http://www.vala.org.au/vala2000/2000pdf/McMillan.PDF

384. Mercury 4 RFID reader manual – www.thingmagic. com

385. Mero, Kerinino P. (2007). Development of Public Libraries in Nagaland. Proceedings of National conference on Public Libraries as Community Information Centers, Bangalore, 6-8 June 2007 edited by P.Y.Rajendrakumar and Mangla, P.B. et.al (eds). Library and Information Services in India: States and Union Territories . New Delhi: Shipra; 2001.

386. Michelson, Avra (1987). "Description and Reference in the Age of Automation." American Archivist 50 (Spring 1987): 192-208.

387. Miller, L Peters, K Pappano, M & Manuel, K. (1999). 'A research view for librarians working with electronic serials and licensing agreements in the age of the Internet and distance education', The Bottom Line: managing library finances, 12 (3), pp113-119.

388. Miller, P. (1996). 'Metadata for the masses', Ariadne [online] no.5, http://www.ariadne.ac.uk/issue5/metadata-masses/

389. Missingham, R. (1999). 'Science and technology: a web of information: impact of the electronic present and future on scientists and libraries', Strategies for the next millennium: proceedings of the ninth Australasian Information Online & On Disc Conference and Exhibition, ALIA, Sydney, pp 219-236.

390. Mirja Ryynänen (1999). 7 th Catalan Congress on Documentation.

The role of libraries in modern society, Report on "The Role of Libraries in the Modern Society".

391. Mitchell, Joan (2013). "Michael Panzer named Editor-in-Chief of the Dewey Decimal Classification system". OCLC Press Release.
392. Morelon, Régis; Rashed, Roshdi (1996). Encyclopedia of the History of Arabic Science 3, Routledge, ISBN 0-415-12410-7
393. Moore, N 'The information society', World Information Report, [online] http://www.unesco.org/webworld/wirerpt/report.htm
394. Muirhead, Graeme A. (1993). "The role of the systems librarian in libraries in the United Kingdom", Journal of Librarianship and Information Science, 25, no.3, (1993): 123-135.
395. Multiple Versions Forum Report: Report from a Meeting Held December 6-8, 1989, Airlie, Virginia. Washington, DC: Network Development and MARC Standards Office, Library of Congress, 1990.
396. Murray, Stuart (2009). The Library: An Illustrated History, Skypoint Press, Chicago, 2009.
397. Natasha Cooper | October 18, 2011 . The Importance of Academic Libraries. http://infospace.ischool.syr.edu/2011/10/18/the-importance-of-academic-libraries/#
398. National Library of Australia Cataloguing Policy. http://www.nla.gov.au/policy-and-planning/cataloguing-policy
399. Naturalis Historia.
400. National Library (2003). http://kblibrary.bih.nic.in/default.htm
401. National Library of Australia. PADI: Preserving Access to Digital Information. http://www.nla.gov.au/padi/
402. National Knowledge Commission. Libraries: Gateways to knowledge. 2007.
403. National Knowledge Commission (2007); Report to the Nation 2006. New Delhi: NKC
404. National Knowledge Commission. Libraries- Gateways to Knowledge (2007). A Roadmap for Revitalization. New Delhi: NKCNATIONAL MISSION ON LIBRARIES, Ministry of Culture, Government of India http://www.nmlindia.nic.in/pages/display/24
405. Needham, Joseph (1986). "Part 7, Military Technology; the Gunpowder Epic". Science and Civilization in China. 5 – Chemistry and Chemical Technology. Taipei: Caves Books Ltd.
406. Neelameghan A, Library is a growing organism – S R Ranganathan, DLIBCO, 2 (8-9) (2007) 2-3.
407. Negroponte, N 1995. Being digital, Hodder and Stoughton, Rydalmere.
408. NJLA: New Jersey Library Association. Web. 01 May 2009. <http://www.njla.org/resources/competencies. html>.

409. Northvegr - Holy Language Lexicon: B

410. Noruzi, Alireza (2004). "Application of Ranganathan's Laws to the Web." Webology, 1(2), Article 8. http://www.webology.org/2004/v1n2/a8.html

411. Oberg, L. R.; And Others. (1992). The role, status, and working conditions of paraprofessionals: A national survey of academic libraries. College & Research Libraries, 53(3), 215-238.

412. Oberg, L. R. (1992). The emergence of the paraprofessional in academic libraries: Perceptions and realities. College & Research Libraries, 53(2), 99-112.

413. "OCLC and The Library Hotel settle trademark complaint". Library Technology Guides. October 24, 2003.

414. OCLC. "Introduction to the Dewey Decimal Classification".

415. O'Connor, M.J. (1981). "Review article: The librarian as manager", Journal of librarianship and information, 13, no.2, (1981): 131-135.

416. Odlyzko, A 1996. 'Tragic loss or good riddance? The impending demise of traditional scholarly journals', in Scholarly publishing: the electronic frontier, R.B. Peek & G.B. Newby, MIT Press.

417. Odlyzko, A 1997. 'The economics of electronic journals', First Monday, 2 (8). http://www.firstmonday.dk

418. Ojedokun, A. A. (2007). Information literacy for tertiary education students in Africa . Ibadan: Third World Information Services Limited.

419. Okorafor, C. N. (2006). Using library catalogue as access to academic library collection in Nigeria. Journal of the Nigerian Library Association, Imo State Chapter 4 (1&2): 37- 43.

420. Opaleke, J. S. (2006). Study on non-print resources in Nigerian libraries. Ilorin: Nathadex Publishers.

421. Opaleke, J. S., Olayemi T. K., & Aina, R. (2006). School library management for teacher librarian. Ilorin: Nathadex publishers.

422. Orbach, Barbara. "Integrating Concepts: Corporate Main Entry and Graphic Materials." Cataloging and Classification Quarterly 8:2 (1987/88): 71-89.

423. Orbach, Barbara. "So That Others May See: Tools for Cataloging Still Images." In Describing Archival Materials: The Use of the MARC AMC Format, edited by Richard P. Smiralgia, 163-191. New York: Haworth Press, 1990. Also published as Cataloging and Classification Quarterly 11:3/4 (1990).

424. Osiobe, S. (1987). Use and relevance of information on the card catalogue for undergraduate students. Library Review 36 (4): 261-267.

425. Oswitch, Pauline A. "The role of the information professional in development",Information Development, 6 no.1, (1990): 28-33.

426. Ostroff, Harriet. "From Clay Tablets to MARC AMC: The Past, Present, and Future of Cataloging Manuscript and Archival Collections." Provenance 4 (Fall 1986): 1-11.

427. P.D. Wightman (1953). The Growth of Scientific Ideas.

428. Palmini, C. C. (1994). The impact of computerization on library support staff: A study of support staff in academic libraries in Wisconsin. College & Research Libraries, 55(2), 119-127.

429. Palmira Juceviciene & Gintare Tautkeviciene. Academic library as a learning environment: how do students perceive it? Paper presented at the European Conference on Educational Research, University of Hamburg, 17-20 September 2003

430. Panda, B D. (1993).Handbook of Public Library System. New Delhi: Anmol.

431. Parekh H, Five laws of library science: continuing foundations in an information society, DLIBCOM , 2 (8-9) (2007) 7-9

432. Parkhi, R.S. Decimal Classification and Colon Classification in Perspective. New York: Asia Publishing House, 1964.

433. Parvez Ahmad and Mohd Yaseen, Librarian. The Role of the Library and Information Science Professionals As Managers: A Comparative Analysis. Electronic Journal of Academic and Special Librarianship, v.10 no.3 (Winter 2009)

434. Patel, Jashu and Krishan Kumar (2004). Libraries and Librarianship in India. Westport: Greenwood, 2004.

435. Ramasamy, R. (2001). Gujarat. In. Library and Information Services in Indian States and Union Territories edited by P.B.Mangla, et.al. New Delhi: Shipra.

436. Paterson, A 1999, 'Ahead of the game: developing academic library staff for the twenty-first century', Librarian Career Development, 7 (12) November, pp143-149.

437. Pattee, Amy (March 2009). Expedient, but a what cost?School Library Journal, 55(3).

438. Pearl, N. & Buthod, C. (1992). Upgrading the McLibrary. Library Journal, 117, 37-41

439. Pearl, Nancy (September 1 1996). Gave 'em what they wanted. Library Journal, 121, 136-38.

440. Peter Binkley. Pre-Modern Encyclopaedic Texts: Proceedings of the Second Comers Congress, Groningen, 1 – July 4, 1996. BRILL. p. 213..

441. Peter Johan Lor. National library services

442. http://lis6010blog.blogspot.in/2008/10/function-of-national-libraries.html

443. Piggott, S 1996, 'Implementing a virtual library: are you ready?' Electronic dream? Virtual nightmare: the reality for libraries:

Conference Proceedings: 1996 VALA Biennial Conference and Exhibition, VALA, Melbourne, pp.181-190.

444. Pinfield, S 1998. 'Managing the hybrid library', SCONUL newsletter, no.14, pp 41-44.

445. Planning Commission India (1952). The First Five year Plan. New Delhi: Planning Commission.

446. Planning Commission India (1956). Second Five Year Plan. New Delhi:Planning Commission.

447. Planning Commission India (1991). 7th Five Year Plan. New Delhi: Planning Commission.

448. Planning Commission India (1992). 8th Five Year Plan. www.planningcommission.nic.in

449. Planning Commission India (1997). 9th Five Year Plan. www.planningcommission.nic.in

450. Planning Commission India (2002). 10th Five Year Plan. www.planningcommission.nic.in

451. Planning strategies and evaluating resources. http://www.library.illinois.edu/export/spx/webct/strategies2. html

452. Pradeep,C& Rama Reddy,E Application of barcode technology for library operations-experience at IGM Library, University of Hydrabad. University News, 36(35),6-9.

453. Primary, Secondary and Tertiary Sources. http://www.lib.umd.edu/tl/welcome/library-skills-guides

454. Pritchard, S. M. (1995, Spring). Librarians: The ultimate moveable type. Moveable Type, 2(2), 3-4.

455. Priyanki R. Vyas, Mr. Bharat D.Patel. Application of Barcode in the LDRP ITR Library, Gandhinagar. http://www.sahityasetu.co.in/issue14/index.php

456. Pollock, A & Hockley, A 1997, 'What's wrong with internet searching', [online] D-Lib Magazine March 1997 http://www.dlib.org/dlib/march97/bt/03pollock. html

457. Posigha Bassil Ebiwolate. The Use of the Library Catalogue by Undergraduate Students in Niger Delta University Library. Library Philosophy and Practice 2010, ISSN 1522-0222

458. Prasad, A.R.D., & Urs, S. (Eds.) (2001). Workshop on digital libraries: Managing convergence, continuity and change. 12 th -16th March 2001. Mysore: University of Mysore.

459. Psion Teklogix handheld reader manual – www. psionteklogix.com

460. Problems with Classification Schemes http://www.hinkelmann.ch/knut/lectures/irko/IRKO-Classification.pdf

461. Public library. Dictionary.com. Dictionary.com Unabridged. Random House, Inc. http://dictionary. reference.com/browse/public library

462. Public Library Information Resources, Facilities, and Services: User Satisfaction with the Edo State Central Library, Benin-City, Nigeria
463. Quinn, B. (2000). McDonaldization of academic libraries? College & Research Libraries, 61, 248-261.
464. Radcliffe, John Bibliotheca chethamensis: Bibliothecae publicae Mancuniensis ab Humfredo Chetham, armigero fundatae catalogus, exhibens libros in varias classas pro varietate argumenti distributos; [begun by John Radcliffe, continued by Thoams Jones]. 5 vols. Mancuni: Harrop, 1791-1863.
465. Rahmatollah Fattahi's. Online Catalogues And Card Catalogues: Identification Of Areas Of Similarities And Differences.
466. Raitt, D. (Ed.) (1987). Libraries for the new millennium: Implication for managers. London: Library Association Publishing.
467. Raju A A N, The seeds for the origin of the Five laws of library, science, DLIBCOM
468. Raju, A.A.N. Decimal Universal Decimal & Colon Classification. Delhi, India: Ajanta Publications, 1984.
469. Ramasamy, R. and Pia de Menezes Rodrigues. (2001). Goa. In. Library and Information Services in Indian States and Union Territories edited by P.B.Mangla, et.al. New Delhi: Shipra.
470. Ranganathan, S.R. The Five Laws of Library Science. 2nd ed. Bangalore, India: Sarada Ranganathan Endowment for Library Science, 1988.
471. Ranganathan, S.R. Colon Classification. Madras, India: Madras Library Association, 1933.
472. Ranganathan, S.R. (1957). The Five Laws of Library Science. Bangalore; Sarada Ranganathan Endowment for Library Science.
473. Ranganathan, S.R. Volume IV The Colon Classification. New Brunswick, NJ: Graduate School of Library Service, Rutgers - the State University, 1965.
474. Ranganathan S R, The five laws of library science, 2nd edn (Asia Publishing House; Bombay), 1957. (Reprinted in 1963 with minor amendments)
475. Rawlinson, N. (1981). Give 'em what they want! Library Journal, 106, 2188-2195.
476. RDA: Resource Description and Access Prospectus http://www.rda-jsc.org/rdaprospectus.html
477. RDA Blog http://resourcedescriptionandaccess. blogspot.com/
478. "Report and Recommendations of the U.S. RDA Test Coordinating Committee on the implementation of RDA—Resource Description & Access". http://www.loc.gov/bibliographic-future/rda/
479. Report on the Green Paper on the Role of Libraries in the Modern World, [online] http://www.public libraries.fi/publications/

report.htm

480. Reference Service and sources. Elmer E. Rasmuson & BioSciences Libraries. http://library.uaf.edu/ls101-reference-services

481. REFERENCE WORKS: PURPOSE & USES. http://www.tarleton.edu/departments/library/library_module/unit3

482. Reference Sources in Libraries. http://www.ipl.org/

483. REFERENCE WORKS: PURPOSE & USES. http://www.tarleton.edu/departments/library/library_module/unit3

484. Reference Sources in Libraries. http://www.ipl.org/

485. Reynolds, L. J., Pickett, C., van Duinkerken, W., Smith, J., Harrell, J., & Tucker, S. (2010). User-driven acquisitions: Allowing patron requests to drive collection development in an academic library. Collection Management, 35(3/4), 244-254.

486. Rice-Livey, M & Racine, J. (1997). 'The role of academic librarians in the era of information technology', Journal of Academic Librarianship, 23 (1), pp 31-41.

487. Rosenzweig, Roy (2006). "Can History Be Open Source? Wikipedia and the Future of the Past". Journal of American History 93 (1): 117–46.

488. Rout, R.K. (2001). Orissa. In. Library and Information Services in Indian States and Union Territories edited by P.B.Mangla, et.al. New Delhi: Shipra.

489. RRRLF : Information Brochure (2004). Kolkata; Raja Rammohun Roy Library Foundation.

490. RRRLF (1997). Books for the Millions at their Doorsteps; Information Manual. Calcutta: RRRLF.

491. Rusbridge, C. (1998). 'Towards the hybrid library', [online] D-Lib Magazine, July/August, http://www.dlib.org/dlib/july98/rusbridge/07rusbridge.html

492. Rubin, Richard E. Foundations of Library and Information Science. 2nd ed. New York: Neal-Schuman Publishers. 2004.

493. Sahib, S. (2003).Library and Literacy Movement for National Development. New Delhi: Concept.

494. Sambasivan, K. (1997). Use of Bar Codes in Libraries. International Library Movement.V.19, N.3 (1997), p. 149-56.

495. Satija, M.P. (1997). "The revision and future of Colon Classification." Knowledge Organization, Vol. 24, No. 1, 1997.

496. Satija, M.P. and Sukhdev Singh. (2001). Panjab. In. Library and Information Services in Indian States and Union Territories edited by P.B.Mangla, et.al. New Delhi: Shipra.

497. Sathikumar, C. S. (1993). Public Library Development in India. In Raman. Nair, R. (Ed.),Public Library Development. New Delhi: Ess Ess.

498. Schachter, D. (2006). An essential function for special libraries. Information Outlook, 10(10): 8–9.

499. School library: purpose. http://schools.natlib.govt.nz/supporting-learners/effective-practice

500. Schmidt-Braul, I. (1999). 'Does culture create new jobs in the information society?: strategic issues and new professional profiles', Librarian Career Development, 7 (12), pp 127-142.

501. Schutz, Herbert, The Carolingians in Central Europe, Their History, Arts, and Architecture Koninklijke Brill NV, Leiden, The Netherlands, 2004, 160-162.

502. Schuyler, M. (1999). 'Prognostications on technology unbound or, the library to come', Computers in Libraries, 19 (5), pp 30-32

503. Sen B K. (2002). Five laws of library science? IASLIC Bulletin, 47 (3) (2002) 121-140

504. Sen, Bharati (2001). Maharashtra. In. Library and Information Services in Indian States and Union Territories edited by P.B.Mangla, et.al. New Delhi: Shipra.

505. Seth, Ved (2001). Sikkim. In. Library and Information Services in Indian States and Union Territories edited by P.B.Mangla, et.al. New Delhi: Shipra.

506. Sharma, Pandey S K (1987). Libraries and Society. New Delhi: Ess Ess.

507. Sharma, Pandey S.K. (1985). Public Libraries in India. New Delhi: Ess Ess.

508. Sharma, J. S. (1965).The Substance of Library Science. Bombay: Asia Publishing.

509. Sharma, S. K. Pandey. (1996). Public Libraries in India: Trends and Status. InPublic Libraries in Developing Countries: Status and Trends. Ed. P.K. Mahapatra, 121-127. New Delhi: Vikas Publishing House.

510. Sharma, Pandey S.K. (1996). Public Libraries in India; Trends and Status. In. Public Libraries in developing Countries: Status and Trends edited by P K Mahapatra and V K Thomas. New Delhi: Vikas. 91

511. Sherman, Jill. 2009. Melvil Dewey: Library Genius. Edina, MN: Abdo Publishing Company. Shiri, A. (2003). Digital library research: Current developments and trends. Library Review 52 (5): 198 - 202

512. SIGNE E. LARSON. Reference and Inforation Services in Special Libraries

513. Simpson, Carol. "Five Laws". Library Media Connection 26 no7 6 Ap/My 2008. http://www.carolsimpson.com/5laws.pdf

514. Singh, Arjun (2001). Madhya Pradesh and Chattisgarh. In. Library and Information Services in Indian States and Union Territories edited by P.B.Mangla, et.al. New Delhi: Shipra.

515. Singh, Dalip and Anjana Chattipahyay (2001). Uttar Pradesh and

Uttaranchal. In

516. Library and Information Services in Indian States and Union Territories edited by P.B.Mangla, et.al. New Delhi: Shipra.
517. Singh, Sukhdev (1999). "Potentialities, limitations and the future of the Colon Classification." Herald of Library Science, Vol. 38, No. 3-4, July-October 1999.
518. Singh, J. (2003). Information democracy and South Asia: Promises and perils of the Web. Ludhiana: Madallion Press.
519. Singh, H Dodendro (2007). Scenario of Public Library Services in Manipur. Proceedings of National conference on Public Libraries as Community Information Centers, Bangalore, 6-8 June 2007 edited by P.Y.Rajendrakumar and V.G.Talwar. Bangalore, Department of Public Libraries, Govt. of Karnataka.
520. Singh, R.S.P. (2007). Brief History of Public Library development in Bihar. Proceedings of National Conference on Public Libraries as Community Information Centers, Bangalore, 6-8 June 2007 edited by P.Y.Rajendrakumar and V.G.Talwar. Bangalore, Department of Public Libraries, Govt. of Karnataka.
521. Smith, Vincent A. (1981). Oxford history of India. 4th. Ed. Delhi: OUP. 92
522. Smart, Laura J. 2004. Making sense of RFID. Library Journal NetConnect 129 (Fall): 4-14.
523. Sood, Sudesh Kumar (2001). Himachal Pradesh. In. Library and Information Services in Indian States and Union Territories edited by P.B.Mangla, et.al. New Delhi: Shipra.
524. Sorcha Carey (2003). "Two Strategies of Encyclopaedism". Pliny's Catalogue of Culture: Art and Empire in the Natural History. Oxford University Press. p. 17..
525. Special Libraries Association. (2003). Competencies for information professionals of the 21st century. http://www.sla.org/content/learn/members/competencies/index.cfm
526. Special Libraries Association. (2009). SLA alignment portal. http://www.sla.org/content/SLA/alignment/portal/index.html
527. Special Libraries. http://www.nalis.gov.tt/Libraries/SpecialLibraries/tabid/65/Default.aspx?Page ContentID=1014
528. Smiralgia, Richard P., ed. Describing Archival Materials: The Use of the MARC AMC Format. New York: Haworth Press, 1990. Also published as Cataloging and Classification Quarterly 11:3/4 (1990).
529. Strout, R.F. (1956), "The development of the catalog and cataloging codes", Library Quarterly, Vol.26 No.4, pp.254–75.
530. Svenonius, Elaine. The Intellectual Foundation of Information Organization. Cambridge, Mass: MIT Press, 2000.

531. Swanson, Edward. "Choice and Form of Access Points According to AACR 2." In Describing Archival Materials: The Use of the MARC AMC Format, edited by Richard P. Smiralgia, 35-61. New York: Haworth Press, 1990. Also published as Cataloging and Classification Quarterly 11:3/4 (1990).

532. Taylor, Insup; Wang Guizhi. "Library Systems in East Asia". McLuhan Studies.

533. Taylor, Archer (1986) Book Catalogues: their varieties and uses; 2nd ed., introductions, corrections and additions by W. P. Barlow, Jr. Winchester: St Paul's Bibliographies (Previous ed.: Chicago: Newberry Library, 1957)

534. Taylor, Arlene G. Wynar's Introduction to Cataloging and Classification. 9th ed. Westport, CT: Libraries Unlimited, 2000.

535. Tillett, Barbara B. "International Shared Resource Records for Controlled Access" in Authority Control in the 21st Century: An Invitational Conference.

536. "Timeline". OCLC.

537. Thaker U and Rawal C, Five laws of library science in new perspectives, DLIBCOM , 2 (8-9) (2007) 11- 14.

538. Thakur, U.M. Public Libraries in Bihar; An Overview. Herald of Library Science v.45 (1-2) Jan-Apr. 2006.

539. The Compact Edition of the Oxford English Dictionary, Volume I A-O. Oxford University Press. 1971. p. 861.

540. The curious tale of the stolen books, by Martin Vennard for BBC News Magazine, April 24, 2013.

541. The salient features of Colon Classification. Susan Kelsch, 407A Cataloging and Classification I, Summer II term August 5, 2003

542. The Dewey Decimal System http://brianhinz.blogspot.in/2012/12/advantages disadvantages.html

543. http://www.library.illinois.edu/export/ugl/about/dewey.html

544. The psycho-biology of language: an introduction to dynamic philology, (Riverside Press; Cambridge), 1935.

545. The School Library Association. http://www.sla.org.uk/pol-school-library-purpose.php

546. The American Association of School Librarians. http://www.ala.org/ala/mgrps/divs/aasl/aaslproftools/positionstatements/aaslposition.cfm

547. The Australian School Library Association. http://www.asla.org.au/policy/p_bor.htm#TopOfPage

548. Thomas, V.K. (1997).Public Libraries in India: Development & Finance. New Delhi: Vikas.

549. Thomas, David H. "Cataloging Sound Recordings Using Archival Methods," 193-212.

550. Tikekar A C, Digvijaya (2007). (global acclaim) of Ranganathan's Five laws of library science, DLIBCOM, 2 (8-9) (2007) 10-11.

551. Trehan, G.L. (1986). Main Problems of Library Legislation in India. In. Library Legislation in India edited by R K Rout. New Delhi: Reliance.

552. Trikha, Sudha (2001). Rajasthan. In. Library and Information Services in Indian States and Union Territories edited by P.B.Mangla, et.al. New Delhi: Shipra.

553. Trotter, Ross (1995). "Electronic Dewey: The CD-ROM Version of the Dewey Decimal Classification". Cataloging & Classification Quarterly 19 (3-4): 213–234. doi:10.1300/J104v19n03_17.

554. Twiss, Thomas M. (2001). A validation of Brief Tests of Collection Strength. Collection Management, 25(3), 23-37.

555. Types of information Sources. http://www.lib.vt.edu/help/research/info-sources.html

556. UHF RFID – Libraries taking the next step into the future – www.Adilam.com.au [http://www.rfidtribe. com/index.php?option=com_content&task=view&id= 350&Itemid=102

557. United States. Bureau of Education. (1876), Public libraries in the United States of America, Washington: Govt. Print. Off., pp. 623–648

558. United States. Office of Education. (1876), Public libraries in the United States of America, Washington: Govt. print. off., p. 628

559. US Digital Library Federation, 1999, 'A working definition of the digital library'. [online] http://www.diglib.org/dlfhomepage.htm

560. Utilizing Barcode Technology in Library System, By Ismalordy | Feb. 2013, http://www.studymode.com/profile/Ismalordy-80139513/

561. Vashishth, C.P. (1991). Indian Library Association. Quoted by Jashu Patel and Krishan Kumar. In. Libraries and Librarianship in India. Westport: Greenwood Press, 2004. p.183.

562. Veaner, A. B. (1994). Paradigm lost, paradigm regained? A persistent personnel issue in academic librarianship, II. College & Research Libraries, 55(5), 389-402.

563. Venkata, Ramana, P. (2006). The changing role of librarian in a challenging dynamic web environment. 4th International Convention Caliber-, Gulbarga, 2-4 February, Inflibnet Centre, Ahmedabad. (2006). Print.

564. Verma, I.N., & Agarawal, U.K. (Eds.) (1994).Public Library Services in India. Udaipur: Himanshu.

565. Vidyavati Devi, N; Ibohal Singh, Ch and Giridhari Singh, N. Development of Public Library System and Services in Manipur. Proceedings of National Seminar on Legislation Based Rural Library service in India. Organised byRanganathan Society for Book Culture, Library and Information Studies, North East Chapter on 8-10

Sept.,2007 at Imphal.

566. Viswanathan, C.G. (2005). Public Library Organization. 4th. Ed. New Delhi: Ess Ess Publications
567. Wainwright, E. (1996). 'Digital libraries: some implications for government and education from the Australian development experience'. [online] http://www.nla.gov.au/nla/staffpaper/ew6.html
568. Walford, A. J., ed. (1981) Walford's Concise Guide to Reference Material. London: Library Association; p. 6
569. Ward, N & Wood, A. (1998). 'Emerging technologies for networked information discovery: beyond Z39.50', Robots to knowbots: the wider information agenda: Conference Proceedings, 1998 VALA Biennial Conference and Exhibition, VALA, Melbourne, pp.377-391. [Also online] http://www.vala.org.au/valaweb/num821.pdf
570. Walsh, S. Padraig (1968). Anglo-American general encyclopedias: a historical bibliography, 1703–1967. New York: Bowker. p. 270.
571. Waters, D. (1998). 'What are digital libraries?' CLIR issues, 4, July/August, p1,5. http://www.clir.org/pubs/issues/issues04.html#dlf
572. Watstein, SB, Calarco, PV & Ghaphery, JS (1999). 'Digital library: keywords', Reference Services Review, 27 (4) pp344-352.
573. Weber, Lisa B. (1987). "Describing Microforms and the MARC Formats: A Discussion Paper." Archival Informatics Newsletter 1:2 (Summer 1987): 9-13.
574. What is a library anymore, anyway? by Michael A. Keller, Victoria A. Reich, and Andrew C. Herkovic. First Monday, Volume 8, Number 5 - 5 May 2003. http://firstmonday.org/ojs/index.php/fm/issue/view/157
575. What is a Reference Source? http://www.library.yorku. ca/cms/scottreference
576. Wiegand, W.A. (1996). Irrepressible Reformer: A Biography of Melvil Dewey. Chicago: ALA Editions. Wiegand, W.A. (1998). The "Amherst Method:" The Origins of the Dewey Decimal Classification Scheme. Libraries & Culture, Vol. 33, No. 2, Spring 1998. Williamsón, C. C. (1971). The Williamson reports of 1921 and 1923, including Training for library work (1921) and Training for library service (1923). Metuchen, NJ: Scarecrow Press.
577. Wood, PA & Walther, J. H. (2000). 'The future of academic libraries: changing formats and changing delivery', The Bottom Line: Managing Library Finances, 13, (4) pp173-181.
578. Workbook for Selection Policy Writing from ALA. http://www.ala.org/advocacy/banned/challenges librarymaterials/essential preparation/workbookslctn
579. What are Primary Sources? http://www.yale.edu/collections_

collaborative/primarysources/primary sources.html

580. What is a primary source. http://www.eduplace.com/ss/hmss/primary.html
581. What is a Reference Source?. http://www.library.yorku. ca/cms/scottreference
582. White, Howard D. (1995). Brief Tests of Collection Strength. Greenwood Publishing Group. http://books.google.com/books?id=z01jExrgAA8C& printsec=frontcover
583. Why libraries are essential. http://www.librariesa reessential.com/
584. Why classify. http://lili.org/forlibs/ce/able/course7/
585. Wiegand, Wayne A. (1996), Irrepressible reformer, Chicago: American Library Association, ISBN 083890680X, 083890680X
586. Wilde, Michelle & Level, Allison (2011). How to drink from a fire hose without drowning: collection assessment in a numbers-driven environment. Collection Management, 36, 217-236.
587. "WorldCat facts and statistics". Online Computer Library Center. 2011.
588. Wright, C. T. Hagberg & Purnell, C. J. Catalogue of the London Library, St. James's Square, London. 10 vols. London, 1913-55. Includes: Supplement: 1913-20. 1920. Supplement: 1920-28. 1929. Supplement: 1928-53. 1953 (in 2 vols). Subject index: (Vol. 1). 1909. Vol. 2: Additions, 1909-22. Vol. 3: Additions, 1923-38. 1938. Vol. 4: (Additions), 1938-53. 1955.
589. WWW Virtual Library: <http://vlib.stanford.edu/Overwiew.html>
590. www.wikipedia.org - Library
591. www.isibang.ac.in/~library/portal/Pages/chp1.pdf Fifty Years of Experience in the Development of Colon Classification
592. Wynar, B.S. (1992). Introduction to Cataloguing and Classification. 8th ed. Littleton, Co.: Libraries Unlimited.
593. Wynar, Bohdan S. (1980). Introduction to cataloguing and classification. 6th ed. Littleton, Colorado : Libraries Unlimited. 1980.
594. Yee, Martha M. "Integration of Nonbook Materials in AACR2." Cataloging and Classification Quarterly 3:4 (Summer 1983): 1-18.
595. Yeo, Richard R. (2001). Encyclopaedic visions : scientific dictionaries and enlightenment culture. Cambridge, New York: Cambridge University Press.
596. Yýlmaz, B. ve Aydýn, H. (2011). Bilgi politikasý konusundaki uluslararasý çalýþmalarda kütüphane kurumuna yaklaþým: Avrupa Birliði Lizbon Stratejisi ile Birleþmiþ Milletler Dünya Bilgi Toplumu Zirvesi. Bilgi Dünyasý, 12(1); ss. 46-69.
597. Yontz, Elaine (1992). "Cataloger/Archivist Cooperation, or, Don't Those People Know What a Series Is?" In Academic Libraries: Acheiving Excellence in Higher Education. Proceedings of the 6th

National Conference of the Association of College and Research Libraries, edited by Thomas Kirk, 128-130. Chicago: ACRL, 1992.

598. Young, P. (1998). 'Librarianship: a changing profession', in Books, bricks & bytes: libraries in the twenty-first century, ed S Graubard & P LeClerc, Transaction Publishers, London, pp103-125.
599. Zahid Ashraf Wani (2008). Development of Public Libraries in India. Library Philosophy and Practice 2008
600. Zipf G K (1949). Human behavior and the principle of least effort; an introduction to human ecology, (Addison –Wesley; Reading, Mass), 1949.